DEDICATION

to Michael, Anna, Madison, Thomas and Owen.

CONTENTS

	Acknowledgments	i
	Preface: The Concept of Papal Greatness	1
	Part One: Papal Primacy	
1	Peter the Apostle, (d. 64)	5
2	Leo I (The Great), (440–461)	10
3	Gregory I (The Great), (590–604)	15
4	Gregory VII (Hildebrand), (1073–1085)	23
5	Innocent III, (1198–1216)	30
	Part Two: The Modern Papacy	43
6	Pius IX, (1846–1877)	45
7	Leo XIII, (1877–1903)	69
8	Benedict XV, (1914–1922)	95
9	John XXII, (1958–1963)	119
10	John Paul II, (1978–2005)	156
	Conclusion	222
	Endnotes	224
	About the Author	253

ACKNOWLEDGEMENTS

We are grateful to the librarians at the following who have been helpful in our work: the College of the Holy Cross, Shepherd University, Fitchburg State University, Hamilton Township Public Library, the New Jersey State Public Library, and Seton Hall University. They represent the best of communities of scholarship.

PAPAL GREATNESS: THE TEN MOST IMPORTANT PONTIFFS

PREFACE:
THE CONCEPT OF PAPAL GREATNESS

For over two thousand years, the papacy has been associated with the highly influential Roman Catholic Church. It is the oldest major elective office in the West, and a major adjudicator of Christian doctrine dealing with moral issues. Not all of the 266 or so popes have been good managers or even good men. A few have made terrible judgments in their time, lost whole empires of souls, engaged in scandalous behavior usually during scandalous times.

But overall, especially recently, the Church has been led by good, kind, concerned clergy, some of whom attained the rare status of saints, that is have lived lives worthy of emulation. Three popes in the earlier periods were called by the people of their time "the Great" usually for their roles in saving the city of Rome.[1] The popes must be able to manage a huge bureaucracy, committing often acts of moral ambiguity, dealing with powerful foes, and barely gaining support, let alone salvation for themselves in the process.

To be a great pope one must have had a major impact on the Church and at times the world. Therefore most great popes had long terms in office, but one did not—John XXIII whose reign last only two and a half years, but who unleashed the fervor of reform and self-criticism called Vatican II. Most popes though lasted twenty to thirty years, too long especially at the end of most of their lives. Few popes would repeat with honesty, Leo XIII's remarks at the end of his life, "If only I had more years, I could reconcile faith and science."[2]

Generally these popes were in secular terms, good managers of a large, heterogeneous voluntary association of faith. Some reform popes recalibrated the vacillating baroque of St. Peter, men like Leo I, Gregory I, Innocent III, and Gregory VII, all of whom were men of powerful egos and deep dedication.

Great crisis often bring forth great popes, but not always. Some popes, like Julius II, were actually warriors leading an Italian city state and acting like the head of conditerri. But not in the later terrible wars of genocide and totalitarian states of the modern era. In World War I, Benedict XV was in the Great War one of the few voices of reason. He refused to jump on the nationalist Italian bandwagon and tried to use his influence to bring peace. Italian soldiers went into the meat grinders of war, crying out, "Hail Benedict."[3]

He was not successful in bringing peace; no leader was. Conflict destroyed the upper layers of European societies, upended five stable empires, and released forces that eventually led to World War II. He tried to broker a peace, and gladly encouraged Woodrow Wilson's efforts--the son of a Presbyterian's minster---who was himself shocked at the carnage the armies had wrought.

Most importantly, it was the usually quiet Benedict who set the pattern for Vatican diplomacy for two generations. He pushed out of obscurity his successor, Pius XI, and established a string of popes who were in a sense his protégés: Popes Pius XI, Pius XII, John XXIII, and his influence extended to Paul VI and Paul's protégé John Paul II. He was not successful in stopping the war, of course, but neither were Woodrow Wilson, Lloyd George, Georges Clemenceau, and before that Czar Nicholas II.[4]

Great American presidents make great errors. Great popes often make terrible decisions too. Clerical infighting and papal weakness lost China, which could have been another Philippines for the Jesuit missionaries, operating in the cities and fields of that great civilization. A Confucian–Catholicism would have been a beneficial balance to Latin Christianity.

The names of some of these influential popes may surprise readers. The first question is one of criteria: what makes a pope great. In some ways, it is the same question I dealt with in my book on presidential greatness in the United States. But an institutional church of course is not a secular polity. The most comprehensive listing of presidential qualities comes from attribute studies, and the most comprehensive list has been done by Robert K. Murray and Tim H. Blessing who have given a laundry list which is some interest to this study.[5] They cite:

Charisma
Intelligence
Integrity
Capacity for growth
Decisiveness
Activeness
Symbolic leadership
Priority setting and implementation
Crisis management
Coalition building
Recruiting good advisers
Ideals and lofty goals

Wisdom

The great British papal historian, Eamon Duffy, who has given a series of lectures on the BBC, lists the most significant popes:[6]

1. St. Peter
2. Leo the Great
3. Gregory the Great
4. Gregory VII
5. Innocent III
6. Paul III
7. Pius IX
8. Pius XII
9. John XXIII
10. John Paul II

Another fine historian of the papacy, American Rev. Richard McBrien, listed the following historically important popes in chronological order:[7]

1. Leo the Great
2. Gregory the Great
3. Gregory VII
4. Innocent III
5. Boniface VIII
6. Pius V
7. Pius IX
8. Leo XIII
9. John XXIII
10. Paul VI
11. John Paul I
12. John Paul II

One other interesting point of departure is in the work of Jesuit Avery Cardinal Dulles. He has argued that the Church has seen several models of organization over the centuries:[8]

The Church as an Institution
The Church as a Mystical community
The Church as Sacrament
The Church as Herald
The Church as Servant
The Church as a Community of Disciples

It seems that the roles of the popes flow from that schema into pastoral, theologian, bureaucrat, and international figure. In our times, especially under intensive public scrutiny, the pope must be holy and wise, as well as well-traveled! A tough job description even if one believes in the guidance of the Holy Spirit.

My list of the top ten popes is a judgment call on my part, and are:
  Peter the Apostle (d. 64)
  Leo I (401-417)
  Gregory I (590-604)
  Gregory VII (Hildebrand, 1073-1085)
  Innocent III (1198-1216)
  Pius IX (1846-1878)
  Leo XIII (1878-1903)
  Benedict XV (1914-1922)
  John XXIII (1958-1963)
  John Paul II (1978-2014)

The first five popes represent the beginning and the establishment of the primacy of the office. After the apex of power and influence in the 13th century under Innocent III, there came a period of decline, corruption, and the Protestant Reformation followed by the defensive Council of Trent.

This book spends much more time on the five modern popes whom we know more about, and their conflicts with secularism, atheism, totalitarianism, democracy, and inequality are much more relevant to our current times and challenges.

CHAPTER ONE
PETER THE APOSTLE (d.64)

Sometime around the age of 30, Jesus of Nazareth began his preaching ministry, probably at first watching John the Baptizer who was demanding forgiveness and penance as he stood in the River Jordan.[1] It was not an unusual message for a Jewish prophet. When Jesus emerged from the crowd for baptism, John demurred and said it was he who should be baptized by his younger cousin, whom he characterized as "the Lamb of God." But according to the Scriptures, Jesus underwent the ritual, and the heavens opened up and bystanders could hear, "This is my beloved son in whom I am well pleased."[2]

According to tradition, the fisherman Andrew was in the crowd and immediately pronounced that Jesus was indeed the Messiah, the Promised One of the Old Testament. He insisted to his brother, Simon, as well as that Jesus was the Messiah; Simon was probably also in some ways a disciple of the Baptizer; he was the son of Jonah and was from the village of Bethsaida in the province of Galilee. Peter's life is related in the four canonical gospels, the Books of Acts, some New Testament letters, the non-canonical gospel according to the Hebrews and other early Church accounts. He was the first named of the disciples called during Jesus' ministry, and at his very first meeting with Jesus he was named "Peter," a pun on the word "rock" (in Greek) or in Syraic or Aramaic "Cephas."[3]

He was a married man, and his wife is frequently known as Febronia. The Scriptures say that he lived in Capernaum with his mother-in-law, whom Jesus had once cured. Peter too was a fisherman along with his brother Andrew and the sons of Zebedee, James and John. Jesus quickly told the men that they would become "fishers of men."[4] In Luke 5:3 Simon Peter owned the boat from which Jesus preached to the multitudes who were crowding him at the shore of Lake Gennesaret. In return, Jesus told the fishermen to lower their nets, and they suddenly caught a huge number of fish. Three of the gospels tell the story of Jesus walking on water, and how Peter tried to imitate him, but sank when his faith grew shaky.[5]

Peter the Rock
In speaking to his disciples, Jesus asked, "Who do people say that the Son of Man is?" The disciples gave various answers, but Simon Peter responded, "You are the Christ, the Son of the living God." Jesus pronounced Peter "blessed" for having recognized him and argued that this knowledge came from divine revelation.[6] Using the pun for rock, Jesus says, "On this rock I will build my church, and the gates of Hell will not prevail against it." Christ also had given Peter the keys of the kingdom of heaven with the right to forgive or to refuse to forgive sin. In ancient times, a distinguished guest was given two keys to a city—one to the treasury and the other to the jails. This allusion may just be a reference to an older tradition.[7] The terminology of the keys of the kingdom of heaven is also remarkably parallel to the commissioning of Eliakim ben Hilkiah in the Book of Isaiah. But Catholic apologists see this expression as giving its Church the institutional power to forgive or not forgive sins.[8] With all these sorts of recognition, it is sometimes difficult to see how Peter could eventually deny Jesus at his greatest moment of peril. Peter may be a rock, but he was an impulsive leader, and also like all of us a weak, forgiven sinner.

Although Peter's preeminence was acknowledged from the beginning, all four canonical gospels recount that Jesus at the Last Supper predicted that Peter would deny him three times before the cock crows (twice in Mark). Rarely do the four gospels agree so closely. It was either that the authors took pride in Peter's humiliation, or that they wished the Christian community to know about forgiveness and penance.[9] Yet three gospels report that when Jesus was arrested, one of his companions, probably Peter, cut off the ear of servant of the High Priest, and was ready for battle. But Jesus touched the ear, and it was restored. This is the last of the thirty-seven miracles attributed to Jesus, although the Scriptures insist that he performed many more than are reported.[10]

The Gospel of John insists that Peter is the first person to enter the tomb, although several women and the "beloved disciple" actually went in first. In Luke, however, it only Peter who goes to check the women's report of an empty tomb, but after seeing the gravesite linens resting there, he goes home, not informing the other disciples. Perhaps he had a difficult time understanding what he had seen. It must be remembered that after the terrible trauma of the Crucifixion and then the Resurrection of their Lord, Peter and several other apostles went back to their occupation, fishing.[11]

Paul relates that Peter was the first to see the resurrected Jesus, and in the Gospel of John Peter tells Jesus three times of his love for him, matching his threefold denial before the Crucifixion.[12]

Peter is frequently listed as the first in rank among the Twelve Apostles in the Book of Acts. He is also mentioned in the Gospels as composing with James, and John, a special group who were present at incidents at which the others were not present, such as the Transfiguration. He is frequent persecuted after the death of Jesus, as if the Roman and Jewish authorities recognized his primacy in their harsh treatment of the followers of Jesus. St Clement of Alexandria (writing about 190 AD) said, "For they saw that Peter and James and John after the ascents of our Savior, as if also preferred by our Lord, strove not after honor, but chose James the Just bishop of Jerusalem." Paul insisted that Peter should be the apostle to the Jews, and he would be the apostle to the Gentiles; when he sought approval for his mission, he went to Jerusalem to talk to the group of three about his plans.[13]

Peter is frequently the spokesman for the early Christian community, and delivered the public sermon during Pentecost, when thousands were converted on the spot.[14] He took the lead in selecting a replacement for Judas Iscariot with the disciple Matthias. Peter was twice arrested with John, and brought before the Sanhedrin. But the captives defied the council, and undertook missionary journeys to Lydda, Joppa, and Caesarea, and there is indirect evidence that Peter also visited Corinth. He gave Paul approval to evangelize the Gentiles, and did not insist on circumcision for their conversion to what was called "The Way" of Jesus, although Paul at times got angry at Peter's deference at Antioch to Jewish converts who insisted on observing the traditional dietary laws and performing circumcision. Tradition has it that Peter became the head of the church in Antioch for seven years.[15]

We know of the extensive writings of Paul to the various Christian communities, although we are not clear which epistles come from his own hand. There are also two epistles, "First Peter" and "Second Peter," which are credited to Peter, but the New Testament describes Peter as illiterate.[16] That may be a reference to his lack of learning, or he may have dictated his memoirs to a secretary. Evidence has been produced that the Gospel of Mark is from the direct testimony of Peter to an evangelist.

Spreading the Good News
Even before Julius Caesar, the Roman city state was remarkably tolerant of the Jews, even though they were a monotheistic religion in a polytheistic empire. It appears that very early on after the Resurrection and Pentecost, there were some Jews who brought back the news of Jesus and his Resurrection to the Jewish colony in Rome. There must

have been an early Christian community there since Paul was addressing them in his epistles. Both Peter and Paul decided, probably separately, that the greatest city in the empire needed the "good news," after both of them had moved through the Mediterranean world preaching and baptizing. We know much of Paul's arduous travels. And we know of Peter's services to Antioch, maybe for as long as seven years where tradition has it he was the "first Patriarch of Antioch." Church records have it that early on in Rome Peter came into conflict with Simon the Magus (a magician) who claimed that he could better Peter in performing miracles.[17] When he threw himself off a building to prove his supernatural powers, he was crushed, proof of his misguided claim against the prime apostle, who was spared harm by God's intercession. Theologians, including Tertullian and Origen, have recorded that "Peter was crucified at Rome with his head downwards, as he himself had desired to suffer." Peter did not consider himself worthy enough to die the same way as his Savior. The record of Peter's times is based in part on the Gospel of Mark.

Peter and Paul were probably casualties around October 13, 64 AD of the persecutions ordered by the insane emperor Nero who blamed the great fire that destroyed Rome on the newly arrived Christians.[18] There is a charming tradition which is probably apocryphal that Peter was fleeing Rome, and was stopped by a stranger saying, "Quo vadis, Domino," "Where are you going, Master?" Peter insisted that he was wanted to avoid execution, to which the stranger, Jesus, responded he was going to Rome to be crucified again. Peter returned to the city to accept martyrdom. That encounter is dramatized in a fine novel by Polish storyteller Henryk Sienkiewicz. In real life, Peter is supposed to have been crucified on the spot now occupied by the Clementine Chapel, and in 1950 human bones were found buried underneath the altar of St. Peter's Basilica. That claim has been strengthened over the years. The bones belonged to a male of about sixty-one years living around the first century. But one archeologist, in 2009, Otto Zwierlein concluded that there was not "a single piece of reliable literary evidence" that Peter was ever in Rome. But the early documents and the long traditional records are fairly strong.

Early authorities, like St. Ignatius of Antioch, implied that both Peter and Paul had a special authority over the Roman church. "I do not command you, as Peter and Paul did," he remarked once. Peter is supposed to have turned over the episcopate of Rome to Linus who Paul mentions in the Epistles to Timothy.

The Church has historically cited Peter as its first "pope," although the term was not even used until centuries later. But the strong evidence of Peter's leadership was given in such expressions, as Jesus' admonition, "Feed my lambs, feed my lambs, feed my sheep." And of course as noted, "I tell you that you are Peter, and on this rock I will build my church, and the gates of Hell will not overcome it. I will give you the keys of the kingdom of heaven; whatever you bind on earth will be bound in heaven, and whatever you loose on earth will be loosed in heaven."

The historical records of the gospels are at times very mixed toward Peter.[19] There are considerable accounts of his weakness if not cowardice. But looking at the distant past, it is Peter who pulled together a very dispirited group of followers after the Crucifixion, and provided them with care and solace during a difficult period. After the Resurrection, he presided over the visitations of Jesus, and from the Pentecost event, he turned a frightened group of poor Palestinians into an evangelical force. He stood against the Roman and Jewish forces who wanted to intimidate the new Christians, and at a critical moment he gave Paul approval to go out to the Gentile world. That became one of the greatest turning points in the history of the Western world. From Paul to Constantine there was an enormous jump that led to the changes in Roman support. Eventually the pope (as he was eventually called) became the major force in the West, replacing the emperor and eventually outlasting the great empire that ended in 451 AD.

There was something in Peter that made men and especially women listen to Christ's message. He was a miracle worker, and a rather remarkable orator. He created a more cohesive church in Rome, because he had one great asset. He was not just preaching the Word, he was a constant companion of Jesus, he ate with him, traveled with him, gave him residence in Capernaum, and eventually proclaimed that he was not just another John the Baptizer, but was indeed in their vocabulary, the Messiah, the son of God. That witness gave him enormous prestige both with Paul and with the Antioch and Roman churches. He became the first vicar of the Christ, Jesus.

CHAPTER TWO
LEO I (THE GREAT), (440–461)

The papacy of Leo I is probably the most significant reign in the early Church, equaling that of the later period of Gregory I. It is not clear in what year he was born, but papal historian Richard McBrien uses the date 401. Leo was born in Tuscany and his father's name was Quintianus. He served as a deacon in the Church under Pope Celestine I (422–32), and had some dealings with authorities in Gaul during the reign of Casianus (430–32). He also had some contact with Cyril of Alexandria, a major theologian of the time who influenced his thinking on the doctrines of the orthodox faith. During the pontificate of Sixtus III (422–40), Leo was sent to Gaul by Emperor Valentinian III to deal with a dispute between his chief military commander of the province and his chief magistrate. It was obviously a sign of great confidence. Sixtus III died in 440 while Leo was still in Gaul, and he was chosen his successor.

The election of Leo was nearly unanimous, and so at the age of 39 he became pontiff and bishop of Rome. The most immediate problem he faced was political—the flood of immigrants from Africa, fleeing the violent Vandal invaders. In 439, the city of Carthage and the proconsul province were then in the hands of a barbarian tribe that was Arian in religion, rather than orthodox Catholic. It was that development that the prestigious bishop of nearby Hippo, St. Augustine, had feared most before his death. As bishop of Rome, Leo began preaching about fifteen sermons on great feasts and ecclesiastical seasons in the Church calendar, spelling out the orthodox faith.[1] At that period of time, Christianity was rooted in the working class districts of the city, with the upper classes embracing it only in the first decades of the fifth century. The city though was dotted with churches and shrines to the martyrs that extended into what was then the suburbs. Emperor Theodosius in 389 ended all pagan holidays, and replaced them with Christian celebrations. By the mid-fourth century, there were 177 festivals with games and circuses. The most important Catholic bishop was Ambrose of Milan in Northern Italy where papal influence was weak at the time.[2] He withstood enormous threats from secular and tribal authorities and baptized Augustine, the most influential theologian for a thousand years.

Understanding Christ

Leo was the first pope to attempt any systematic program of theological pronouncements on major issues of faith. He even published some of his sermons, an incredible venture in that era. He did not look to the monastic ideas of Christian life, but was influenced by Ambrose as he blended together virtue and utility, into a workable message. Leo saw the Church's mission as universal, meant for all, a broader mandate than even his contemporary Augustine of Hippo proclaimed. Christ was the Mediator between God and man, emphasizing a communion of love.[3] He was profoundly influenced by the writings of both Augustine and Cyril of Alexandria, the stalwart champions of orthodox Catholicism.

Leo's central preoccupation in proclaiming the faith was trying to delineate the two natures of Jesus Christ's personality—the second person of the Blessed Trinity in the Godhead, and the flesh and blood martyr of human experience. These views were directly opposed by the Arians who believed that Jesus Christ was not divine. The attempt to export the Arian cult to Rome in the next century and a half was not successful, due in large part to the intense opposition of both pagan and Christian emperors. The new pope proved to be a bulwark of orthodoxy, both in Rome and outside the city throughout the empire, especially in the western part. He worked closely with the civil powers and called for a composite court of clergy and members of the Senate to assist him to protect the tenets of the early faith.

Leo specifically addressed the advances of another popular heresy called the Manicheans, who regarded their founder Mani as a manifestation of the Holy Ghost. They were often recognized by their grim asceticism, their repudiation of baptism, and their observance of Sunday and Monday as days of fasting in honor of the sun and the moon. Despite Leo's careful eye on the Manichean forces and faithful, they were a powerful faith group, even at one time including in their ranks the young Augustine. Leo used the powers of the state to force them out of the city of Rome. The pope than appealed to neighboring bishops to help in his efforts. His action is probably the first known example of a Church-state partnership engaging in religious persecution.[4]

Leo emphasized the symbolic importance of marking the Church's presence with greater public spaces as testimony to the power and traditions of the faith. First, he began a restoration of the Basilica of St. Peter, which remained somewhat the same with some alterations until the major new structural edifice sponsored by Pope Gregory IX. Leo then created the famed Archway at St. Paul's Outside the Walls, and he built the church of St. Stephen on the *Via Latina.* Like his successor, Gregory I, he was associated with important liturgical changes as well.[5]

Leo held a very enhanced view of his office, seeing himself as embracing "Peter in Peter's see." He found that Peter's faith rested on the firm belief in the Incarnation and its definition of Christ the Son. In his eyes, what made Peter different from the other apostles was the universality of the authority of the Roman see. Leo employed that reasoning to intervene in the affairs of other dioceses, especially in nearby Italy and Sicily.

Leo's major biographer in English, Trevor Julland, finds that his view of the Petrine authority is direct and simple. But neither he nor his predecessors could prove its historical veracity. Still Leo exercised great personal prestige in the office and provided stability and a sense of permanence against the barbarians and the Byzantines.[6]

As metropolitan of the Roman Province, he dealt also with abuses regarding holy orders: especially the practice of ordaining men of inferior social standing, priests who were widowers, and the practice of usury. He opposed another heresy, the Pelegian heresy, which insisted that individuals were not tainted by original sin or needed grace. He argued, "Grace is not actually given *gratis....*"[7]

As a good bureaucrat, he was concerned about the organization of churches, especially in Gaul. The church was rather weak in northern Gaul and Britain, far from the Roman capital and the pope's sway. There is a vague tradition that St. Patrick of Ireland made a trip to Rome at that time to talk about the conversion of the Celtic peoples. As one moved East, the general authority of Rome was recognized, but Constantinople became the center for settlement of disputes, not Rome. It must be remembered that it was the Eastern Church then that provided the intellectual backbone of the creeds of the faith and some of its greatest theologians. The Nicene Creed, the very essence of doctrinal unity, was to a large extent the creation of the East and Emperor Constantine sitting in attendance. Today tenets of that council are still a part of the Catholic statement of theology said at every Mass. But the eastern patriarchs were concerned about the prestige of the historic sees of Constantinople, Alexandria, and Antioch in their competition with Rome. A great blow to Constantinople was the deposition and banishment of its bishop, Nestorius, and the establishment of Alexandrine Christology. The latter emphasized the union of the Godhead and the Manhood of Christ. That position was defended most particularly by Cyril of Alexandria, and was the view adopted by Leo in trying to explain the most complex issue of Christianity. Cyril prevailed, and so did Leo, and Nestorius became the patron of another forgotten heresy.[8]

Heresies and Invasions

At the synod at Constantinople, the Nestorian controversy continued, and Leo was much annoyed that he had not received a record of the proceedings of that group from the orthodox Catholics. As the matter progressed, Leo wrote his famed, "Tome to Flavian." He recalled Peter's famous response to Jesus who asked him who he was. Peter's response was a reassuring, "Thou are the Christ, the Son of the Living God." The see of Peter, the see of Rome, was the final authority on matters of doctrine. But as Bernard Green has argued, Leo may have misunderstood what he was criticizing. In fact, a more disciplined and clear treatment of the issue came as he matured in his treatment of the dispute. Earlier in the Council of Chalcedon, in 451, which hosted over 500 Christian bishops—more than any other previous council, and only a little short of the number at Vatican I in 1870—the overwhelming majority supported Leo's view. "This is the faith of our Fathers, the faith of the Apostle. We all believe thus, the orthodox believe so! Anathema to him who believes otherwise! Peter has thus spoken through Leo! The Apostles taught us! Cyril has taught the same thing! Anathema to him who teaches otherwise!"[9]

The essence of Leo's teaching was that Jesus had two natures: "inconfusedly, unchangeable, indivisibly, in separately." While Leo and his allies won an important victory in doctrine, the council seemed to give more authority and jurisdiction to the see of Constantinople, a development Leo opposed. It was another step toward the aggrandizement of "the New Rome," the eastern capital in the imperial court, in his view.[10]

Leo's refusal in approving Constantinople's religious ambitions, meant to match its new civic status in the empire, furthered the division of the two sees which widening a gulf that in 1054 became a total historical breach. Leo sought to intervene with the administration of the church of Constantinople, but he insisted that Rome needed to be "the guardian of the Catholic faith and of the decrees of the Fathers."[11]

Leo was also involved in setting the date of Easter, insisting that it must fall between March 22 and April 21, while Alexandria proclaimed that the end date be April 25. This was an old, weary controversy which to the Roman see was an important example of its authority. Leo tried though to pressure the Alexandrians, but changed his mind. The early Church had yoked the Easter date to the Jewish date set for Passover. Later there were erudite calculations of different calendars that affected Easter time.[12]

In 452 AD, the frightening news arrived that Attila the Hun was moving across the Roman landscape and then southward. The Roman civic leadership appeared increasingly lethargic to the threat. Leo, the defender of doctrine, now was forced to become an ambassador for the security of Western Europe. Soon the regally clad clergyman with a train of others, including some courageous senators, appeared before Attila. He was a barbarian, it is true, but he was no fool. He did not disdain other men's gods or their representatives. Meeting him on the outskirts of the city, the pope seemed most impressive as an unarmed holy man. Attila turned back from Rome, and a year later the Hun died.

Later the Vandals under Gaiseric (Genseric) landed in Italy and marched on the capital. The emperor moved on, and the city was totally defenseless, and was conquered. Again Leo met the tribal leader and got him to consider sparing the capital from fire, massacre, and torture. Still after 14 days, the Vandals plundered works of art, and other treasures. The large basilicas were spared, probably thanks to Leo, but the local churches were sacked and often destroyed. Finally after his death, Leo I was hailed as the Great because he like Gregory was the savior of his city.

He was a bastion of orthodox Catholicism, especially on the question of the divine personhood of Jesus Christ. He was not a great theologian of the caliber of Paul the Apostle or Augustine of Hippo. His theology was well-grounded however in the Scriptures, in the wisdom of the accepted Church fathers and the early councils of the Church. He praised the opportunity that the faithful have to go to heaven, denounced sin, did battle against a host of heresies, and emphasized what was the nature of personal expressions of charity. He believed in the power of hope and love, and was a frequent and eloquent orator, leaving behind for history some of his works of faith. His allies said simply, he fought "Satan and his deceits."[13]

CHAPTER THREE
GREGORY I (THE GREAT), (590-604)

The late sixth and early seventh century marked for Rome a period of deep decline and institutional decay. The population severely tumbled, and the environment was marked by famines and plagues. Politically, Rome has been labeled at this time "a backwater"—historically central, but removed from the mainstream of imperial policy and strategy. The Ostrogothic kings were in charge, and they tried to keep the old Roman bureaucratic system intact, continued policies of religious toleration, insisted on law and order, encouraged peace and prosperity, and struggled to establish harmony between the Goths and the Romans. The emperors of the east, especially Justinian, sought to re-establish imperial rule over Italy, but the conflicts and more famine took their tolls on the pope and the Roman Church.[1]

The Chaos of Rome
Amidst all that chaos, Gregory the Great was born of a devout and aristocratic Roman family, probably in 540. It was said once that he was a saint born in a family of saints. This era revolved around the massive attacks of the Lombard tribes, a collection of barbaric Germanic clans from Pannonia, ruled by an elective king, and committed to the Arian brand of Christianity. The historian Jeffrey Richards records that the city of Rome was visited by plagues, famines, soothsayers, magicians, and heretics. In terms of religion, Richards proclaimed, "From the profound to the trivial, paganism dominated everything."[2]

To counter that movement Catholicism began to emphasize even more the role of "holy men," their noteworthy lives and the work of saints as intercessors. Concomitant with the rise of saints was the recognition of relics of the holy life.[3]

In 590 Gregory gave a sermon in which he preached, "What happiness is there left in the world? Everywhere we see war. Everywhere we hear groans...Yet the scourge of divine justice has no end."

Gregory's family though was fairly affluent in the declining city. They owned a palatial home on Caelian hill and extensive estates in Sicily and in the neighborhood of Rome itself. He was related to a variety of popes, including his great-great-grandfather, Pope Felix III. He was well educated considering the time, probably trained in the law, but deficient in classic Greek. He believed that the liberal arts led one to a more accurate knowledge of God's Word. Gregory was in charge of the family estates, which turned out to be good training for when he had to manage the Holy See's patrimony. Gregory was probably a city prefect, or at least a city *praetor,* and exhibited all the behavior associated with the Roman aristocracy.[4]

He became increasingly influenced though by the monastic life at St. Andrew's monastery and may have committed himself personally to the vows of poverty, chastity, simplicity, obedience to the abbot, and soon Gregory came to believe that he had a religious vocation.[5]

But he was summoned by the pope, Pelagius II, to leave St. Andrew's and be ordained a deacon, probably in 578. He was assigned to be a papal ambassador to Constantinople. The pope desperately needed help from the forces of Rome and had previously appealed to the exarch in Ravenna and to the Frankish king. Unfortunately while in Constantinople, Gregory got involved in a theological dispute with the patriarch of that city on whether Jesus' body at the Resurrection was still palpable. In the end, Gregory was not successful in getting troops to protect Rome.

Servant of the Servants of God

The pope then asked him to negotiate with the Istrian schematics. Back home, the city was hard hit by floods and the plague, taking the life of pope Pelagius II who died in Feb 8, 590. In the ensuing conclave the electors (then composed of clergy, nobles and some lay people) turned unanimously to Gregory. To his contemporaries, he was a saintly ascetic and a model administrator, but he did not want the office, and he appealed to the emperor to veto his election. Gregory's brother intercepted his letter to the emperor, destroyed it, and simply announced to the emperor that Gregory was the elected choice, and the emperor approved it.

As he waited for the emperor's response, Gregory took control of the city, and appealed to God to accept the people's penance for their sins. For three days the populace prayed and sang psalms as a massive procession took place meeting at St. Maria Maggiore. Hearing of his election as pope and the emperor's concurrence, Gregory according to tradition fled the city, but was brought back to St. Peter's Basilica. He was a reluctant pope. He glumly concluded "the Emperor has ordered an ape to become a lion."

The Power of a Pope
His contemporaries said he was of middling height, was nearly bald, had thick lips and suffered from pain from his digestive system, probably due to his severe asceticism and limited diet. Despite his insistence on retaining and augmenting the office of the papacy, he was a man of humility and called himself, "The servant of the servants of God." Yet he could be waspishly bad-tempered with a bitter, sarcastic sense of humor. And like many clergymen, he loved gossip. One biographer has summarized him as a conservative, an authoritarian, and a legalist," an old fashioned Roman of the best kind—a devoted public servant and dedicated paterfamilias," He believed in discipline "since it is proper to restrain men from illicit deeds...the punishment system must be studiously preserved."[6]

He lamented as a true Roman the decline of the city and of the Western empire in general, comparing the city to an old eagle that had lost its plumage. He believed the end of the world was near, and he prepared for the Second Coming of Christ. He looked for guidance not in secular learning, but in the Bible and the works of the Church Fathers. He believed in mortification, good works, and contemplation.

Gregory insisted that kings, even if they had to be obeyed by subjects, and also other major church sees of Christianity, acknowledge the primacy of Rome. But he personally insisted on humility of the pope himself. Even Emperor Constantine the Great recognized his obligation to the Catholic Church when he concluded in 313, "You are bishops for all which is internal to the church. I am bishop for all external affairs of the church. It is the duty of the emperor to protect the church and preserve the unity of the church."[7]

As pope Gregory still lived the monastic life and his reforms of the Latin Church exhibited that policy and style. In 595, he instituted that commitment by excluding lay attendants from his residence in the Lateran Place. In making appointments he appointed monks, and Gregory removed all laymen from his councils. Gregory sent men with monk backgrounds on missionary expeditions. His major modern biographer, Jeffrey Richards, judged that these developments were "a decisive bid to reshape the papal power structure along monastic lines and to use the papal household rather than the burgeoning clerical administrative centre."[8]

It was the monastic influence that lent credence to mandatory priestly celibacy in the West. After Gregory's death, his successor returned the clergy to positions of responsibility, once monopolized by the monks. But his reign was short, and finally Boniface IV reestablished Gregory's policies. By the eighth century sole monastic control was over, but celibacy remained in the West as the standard practice.

With the decline of Rome, the city had to face the development that even imperial political power had moved to Ravenna. On one occasion Gregory insisted that the Lombards were kinder than the imperial governors in Ravenna, and once sarcastically called himself, "The paymaster of the Lombards." The pope ended up mobilizing troops, negotiating treaties, paying troops, and even directing the imperial generals. Necessity distracted him from his pastoral duties. It was essential to "prevent wolves from destroying the flocks committed to my care." He requested grain supplies from the officials in Sicily, and the church in the city ran its own food distribution centers. Gregory worried about the water supply system, and moved against corrupt imperial officials. Gregory even dealt with the issues of immigration and refugee problems in the region.[9]

Gregory curtailed the plurality of offices held by one individual in the Church. He gave out the substantial resources of the Holy See to the needy, often raising funds based on taxing more heavily the rich. Many bishops left their jurisdictions to run for safety from the invaders. In the diocese of Spoletto only one bishop was left. Some priests lived with Lombard women, ignoring the celibacy requirement. But by the seventh century, the Lombards were beginning to convert to orthodox Catholicism, and the Church's influence slowly mounted.[10]

Administration of the Church

In the time of Gregory I there was no codified body of canon law. There were collections of decisions of church councils, papal jurisdictional documents, and imperial laws which sometimes filled the gap. Gregory was committed to the traditional behavior and principles of the classical Roman juridical mentality. But also being heavily influenced by monastic practices, he insisted that southern Italy observe celibacy, making it obligatory for bishops, deacons and priests—a practice since Pope Siricus (385–99)—and for subdeacons (in practice since Leo the Great). He granted the palium (a woolen vestment with crosses worn over other vestments) to bishops as a sign of their unique office. He rigorously opposed any abridgment of the rights and privileges of the Roman Church, and deposed bishops for a variety of causes, including embezzlement, keeping concubines, and other acts of misbehavior. He even set up a special bureau to deal with troubling complaints coming out of the island of Sardinia. And Gregory, of course, made some major changes in the liturgy of the Mass. He was a fine administrator, and managed carefully the papal lands which were a major source of revenue for the Roman churches.

More contemporary historians have examined in depth Gregory's complex leadership styles. George E. Demacopulos argues that the pope's behavior sought to integrate his ascetic side with this pastoral theology into a synthesis that explains not just his personal temperament, but his far reaching attempt to reform the Roman Church. Carole Straw maintains that Gregory sought to promote a life of perfection especially emphasizing honesty. At odds with the Byzantines and the Lombards, the papacy became increasingly autonomous. Eventually the papacy undertook aqueducts, grain supplies, food distribution and hundreds of acts of personal charity. In many ways, Gregory retained the public service attitudes of being the urban prefect. He insisted on living in the world, but living a life of perfection in an imperfect environment. Gregory especially was concerned with the "shame-faced" poor.

At the time of his accession, there were fifteen separate patrimonies, and peasants on the estates were leaving as the entire city and its environs continued to lose population. The resident estates of the papacy were in Sicily, and food reserves were important to feeding the people and the upkeep of the Church. He was careful of the activities of his managers, "rectors," and Gregory extended his direct control by appointing clerics to administer them. In the midst of chaos and imperial neglect and barbarian upheavals, Gregory and his bishops became the main sources of local government the people counted on. The bishops listened to people's complaints, cared for the orphans, foundlings and lunatics, created public works and aqueducts, maintained law and order, and supplied food to the troops. Critics of the papacy have criticized its expansion, but it was not ambition but genuine practical demands and civic care which demanded its growth. Power abhors a vacuum. Bishops were selected by clergy, nobles and some faithful people with the first being the most important. The popes could influence and on rare occasions veto an election on canonical grounds, but it was still a local situation in many ways.

Gregory wrote a book on the ideal bishop, *Regula Paseralis*. Its themes reflected his values and his administrative preoccupations. The main concern must be the character of the candidate, "for no one does more harm than one who has the name and rank of sanctity while he acts perversely." He should be "solicitous for the safety of souls but also for the external advantage and security of his subjects." A bishop should be "dead to all fleshly passions, already spiritually; who disregards worldly prosperity; who fears no adversity; who desires only spiritual things."[11]

Outside of Rome
For the first five years of his pontificate, Gregory, was involved actively in intervention on the mainland of Italy. Some of the major dioceses such as Milan resented his intrusions. With all of these burdens, Gregory still had as a stark backdrop the presence of the Lombards. He pushed for a peace treaty between the empire and the Lombards, and moved toward the conversion of the Lombards to Catholicism. Gregory got little support from the exarch of Ravenna, representing the empire, and the pope left to his own devices paid the Lombard chief to withdraw from the city of Rome. But soon the Lombards returned, and they wreaked havoc on the farms and continued to do battle. Again Gregory resorted to a bribe, and the tribes returned to Milan. Unbelievable, the emperor castigated him for interfering in matters of state.

Gregory continued his policy of treaty and bribes, and he tried to get the Lombard king to convert to Catholicism. Some Lombards were Aryan, some were pagan, and some were just crude barbarians. To quiet the restive troops he paid them out of his own resources.

As with the Lombards, Gregory continued his evangelical efforts in Western Germanic areas and in England. In the North African provinces of the west, Pope Gregory had to confront another heresy—the Donatists in Numidia. At the time, the hierarchies of the Catholic and Donatist churches were "peacefully co-existing." Gregory tried to get the civil authorities to side with his church, but to little effect. Gregory took that laxity as due to bribery, saying that in Africa "the Catholic faith is publicly put up for sale."[11]

It is probable that Gregory was just not successful, but that in the mists of history Donatism just vanished. Papal authority was nonexistent in North Africa, and in at least one instance, Gregory got himself in a nasty confrontation over the choice of a new bishop there, and threatened excommunication to those who did not support his candidate.

Perhaps considering his high-handedness one can understand why bishops in Greece and the Balkans referred matters not to Rome, but to nearby Constantinople and the emperor. Meanwhile in Gaul, the Visigoths had concluded a treaty with the emperor and converted from Arianism to Catholicism. But they too kept the pope and his successors at arm's length. In 599, Gregory sent his envoy to Gaul to attend a church council, with the pope urging the delegation to oppose simony, concubinage, and lay ordination. But the outcome was unclear. He tried again in 601. The papacy was in these years also dealing with the tribes both in France and Spain in the empire.[12]

But the emperor lay in the east, and Gregory continued to insist on the primacy of Rome over Constantinople, and his opposition to the use of the expression "Oecumenical Patriarch" to describe the imperial capital. The popes insisted that Rome be the court of final result, in ecclesiastical disputes. Gregory sought to enlist the support of the Alexandria and Antioch dioceses in acknowledging he was the "universal pope." He called Patriarch John IV "Lucifer." Actually it may have been a misunderstanding. The title Oecumenical Patriarch was granted to both sees in the sixth and the seventh centuries when Gregory invited Constantive IV "to attend the General Council of the Church." The patriarchs of Alexandria and Antioch affirmed that Gregory was mistaken in the context the expression was used.

Although Gregory had respect for the east, there was little contact with that Church there. In a day of no mass direct communications, distance was the determining fact in the efficacy of messages. At times, Gregory had to accept the emperor's concerns even on dogmatic matters, like the so-called "Three Letters" which dealt with the Nestorian heresy (that Jesus was two distinct persons). Gregory tried to keep the emperor and the Church in harmony, knowing well his own weaknesses in a world of invaders, barbarians, heretics, and corrupt officials.

Gregory retained the general policy of toleration toward the Jews, whom he regarded not as a religion but as a superstition. Jews were not persecuted under Roman law, but did suffer legal disabilities. They were not to own Christian slaves, and the pope insisted on vigorous persuasion to convert them. With regard to dissident Christians, he was not above requesting imperial approved troops to deal with schisms. But even in Rome, paganism remained despite Christianity being the official religion. Gregory angrily wrote, "We are aware that, owing to the absence of priests, there are still pagans there, living like wild beasts and entirely ignorant of the worship of God."

The most famous episode involving Gregory's outreach occurred in Rome before he was chosen pope. He saw some fair-skinned, light-haired people from England, and observers remarked that they were beautiful youth and called them "Angles." Gregory said, "No, they are angels of God," and he asked the pope for permission to go and convert England, but the Romans objected. Eventually when he was pope, he sent St. Augustine to begin the missionary efforts there. The Anglo Saxons were pagans, who venerated Woden, the god of strife, and Thor, the thunder god. Gregory sent Augustine (pastor of St. Andrew's) and forty monks to bring the faith. Augustine became eventually the Archbishop of Canterbury. Gregory insisted that he adapt the accepted Roman rites to British customs. "For things are not to be loved for the sake of places, but places for the sake of good things." He felt that the

English needed converting, and the Frankish bishops neglected the task. The pope knew little about the activities of the Welsh or the Irish churches.

The conversations by Augustine and his colleagues were influenced by the practices of monasticism that Gregory himself was so devoted to. The origins of monasticism began in the deserts of Egypt in the early fourth century with a community of hermits adopting the Rule of St. Basil. By the end of the fifth century, monasteries became established as a respected way of ecclesiastical life across the continents.

Burdened with pain and just weary of office, Gregory died in 604. The truce with the Lombards was soon broken. He was buried in St. Peter's, as the city experienced famine again, and a mob moved to even burn Gregory's books in protest for their plight. Only in the ninth century was he rediscovered in Church history, although he was venerated by the English as "their apostle." It has been said that the "nowhere did he promulgate an original thought; he has rather persevered in everything with traditional doctrine." His correspondence gives amply witness to how he ran a complex multicultural papal administration. His major works shows that he was a man of profound Christianity.[13]

Yet Gregory's impact is in some historical ways more profound. From his reign to Vatican Council II, the basic outlines of the Church were set. His emphasis was on a highly legalistic, bureaucratic Church, one with complicated rituals, staffed by celibate men, led by a belligerent papal expression of authority, with an insistence that civil authority support the Church in endless disputes in the secular world. Yet it continued with its mission to serve the poor and vulnerable, often in various guises by very different types of personalities. For better or worse, Gregory I was a hallmark in the development of an institution for over 1500 years.

CHAPTER FOUR
GREGORY VII (HILDEBRAND), (1073–1085)

The increase in wealth and power brought forth the very worse in the Roman Catholic Church. The Church once so vibrantly healthy was seriously divided on matters of discipline and even dogma. Against the Church of Rome were duchies, kingdoms and empires of barely civilized semi-literate leaders. The Church sat in a crumbling city of Rome and had continuing conflicts with the eastern branch of Christianity.

By the end of the tenth century and the beginning of the eleventh, the Church was desperately in need of a new reforming pope, and found it in the personality of Hildebrand. A man of intense belief and implacable character, he was in the words of one of his major biographers, "the most hated man of his time." In that period, escalating chaos had led to three popes at the same time: Benedict, Gregory, and Sylvester. Finally from a church council concerned about the future of the Church, the faithful appealed to the pious and honorable emperor Henry III who called a new council to examine specifically the claims of the three pontiffs. A totally new pope was chosen, and yet controversy and counterclaims continued. Hildebrand, a young church administrator was appointed cardinal-sub deacon and rector of the monastery of St. Paul. He was a smallish built person, a homely figure who undertook important diplomatic expeditions on behalf of popes Leo and Victor. It was on one of those trips that he experienced the great reforms at the monastery at Cluny although he was not himself a monk.

The Reform Agenda

Hildebrand was an able administrator, but in that period the emperor used his influence to control the election of a pope and cardinal-bishops. Emphasis at the electoral meeting was re-directed to enhance Italian interests and to restrict elections to Italian candidates. Hildebrand's work at the time revolved around forging alliances with the Normans, both with William the Conqueror and the Norman forces in Southern Italy, but he was not a viable candidate for pope.[1]

From 1061–1073, the bishop of Lucca, Anselm of Lucca (Alexander II) reigned as pope. When he died, support built up for the election of Hildebrand. At one point, some of the populace in Rome actually cried out his name, "It is the will of St. Peter, Hildebrand is pope!" He was clearly startled at the vehemence of the population's support and the cry for his election. It was in his words, "the hidden dispensation of God."[2]

Hildebrand took the name of Gregory, out of respect for the great reforms of Gregory I, who by the eleventh century finally was seen as a saintly reformer. Hildebrand's election had not been initially approved by the king of the Germans, Henry IV, as was the custom of the time, but his name was finally accepted. Gregory moved toward firming up communications with various factions of the Normans then encircling Rome. He sought allies where he could find them, and was recognized by Richard of Capua who promised his fealty to the pope. But the Holy See's legions of enemies multiplied. Popes of this period calculated correctly that what they lacked in military strength, they could make up by using the punitive instruments of the Church against its enemies such as excommunication, an interdict, and a denial of salvation for the recalcitrant. But those tools were limited, and eventually resented by the faithful as high-handed and too secular for a pope to constantly resort to. The medieval popes could not accept the admonitions of giving to Caesar what is legitimately his. And the monarchs wanted to control their new nations, including the most powerful institution in it, usually the Church. They formed shaky alliances, like any other prince, especially in the disjointed and vulnerable Italian peninsula. As the papal possessions grew, the popes had to become more preoccupied with secular alliances. Even before Gregory VII, some popes took up arms personally, although not to the extent that the warrior pope and patron of Michelangelo during the Renaissance, Pope Julius II.[3]

The early great reform popes focused on two special abuses: simony and violations of celibacy. There were good spiritual reasons for opposing each, but there were also compelling political rationales. To buy and sell ecclesiastical positions and to allow the collection of Church offices gave tremendous leverage to wealthy secular princes, nobles, kings and later Renaissance merchants. In terms of clerical celibacy, it was frequently ignored by priests and even bishops in this period of Church history. Celibacy was a way for the Holy See and its hierarchy to control the disposition of land frequently given not to the Church, but to individual priests, for it was the priest who baptized and helped the wealthy face death.

Hildebrand was a pious, law-driven cleric who was the son of a goat herder, and like many self-made men he made his way up the ladder of preferment in leaps and bounds. As pope in the year 1073, he decided to launch a verbal offensive against the rulers of the kingdom of France, especially Philip I (1060–1108) for the practice of simony. He bluntly wrote the king of his "detestable guilt," in opposing the churches in his kingdom, and he eventually threatened to place the kingdom under an interdict (denying the sacraments to the whole nation).

But the attitude of Hildebrand, remarkably a capable diplomat when younger, generally exhibited a sour outlook toward life. "The rulers and princes of the world oppress the Church as if she were a vile slave. They do not cover her with confusion, but only they can satisfy their own cupidity." He also chastised the clergy who were more interested in worldly gain, in "presumptuous pomp and foolish expenses."[4]

To further his agenda, he called together a synod in 1074. The issue of celibacy immediately came to the forefront, for it was blatantly ignored in Naples, Milan, Rome, and especially in Germany. A married clergy was one of the bonds between the emperor and the Lombard clergy, so he was reluctant to antagonize them. Gregory's immediate predecessors had reaffirmed that principle of celibacy, but this pope just denounced its violations with a vigor that was pronounced.[5]

The synod in 1074 demanded that married clergy be banned from saying Mass. Lay leaders who employed such priests were to be excommunicated. That decision led to major revolt in some areas, for a married clergy had been the norm in some regions. In Germany, a local synod at Erfurt declared the pope "a heretic… a mad man. He would compel all men to live like angels." Some left the priesthood rather than abandon their marriages. The pope had called the marriage of priests "a plague."[6]

Battling Henry IV

In 1074, Gregory was approached about the possible absolution of Henry IV of Germany in order to seek some nominal reconciliation. Henry had only confessed to a few marginal offenses, such as "a lack of respect to the Holy See," simony, and to nominating unworthy persons to bishoprics. While that temporary truce with Henry was occurring, the pope continued his offensive against the king of France, calling him "a bandit among kings." He even encouraged King Svend of Denmark, to wage battle to force Normans out of a sea coast province.[7]

Gregory desired to create a Christian army to fight for control of the Holy Land. In one sense he can be seen as the first papal supporter of the Crusades. His dream was to conquer Byzantium, unite the Eastern and

Western Churches under one head, and drive the Saracens from the Holy Land. But by 1075, getting little support from the lay authorities, he recognized the futility of this ambitious plan.

The great epic battle that Gregory was intertwined in for years was his bitter conflict with Henry IV of Germany. The central issue was the question of "investiture" or the relationship between the secular and the religious authorities in the appointments of high ecclesiastical positions. As historian Arnold H. Mathew summarized it, "The German Popes appointed by the powerful Emperor could hardly hope to oppose the Imperial nomination of bishops." In one letter Gregory praised Henry IV as a "most glorious King" and cited his opposition to certifying the simoniacs and his support for clerical chastity, concluding that Henry's virtues shone with a brilliant luster.[8]

Henry wished to be crowned publicly by the pope as emperor. At first, Gregory seemed disposed to the arrogant monarch, but he first insisted that the secular authority had to recognize more the interests and honor for "St. Peter or us." Ignoring the pope Henry moved to appoint his own choices, even in the sees in Italy. Meanwhile, seeing his problems with Gregory, his Saxon critics compiled a whole list of alleged crimes committed by the emperor.[9]

Henry who was so praised by Gregory before, now found that the pope was demanding that he do penance for his sins or lose control of his kingdom in Germany. Relations deteriorated between the two, and to protect his position, Henry called a synod of twenty-six bishops at Worms. There was a synod four years later which certified that the pope was insisting on seizing offices and denying all right and all justice. Critics charged that the pope took powers granted from the grace of the Holy Spirit which belonged to the bishops, and had given scandal by his relationship with a married woman, probably Countess Matilda of Tuscany. Henry added now his letter to Hildebrand that he was no longer pope, "but a false monk." Gregory had threatened to rob the king of his royal power, to take money from the throne, and use the power of the sword to destroy peace, arming subjects against their rulers. Henry demanded that Hildebrand gave up the chair of St. Peter. He insisted that Gregory had denied him coronation as emperor and tried to deprive him of control over the kingdom of Italy. Both men saw their solution as simply the resignation of the office by the other. In the process, they had created one of the great power struggles of the Middle Ages.[10]

The pope's response was to excommunicate the king and to free all his subjects from obedience and allegiance. The consequences became an immense spiritual and political power struggle, and Henry faced more and more isolation. His subordinates worried about their own souls, and began to desert the monarch. The Saxon princes were especially delighted at the pope's decision. The exact source of a pope's power to depose kings was unclear—what the pope provided were scraps of historical precedents, including one that was an actual forgery. But Gregory insisted, "Why is the King alone excepted from the universal flock committed to St. Peter."[11]

When some princes asked the pope to come to Germany to settle a dispute, Henry seized the initiative. In the midst of a very severe winter, Henry crossed the Alps and appeared in the snow at Canossa dressed in the humble garb of a penitent with bare feet. Unexpectedly, Henry came seeking absolution—a request that no priest could ignore. For three frozen days he waited outside the castle, and Henry was finally absolved almost without condition. The triumph of Gregory was more complicated than assumed by some historians, then and now. And it also was one chapter in a long chronicle of disputes involving the papacy and secular authority.

One of the major sources of opposition to Henry was Rudolph of Swabia who had briefly married Henry's sister. He appealed to the pope in his battle with Henry, and Rudolph took the occasion of Henry's problems to have himself crowned. The pope did not seem to encourage or discourage Rudolph's random action. The pontiff wished to be an arbitrator in their dispute, probably more as a way to assert his own authority than to promote a cause or particular person. The pope abandoned his hope to travel to Germany and instead wished the dispute with the "two kings," as he labeled them, be resolved by his own papal delegates. Negotiations eventually gave way to more confusing disputes.

Endless Conflict

At a church council in March 1080 held at the Lateran, the participants laid out procedures for the election of bishops. There was also another discussion of lay investiture. A bishop would be elected by the combined actions of clergy and the faithful of a diocese without a "secular prince naming a candidate….a bishop, representing the Pope or the Metropolitan to direct…the election."[12]

At the council, an interdict was laid down against the Normans who dared to pillage the "lands of St. Peter." And once again the pope excommunicated Henry. He rejected his control over lucrative church offices, and went on to list Henry's crimes, but insisted that he would never support either side in the German strife. He complained that Henry had threatened to depose him, and to some observers Gregory' remarks had the scent of personal revenge toward Henry. After acknowledging Henry's disdain even after Canossa, he turned toward Rudolph's dubious election, but a few months after the pope's ban Rudolph died. Henry was to continue to retain his kingdom. The pope then prophesized that if Henry did not submit, he and his circle would be deposed after the feast day of St. Peter.

Henry's response was to call forth the prelates of the German church to depose Gregory and elect a new head of the Church. A synod at Brixen of thirty bishops denounced the "false monk Hildebrand." They rejected his method of selection as pope and his "insane fury." He inappropriately even wore a monk's habit. He intruded himself into the throne of Peter "by force, by fraud, and by bribery." Hildebrand, they charged, had made war to the death, sowing discord, permitting scandals and divorces, and even accepting heresy. Archbishop Gilbert of Ravenna was chosen as his replacement.[13]

Gregory who had so often denounced the Normans was forced to make a treaty with them, a group he had once excommunicated and labeled as "worse [than] Jews and Pagans." The pope patiently endured their possession of Salerno, Amalfi, and part of the Marches of Ferno. But the Normans were strong in the field, and Gregory needed their forces to prevail. Gregory moved to force Guibert out of Ravenna, and the Normans were back as allies. The pope then encouraged the bishop, the clergy, and laity to choose a successor to Archbishop Guibert who had gone on to be Henry's "pope." But Henry had different plans. He marched on Rome, enthroned Guibert as his new pope, and then in turn receive from that new pope the crown of the empire. So four years after Canossa, Henry re-crossed the Alps with very different results.

As Henry seized Rome, he still could not force Gregory from the impregnable fortress. Henry later retreated under the heat of the summer, but Gregory ended up at the Castle of St. Agnes. Henry called a synod and it excommunicated the pope, deposed Gregory, and declared Guibert his successor. His took the name Clement III. A week later Clement crowned Henry IV as emperor. One good deed deserved another! Meanwhile Robert Guiscard was advancing with his army toward Rome to rescue the pope.[14]

Facing these odds, Henry withdrew from Rome again, and the Norman army reappeared. The Normans brought hope immediately, and the pope and his entourage returned to the Lateran Palace. But Robert Guiscard's forces pillaged the city and murdered a number of the population. Some of the Romans were killed, raped, and even sold into slavery. The populace turned against Gregory, for he had abandoned the city to those allies.[15]

In one sense, Gregory had saved his beloved Rome from waves of barbarians. In the end though, he had opened up the city to his brutal allies to restore his regime from his long-time German foe. Gregory could not walk the streets of Rome without body guards. He ended up in exile in Salerno, and in May 1085 he died. Meanwhile Robert Guiscard was preoccupied with the idea of taking control of the empire in the East.

Gregory is supposed to have ended his life, saying, "I have loved justice and hated inequality, therefore I die in exile."[16] He was a superb rhetorician and had an extensive knowledge of theology. Sometimes, however, he seemed to lack a sense of good judgment and was often not a good analyst of character, a problem almost all of us have. He was firm, resolute, but at critical times he seemed to vacillate and was lacking in basic intuition about people at which he had excelled during his younger years. He desperately tried to restore the piety and integrity of the medieval church, and with the other reform popes, he often failed. Some felt that he was too severe in dealing with his enemies and too lenient to his friends. He had an exaggerated view of the papacy, which all Christians should obey above all others.[17]

He insisted on uniformity in method and in administration across a complex, disorganized Church. He tried to use the secular powers of the princes to keep his own priests in line, an approach that alienated his own fellow bishops. In Gregory's words he wanted a Church "free, chaste, and Catholic with the pope as unquestionably supreme." He opposed with all his efforts lay investiture, simony, and the marriage of clergy. He assumed the right to depose powerful kings, and the necessity of an alliance with the much maligned Normans against the German Henry which in turn led him into an impossible and self-defeating situation.

He lived in a word of crude, brutal, unbelieving barbarians. A man of God, even a man of great wisdom and shrewdness, will always be at a disadvantage in that sort of secular world. But even his failures were instrumental in setting the tone and philosophy of his great successor, Innocent III.

CHAPTER FIVE
INNOCENT III, (1198–1216)

Innocent III, the most formidable pope in history, was born Lothar dei Conti di Segni in the year 1160 or 1161 at Gavignano. His mother, Claricia, belonged to the powerful Romani de Scotta clan, and Pope Clement III (1187–91) was his uncle. On his father's side were the Conti of Segni, wealthy landowners from the Anagni region southeast of Rome, who were descended from a German family that had settled in the Latium area and prospered. He was probably educated at a Benedictine abbey in St. Andrea al Celio and was the second or a younger son of the family. Thus, he was destined for the Church, rather than being sent to manage the family's estates in the Romanga.

The Young Pope

In his youth the great center of advanced thought was Paris, where a university was beginning to develop and where St. Victor and Peter Abelard, among others, had acquired wide-spread visibility. Lothar was probably the first pope to have been educated in Paris, and he retained throughout his life a deep respect and affection for that nascent university, its academic traditions, and many of his teachers. During his stay, he crossed the English Channel and visited the shrine of the martyr St. Thomas à Becket at Canterbury. There the heroic bishop had met his fate defending the Church against the aggressions of a temporal lord, King Henry II, in the year 1170.[1]

What his exact course of studies was is unclear. He apparently had some knowledge of science and medicine as well as the expected philosophy and theology. There is also some evidence that he studied law at the university in Bologna between 1187-1189, by the end of which he had been made a subdeacon by Pope Gregory VIII (1187), during the latter's brief seven-week reign; later he was named a cardinal deacon by his uncle, Pope Clement III. After Bologna, he probably studied under

Master Huguccio of Pisa who was well regarded for his scholarly approach which linked theology with canonistics. Those studies and the work of other canon law experts seem to have played an important role in forming Innocent's conceptualization about the nature of the medieval papacy.

It has been argued that under Pope Celestine III (1191–1198) who was related to the rival Orsini family, Lothar's star was in descent and that he suffered a sort of political exile. Sometime during this period, he authored several commonplace essays on the misery of the human condition and the vanity of all earthly glory. No modern authority has come forth to praise those works, for they are not insightful or profound, but rather are a part of the general shopworn themes of devotional literature of the time.

The elder Celestine, who was elected at age 85, sought to name as his successor Giovanni of Sao Paolo, and even offered to retire to make way for him. But the College of Cardinals refused to agree and waited patiently for the elderly pontiff to pass on, which he did in 1198. Fearing interference in the election, the cardinals moved the site of the conclave to the elevated fortress of Septizodium of Septimius Severus and chose the youngest of its members on the second ballot.[2]

Lothar was only thirty-seven at the time of his election. Some nineteen or twenty cardinals participated in the choice, and they undoubtedly wanted a man of energy and learning to succeed the previous pope. One observer concluded, "Although young in age, he was old in behavior and manner, endowed with knowledge of learning and prudent by nature." The cardinals also needed to elect a man, preferably a Roman, who would be acceptable to the often fickle and vicious crowds in the city. Generally Innocent was little known outside of the Curia, indeed, one German chronicler exclaimed, "Oh, the Pope is so young! Lord, help your Church." After his election, the new pontiff himself is supposed to have objected to the calls, "weeping, lamenting and resisting them."

Lothar, in fact, was only a deacon, and had not even been ordained a priest yet, let alone a bishop. Six weeks after his election, within the four ember days according to Church custom, he was ordained a priest, and the next morning he was consecrated a bishop.

Innocent's relationship with Rome once he became pontiff started immediately with the populace's traditional demand for gold from a newly elected pontiff. The once proud imperial capital had become by the year 1200 a contentious village of 35,000 people. Innocent was unwilling to contribute at first, but he ended up yielding and giving liberally to them as he asserted his new authority. Immediately, he sought to establish his primacy by requesting the resignation of the city's prefect and having him formally take an oath of vassalage to the pontiff before he was reappointed. Innocent also required the single remaining senator of Rome to take an oath of vassalage to "My Lord, Pope Innocent."[3]

By February, Rome and the vassals in Campania, Marittima, Sabina, and Tuscany recognized his rule. He was the sovereign within the boundaries of the Roman duchy. He soon began to be seen also as an "Italian" patriot, and a check upon the ambitions of the hostile German house of Hohenstaufen, which under the recently deceased Henry VI had started to establish an empire in Italy, focusing on Sicily. Innocent was now the liberator of Italy, the bold new prince from Rome. Seeking to weaken any rival temporal power near him, Innocent III played on the sentiments of those in Tuscany, the Romagna, and the Marches to oppose the influence of the German nobles.

The history of Rome at this time was the history of violence, clan warfare, and endless intrigue. The democratic element, led by Benedetto Carushomo, supported the constitution of 1188 and opposed the pope's control over the Senate. They argued that the pontiff had "plucked her as the hawk plucks the hen." To gain their approval, Innocent reluctantly supported his city against one of its traditional enemies, although he had real reservations about the conflict. The pope declared his preference for Rome in its war against Viterbo, and his brother Richard lent money for Roman troops. Finally at the end of 1200 or the beginning of the next year, the pope brokered a peace which ended up subjecting Viterbo citizenry to the Senate and the Roman people.

As with some of his predecessors, Innocent relied on the power of his family and rewarded members with offices and riches, including extensive land holdings. Celestine III had helped to found the fortunes of the Orsini family, bestowing territories on his kinsmen which increased its fortunes until it went extinct in 1808.

The Vicar of Christ
It is rare that the leader of an established bureaucracy can define in very specific terms the jobs he holds and even mint the vocabularies that will be used in describing it. But such was the case with Innocent, who almost immediately on taking office, called the pope "the Vicar of Christ." That term had been used before, but never as unequivocally asserted in describing the papacy which had been termed more frequently "the Vicar of St. Peter"—an expression which even the powerful Pope Gregory VII employed.

Innocent went further in defining his position when he maintained that the pope was "the mediator between God and Man, placed below God but above men, less than God but greater than man." His rhetoric was so inflated that it is sometimes forgotten that Innocent was a rather conservative, even pragmatic, leader unlike some of the popes before and after him.[4] It is apparent from the historical record, Innocent III rejected the "two sword" theory popularized by St. Bernard of Clairvaux who maintained that God had not just given the popes spiritual authority, but also permitted them to grant temporal authority to monarchs. Pope Gregory VII would make this argument before Innocent's time, and Pope Boniface VIII (1295–1303) would assert it a century later. But the more moderate Innocent argued that God conferred temporal authority on the kings directly, although spiritual power was of a higher order. Only when there was some major unadjudicated conflict or when a question of "sin" was raised should the pope become involved in worldly disputes.

Indeed, Innocent was to maintain that an individual should obey his conscience, even when it was contrary to the Church's or the pope's views. However, that person had to accept the consequences of such claims if need be. And the pope acknowledged that the law of God and directives of the Church might be contradictory. In one instance, Innocent ruled that a wife's right to her husband's affections—a man who had also been ordained a subdeacon—was of divine origin, and thus took precedence over the Church's regulations on clerical celibacy.

The new pope was also quick to insist on the pre-eminence of the bishop of Rome over other bishops. In ancient times a bishop was seen as married to his diocese, and his ring symbolized that union. Innocent, however, maintained that God had permitted his vicar to dissolve such a bond, and he insisted the pope had a right to transfer bishops, or that he even could force one to resign. Even the most pro-papal canonists were reluctant to subject the bishops completely to papal authority. Innocent, in fact, had called bishops, and not just the pope, "Vicars of Christ," thus adding to the complexity of the debate. For the Catholic Church, though, its earliest decrees did not grant simple carte blanche to statements embracing ecclesiastical absolutism. The early Church especially had a strong tradition of apostolic collegiality that was a matter of historical and revered record. In addition, there were major strands of medieval philosophy concerning kingship that limited claims and powers. It has been said by historian Brian Tierney that by the eleventh century, though, the Church was "a rigid hierarchy of inviolable jurisdictions," which underscores both the centralizing and decentralizing components of that institution.[5]

Reaffirming the Papacy

Popes like other leaders have role models who help them understand their positions and enlighten them how to conduct themselves. It is probable that the young Innocent was rather familiar and comfortable with the views of Pope Gregory VII (Hildebrand). Those two medieval giants both faced somewhat the same problems in many ways and resorted to many of the same strategies and justifications, although they were separated by over a hundred years.

For a century and half before Innocent III, the Church had gone through a wrenching period of reform and serious schism. As historian I. S. Robinson has argued, before the middle of the eleventh century the pope was far from being an active leader of the Church. He was restricted to the local concerns of the diocese of Rome and was virtually ignored by the outside world. But in the period starting with Leo IX (1049–54), Alexander II (1061–73), and Gregory VII (1073–85), the reform popes moved to cleanse the Church of simony and clerical marriages and to assert more centralized and uniform control. Simony, or the sale of Church offices, was seen as linked to royal control over ecclesiastical appointments. The second great scandal was the three papal schisms that led to anti-popes and terrible public confusion.

Innocent III came to the papacy after the declining years of Celestine, and had to deal with some of the same problems that had preoccupied Gregory VII. He moved against simony, multiple office holding, clerical concubinage, laxity in the monasteries, and nepotism among other evils. In 1199 he wrote to Hubert Walter, the Archbishop of Canterbury, that his clergy with "their mouths watering for evil gains were panting after simony under another name, saying in effect that by changing the name of the sin the guilt and punishment could be evaded." As for nepotism, Innocent probably agreed with his predecessor, Alexander II (1061–73), who concluded "when God deprived bishops of sons, the devil gave them nephews."

Papal Laws

Innocent III was by training and by profession a curial bureaucrat. His legalistic style of expression and his world view were heavily influenced by the notion that the Roman Catholic Church was a hierarchy, held together not just by faith, but by law, precedent, and custom. Quite probably he was also a canon lawyer, and as pope he sat in judicial judgment three times a week. Some of his judgments are preserved, and one can see in them an alert, lively, prudent, and at times even humorist bent.

The ascendancy of the papacy and its centralization of ecclesiastical authority meant an increase in the power of the papal Curia as well. As with many secular kingdoms of the era, the origins of bureaucracy lie in the royal household. The papal household of the time included the chapel, chancery, and chamber which, according to historian Jane Sayers, became the Curia of the early twelfth century. The Curia functioned at times as a sort of supreme court, hearing cases and giving life to the Church's common law and papal decretals. The offices of government were at that time housed in the Lateran Palace, and the chancery became the specific office through which the clerks or notaries passed on papal documents to the outside world.[6]

Innocent also increased the power of the College of Cardinals who frequently sat with him to hear those cases. Often cases were actually delegated to cardinals, and other members of the college were sent by Innocent as his legates or ambassadors to foreign courts. The pope tended to favor men trained at universities and those who were monks. Nearly fifty percent of the thirty-two cardinals created by Innocent III were masters trained at the academy.

At that time, most of the laws of the Church were statements from the popes called decretals. Those declarations became for judges and scholars a sort of common law based on precedents. Those letters would be responses to particular legal points which had been raised by cases or controversies. The first major collection was compiled under the name of *Gratian*, and came out in the early 1140s in Bologna, the site of the greatest law school of the Middle Ages. Highly influenced by the traditions of Roman law, the Catholic Church also became a law-based organization. Thus, a legalistic pope met the right mood at the right time.

The establishment of a strong canon law system in Church courts also undergirded the power of the Church in having its clergy tried for offenses under its own system of justice rather than in secular courts. But the pope was not unaware of the abuses that undermined the Church. Innocent pushed for greater dedication on the part of local parish clergy in performing their pastoral duties. As noted, the pontiff especially fought the sin of simony and the lapse from mandatory celibacy in the West, just as Gregory VII had over a century ago. The pope also vigorously opposed clergy shedding blood in conflicts and disapproved of their involvement in the "ordeal" and the "duel"—primitive methods used in ascertaining proof from witnesses. The Fourth Lateran Council called by Innocent condemned those practices, and the prohibition by the Church added support to ending those barbaric practices in secular courts.

One of the major areas of legalistic activity then and now in the Catholic Church is the disposition of cases involving marriage. The Catholic Church has historically opposed divorce, although it has permitted various categories of annulment. Those disputes were especially important when they involved powerful monarchs. For example, Innocent considered the case of Philip Augustus, the king of France, who had put aside his wife, Ingeborg, who in turn appealed directly to the pope for support. In a powerful defense of Catholic principles, Innocent refused to accept Philip's justification and ordered him to take back his wife or be excommunicated. In 1201 the king capitulated, but the pope turned around and allowed Philip's children by his then current "wife," Agnes de Meran, to be declared legitimate. He also denied the request for divorce from one of his most loyal allies, Pedro II of Aragon. In another important case, involving Count William of Montpellier, Innocent outlined clearly that the pope was the final authority on matrimonial affairs, while turning down his appeal.

The pope sought to delegate more of the lesser controversies to others. As for Innocent himself, observers have left us the impressions of a witness watching the pope's activities. It was said that Innocent argued convincingly, was sharp on cross-examination, could be sometimes sarcastic in his observations, and had a genuine zeal for justice. He dealt with the rules of evidence and tightened up the standards for canonization as well

The ultimate expression of Innocent's bureaucratization was his calling of the Fourth Lateran Council. In April 1213, his bull *Vineam Domini* summoned a council to meet in Rome on November 1, 1215. The purposes of the council were the convening of another crusade to recover the Holy Land and the need to reform the internal operations of the universal Church. It has been estimated that some 1200 participants attended the council. The council went on to condemn the teachings of Abbot Joachim of Fiore, who had proposed that there were four rather than three persons in the Trinity, and also the heretical views of the Cathars and Waldensians. The council insisted that secular rulers and bishops had an obligation to fight heresy aggressively in their provinces.[7]

This council was the first in history to include lay representatives as well as clergy, with agents of Frederick II of Sicily, the emperor of Constantinople, and the kings of France, England, Hungary, Jerusalem, Cyprus, and Aragon attending. The council sat for only three sessions in two weeks' time during which seventy-one decrees were approved. The council re-affirmed the doctrine of transubstantiation and mandated annual confession and communion for all Christians. Clerical education was upgraded, and annual provincial councils were required. The council in a triumph of intolerance also insisted on identifiable clothing for Moslems and Jews living in Christian areas, and embraced other anti-Semitic expressions. And it forbade the establishment of new religious communities, preferring that individuals enter established ones instead, although Innocent III rejected that recommendation when he approved the new Franciscans and the Dominicans during his reign. As expected, the Council Fathers finally approved, with varying degrees of enthusiasm, the waging of another crusade, "the taking of the cross," as it was expressed.

Father of the Church
Innocent's autocracy was wrapped in a powerful paternalistic assumption that, as the father of the Church temporal, he was guided above all by the good of the flock. Innocent's behavior then was muted and transfixed into an ideology of care as well as command and control.

His world was one of authority, deference, and obedience. Of course, Innocent was pope during a time in which the Church was in ascendancy politically and socially, in which the threat of Henry VI had passed, and in which German and Italian nobles were often unable to reach agreements, and thus left the papacy less challenged. The question, however, is not that the pope prevailed because he was unusually powerful in the early thirteenth century, but why was he so powerful after centuries of papal weakness?

Innocent generally avoided the arrogance that seems to go with such broad grants of power, and he usually refused to personalize disputes. To achieve his ends, he was willing to excommunicate rulers, support their rivals, and declare interdicts over their lands and peoples. But he always welcomed, encouraged, and bargained for their reconciliation to the Church. He was slow to take the final step, to force confrontation, or to abandon diplomacy.

Innocent was a papal monarch, an ecclesiastical autocrat, a determined Church partisan at times. Like other popes of his era, he was even guilty of nepotism—in part to enrich his family, but more importantly to guarantee a dependable source of allies in the vicious Roman environment, especially in the early years of his reign. But again and again, he acted as a pastor, forgiving wayward kings, forgetting their previous betrayals, and blessing crowds in Rome that previously had cursed him and actually forced him once into exile.

It has been said that the Catholic Church of the thirteenth century faced a philosophical dichotomy best epitomized by the wily bureaucratic Innocent III and the devout simplicity of St. Francis of Assisi. But in fact, the pope after some misgivings approved St. Francis' new mendicant order and also encouraged St. Dominic and his Friars Preachers. It was also Innocent who carefully instructed the radical Humiliati how to garner the Church's (and his) approval. Innocent III saw himself as a true reform pope like Gregory the Great and Gregory VII, relying on religious orders, promoting the best aspects of monastic life, and encouraging religious fervor and enthusiasm in the Church within limits.[8]

He was not a philosopher nor a mystic; the office does not easily lend itself to such folks. But his authority, which could be powerful, and his judgments, which could be harsh, were cast in symbols and themes that accentuated not simply the corporate Church, but the Church faithful. In the *Gesta Innocentii*, he was described as being harsh with the disobedient and obstinate, kind to the modest and loyal, humble in prosperity and patient in adversity, a little prone to anger, but quick to forgive.

Innocent knew his responsibilities and promoted an even more aggressive papacy than was normal for that time. He was not enamored with the need to please and plead. He was a man of compelling logic who would take time, however, to explain his decisions. Innocent was by training a lawyer and man of decrees and decisions. But still he never misunderstood the culture of the leadership ethos of that era.

By its very nature, politics is grounded in limitations. For it is the bargaining, the brokering, the coalition building that is the untidy stuff of politics. At first glance, one can argue that Innocent III never had a need to acknowledge limitations or engage in bargaining. The history of his pontificate is the chronicle of such long and tedious negotiations with kings, princes, and prelates of his own Church. What is striking is the skill with which he played the game—a game he publicly identified with the greater glory of God and his Church.

Like any astute politician, Innocent III knew what his major resources were. His communications—written, informal, diplomatic and clandestine—gave him important leverage in any dispute. It is remarkable how often local and national bishops, when faced with the choice between disobeying their pope or betraying their monarch, chose the latter course. Such loyalty to the Church could prove very dangerous, as any devotee of the life of Becket could testify. Still, in a time when the life span was short and the swiftness of death easily witnessed, few Christian nobles and even fewer clergymen could sanguinely face the prospect of dying in an excommunicated state. And despite the powers of kings over their subjects, the threat of interdicting a region or a whole kingdom was a powerful deterrent to secular leaders.

But this pope was not just willing to use the Church's penalties to gain compliance, he was willing as a secular monarch, as seen in his control over Rome and the Papal State, to raise armies, hire mercenaries, build alliances, increase taxes, and even inspire the troops. These activities are most obvious in Innocent's first ten years when he gained control first over Rome and then over the old papal territories. And in his reign, he opposed kings and nobles in Italy, Germany, Aragon, Hungary, Norway, and even England. His threat of an interdict in the last realm brought King John to his knees in 1213.[8]

Among his many achievements, Innocent became the true founder of the Papal State. Surely before his reign, popes were involved in asserting and seeking to consolidate the patrimony that came to them from various donations—the most important being those of Pepin (754), Charlemagne (774), Louis the Pious (817), Otto I (962), and the lands of Countess Matilda of Tuscany (1102).

Almost immediately Innocent faced a power vacuum after the death of the thirty-two-year-old Henry VI in September 1197. Through the skillful use of anti-imperial sentiment and anti-German propaganda, the new pope quickly became the true heir of Henry in southern Italy. Innocent added to his sway by seeking to decide the dispute over the election of a new emperor, and then later claiming suzerainty over the kingdom of Naples. By the end of 1199, he was the guardian of Henry's young son, Frederick, the heir to the Sicilian throne.

The new pope was aided by the powerful position of his family and their extensive holdings in the Campagna region. He quickly demanded that the prefect, justices, and local barons swear fealty to his rule. He sent papal diplomats, or legates, throughout the patrimony to assert his interests.

Fearful of augmenting another center of power, Innocent initially abandoned Celestine III's support for the Tuscan League. The pope encouraged cooperation, however, with the strongly independent communes and tried to deal gingerly with the haughty Roman political establishment that he knew so well.

More important to Innocent was the need to garner imperial recognition for his conquests and re-conquests in the area. For this reason he supported Otto of Brunswick's claim over Philip of Swabia as emperor. Otto IV, as he became known, promised to respect the Papal States and also to protect the pope's interests in the future—guarantees he soon abandoned right after his coronation.

Such was the problem that Italians knew so well—that of having to trust strangers who are not part of the family. For this reason and for the usual reasons that other popes engaged in, Innocent supported his family—the Scotta—over the Orsini, Celestine III's relations. He relied on and promoted his powerful brother Richard, arranged a marriage between his nephew and Philip's daughter, and made his cousin a papal marshal and rector in the Patrimony.

In seeking allegiances, Innocent resorted to the heavy symbolism of the time. He demanded oaths of obedience from feudatories and officers of communes, heard petitions and quarrels, and established statutes for his papal subjects. He excommunicated his foes, placed hostile lands under interdict, and crowned his allies. On the occasion of the death of his one-time ally Philip, he pronounced that it was a divine punishment. He supported Otto at first, excommunicated him in 1210, and later moved to have him deposed. In 1212 Innocent recognized the claim of Frederick of Hohenstaufen as king of the Romans. In 1216, Frederick pledged that his son Henry would reign over the Sicilian kingdom as a papal vassal, so that he could lead the Fourth Crusade to the Holy Land, but by then Innocent had died in Perugia, probably of malaria. There he was laid out in elegant vestments and left alone. The next day his corpse was found stripped naked and decomposing, another example of his own youthful observations of how fleeting is all glory in this brief life.

It is clear that Innocent's overall objectives were two-fold: to assert the historical papal claims to territories by weakening potential rivals, and to destroy the influence of kings and nobles over Church appointments and operations. Critical to the papal strategy was the desire to have a veto or a check on the election of the German emperor—the descendant to the old Holy Roman emperors. Innocent argued that the empire belonged first and last to the papacy since it was Pope Leo III (795–816) who had the focus of that empire shifted from east to west. And it was the popes who historically crowned the emperors, making them, in the vocabulary of feudal times, pledged to the pope.

In the contest between Otto and Philip, Innocent frankly stalled as long as he could to avoid taking sides. The German princes who supported Philip resented the pope's eventual intrusion on Otto's side, but he insisted that while he respected their right to elect an emperor, it was the papacy that extended that right to them in the first place, and it was the pope who ended up crowning the emperor. Thus, they had to expect that the pope would consider the candidate's fitness before such an installation.

The pope was not, though, just another player on the international stage. He was often regarded as an honest and impartial broker in an age of increasing dynastic princes and vigorous aggrandizement. When Innocent told King Richard of England to release a prisoner, the monarch quickly complied. When his brother, King John, tried to interfere in Innocent's choice of the archbishop of Canterbury, the pope laid an interdict on the entire island and later excommunicated him, finally forcing the king to back down. However, the pontiff sided with King John in 1215 against the barons in annulling the Magna Carta, even going as far as to excommunicate them, but he was ignored.[9]

One well known example of the power and limits of Innocent was his call for another crusade to free the Holy Land from Moslem control. Such calls were not unique to Innocent, since the expeditions began with Pope Urban II in the year 1095. But Innocent commanded and supported, with Church approval, the establishment of a powerful fourth religious crusade headed by some major Christian princes. Instead of freeing the Holy Land, however, the forces encouraged, or were hood-winked by the Venetians, into capturing and plundering Constantinople. To pacify the pope, they promised Innocent that such a step would lead to the end of the great schism of 1054 and a reunion of the east with the Church of Rome. Instead of accomplishing those religious objectives, they ended up antagonizing the Byzantines even more.

He offered the traditional indulgences to Crusaders, flattered their leaders, pronounced excommunications on the venal Venetians, and tried to re-establish ties with the eastern Church. But far away from the action, he had little to offer, little with which to bargain. Constantinople saw itself as the "Second Rome," and its people and priests did not want reunion with the clergy of the West. The Children's Crusade in 1211–12 was the ultimate collapse of his dreams of bringing the Holy Land back into the fold.

The same political dilemma surrounded him in another action—his insistence on fighting heresy, especially the Albigensian movement in southern France. For nearly ten years, Innocent had warned, cajoled, and persuaded nobles to stop the spread of those Manichaean doctrines. Under his leadership, the Church began to insist that the secular authorities defend the faith by forcing the heretics out of their lands. While the pontiff had encouraged moderation, his legates became more extreme and supported the slaughter of the heretics. In 1207, Innocent ordered that the houses of the Cathars be destroyed and that their goods confiscated. And he bitterly denounced Count Raymond VI of Toulouse, who was not supportive of the pontiff, calling him a "pestilent man." It was a sign of the bankruptcy of missionary work that the pope and his Curia had to threaten nobles with excommunication if they did not vigorously prosecute the heretical and the unorthodox. In some ways, this brilliant pope of ideas became the godfather of the spirit of the Inquisition.

To support his causes, Innocent taxed the papacy, the Curia, the national hierarchies, and the monasteries. He supported his brother and his armies early in his pontificate and insisted that the local bishops use their influence to promulgate his policies and to underscore the pontiff's political decisions. His leverage and his bargaining powers were limited, for his objectives were so broad and crosscutting. Still, no monarch was as successful in creating alliances, supporting kings, and deposing or crippling authorities as Innocent III.[10] Thus, Innocent III had a variety of sources of power, as he promoted the political objectives of his office. Central, of course, was the august office, its symbolism, its history, its lineage to St. Peter, and thus to Jesus. The papacy had other more worldly advantages as well. The pontiffs had the only real international system of communication with its faithful clergy, its bureaucracy, its extensive written and respected statements, and its diplomatic legates. No prince or monarch could compete on that basis. The pontiff, of course, was capable of being moved by ambition or envy just as any prince, but he could appeal to a far more compelling and higher rationale—to protect God's church here on earth. No prince could compete with that vision.

In addition, the political skills of this one pope were rather obvious as nearly everyone acknowledged. Innocent III was a gifted politician, with a rather fine sense of timing, a good knack for publicity and command, and a sophisticated sense of delegation of authority. And as Machiavelli was to observe several centuries later, it is better for a leader to be feared than to be loved. For all of his achievements, the Church has never called Innocent "the Great" and never canonized him a saint. Like his predecessor, Gregory VII, he directed the major advances of the Middle Ages Church and lived too fully in the conflicts of the world.[11]

PART TWO
THE MODERN PAPACY

The medieval papacy represents the pinnacle of political, economic, and cultural ascendency. But power does indeed corrupt, and the Church went through waves of corruption, malfeasance, devotion, and true reform. More and more power shifted from the Church councils and the lower hierarchy to the papacy. From the Council of Trent sessions and into the nineteenth century, there were intense efforts at more aggressive reform, but the waves of secularism, liberalism, and political democracy were strong.

The Church had once provided the intellectual class with a vocabulary and a strong set of dogmas and beliefs that enticed the brightest philosophers and scientists. But the secular forces in the West created great discontent toward the powers and privileges of the Church. The actions of Napoleon Bonaparte and the post-Napoleonic worlds were often directed against the Catholic Church, even to the extent of imprisoning the pope. But the forces of genocidal war and economic depression in the early and mid-twentieth century upended the naive Western versions of inevitable progress, and gave way to terrible violence and the curtailment of tradition, class distinctions, and general civility.

The twentieth century will be remembered in the long annals of history for two happenings: the landing on the moon by the American astronauts in 1969, and the Holocaust in World War II. Together they shared the true dimensions of human nature: the emergence of science and its harsher sister technology, and the bloody parade of evil with its rawest human focus.

In all those times, institutions were destroyed, and empires crumbled, only the papacy continued on, but in very different forms. In these eras there are more credible sources for historians to understand these popes, so these sections are much longer than the earlier sections. And these popes are more relevant to our times than Gregory I and Innocent III.

PAPAL GREATNESS: THE TEN MOST IMPORTANT PONTIFFS

CHAPTER SIX
PIUS IX, (1846–1877)

The Catholic faithful like to believe that the inspiration of the Holy Spirit guides the secret deliberations of the conclave that elects a pope. Skeptics brush away that reassurance as romantic nonsense. But in the conclave of 1846, it must have seemed rather remarkable that a College of Cardinals, appointed mainly by rigidly conservative popes, would reject the reactionary candidates and choose one of its more liberal members to succeed to the chair of St. Peter. The recently deceased pontiff, Gregory XVI, had reigned for about sixteen years (1831–46). The Italian historian Adolfo Omodeo wrote, "Reactionary, stubborn, and inert, opposed to every sort of innovation, even to the building of railroads, Gregory XVI died after sixteen years of bad government, leaving a difficult heritage to his successor."[1]

In his time, Gregory XVI had established himself as a close political ally of the brilliant diplomat Klems von Metternich, Chancellor of the Austro-Hungarian Empire. Metternich sought to establish a conservative balance of power in Europe, restore the stability of the old order, and chase away the nightmares of the Napoleonic reign. In the process, he guaranteed the continuation of the temporal rule of the popes over the Papal States, which after 1815 included the Patrimony of Saint Peter's (most especially Rome and its environs), the Marches, the Umbria Region, and Romagna (or the Legations).

The Catholic Church in the eighth century had taken over control of the central part of Italy after the Byzantine rulers left the West, and the popes were compelled to look to the French princes for protection against the invading Lombards in the North. At the height of its temporal power in the thirteenth century, the papacy controlled most of the peninsula, including at times even Naples and Sicily. And later in the sixteenth century, the papacy was occupied by warriors, diplomats, and builders who helped restore Rome and further extend the papal sway. But as the glory increased, so did the taxes and the administrative problems, and by the time of Gregory XVI, the Papal States were seen as clerical monopolies riddled with corruption, nepotism, and unenlightened leadership. Gregory, in turn, proved to be a faithful ally of Metternich, and consequently denounced any evidence of democracy in France, Germany, and Italy. But as he left to meet his Maker for whom he so labored, his position was taken by a man with a different background, one who was thought to have a very different orientation toward the world.

The "Liberal" Pope

Giovanni Maria Mastai-Ferretti came from a mildly liberal home with parents from the lower nobility, who were termed "enlightened" within the context of those times. As a boy, he had suffered an epileptic seizure, but later seemed cured. After being educated by the Jesuits, Mastai-Ferretti was ordained and became deeply involved in pastoral activities, and worked for an orphanage. He then went to Latin America as an auditor, and became personally committed to missionary work. After he returned to Rome, he headed up a hospice, later was chosen archbishop of Spoleto, and finally was appointed to the more important bishopric in the diocese of Imola.

One critical historian, E. Llewellyn Woodward, bitterly concluded that while at Imola "he lived an easy, pleasant life and gained a reputation as an eloquent, emotional preacher after the fashion of the sugar-sweet practices of modern Italian devotion. The doctrinal liberalism of his neighbor, Count Pasolini, suited the bishop's sentimental, shallow nature, while the spectacle of the misgovernment of the Papal States confirmed his political views. His liberalism had no real aim, no intellectual foundation; it was as much a reaction of the senses as his later conservatism. His weak goodness of heart was joined to a curious vanity, a vanity which always claimed for itself a knowledge of a higher kind than was open to his fellows; as pope he 'felt' his own infallibility. He was never cynical because he never saw the consequences of his acts, just as he never seemed to regret his friends or servants after they were dead. He was always greedy for adulation; his emotional nature needed excitement, and this excitement was gained most easily under the stimulus of applause from the crowd." [2]

At first, the opinion of the time was much more positive from those who knew him best. Later during his reign as pope, it would change drastically. At the diocesan level, he proved overall to be a well-regarded Church leader, and in 1840 was named a cardinal, although the pope himself probably talked to him about his criticisms of the administration of the Papal States. He was elected at a two-day conclave in 1846, in part because he was seen as a moderate progressive, especially when compared to the leading alternative, powerful reactionary cardinal, Luigi Lambruschini. Metternich lamented, "We have foreseen everything except a liberal pope." The Master of Balliol in Oxford, however, called him "a capital fellow," while more conservative Englishmen called him "a radical pope," and "a pontifical Robespierre."[3]

Taking the name of Pius IX (Pio Nono, as he was called), the new pope seemed at first to live up to his liberal reputation. He signed an amnesty degree that released 1,000 captives held in the Papal States, and allowed hundreds of exiles to return home. The decree was placarded on the walls of Rome on July 17, and it marked a new beginning. Metternich observed in disgust that such an amnesty was a change of principles, and he counseled, "God never grants amnesty, God pardons."[4]

Previously, the Papal States had been run by an oftentimes harsh group of ecclesiastics and their sympathizers. More importantly, those areas were seen as battlegrounds in the political hostilities between France and Austria, which had dated back to the medieval rivalry of the Hapsburgs and the Valois in Italy.[5] Soon, the creation and the maintenance of the Papal States became a European issue, and it invited outside intervention. Some leaders of the revolutionary movements had designs on creating a unified Italy, and those attentions were accentuated by the beginning of a fervent nationalist consciousness called the Italian "Risorgimento," under the dedicated and fiery leadership of Giuseppe Mazzini, which sought to bring all of the peninsula under one government.

Pius IX had not learned a basic fact of political life—that liberalization generates greater discontent than it pacifies. It makes the unhappy more disenchanted, it recharges their negative enthusiasms, and reinforces their agitations. Moderate reform is more often killed by the extremes of liberalism than by the lumbering weight of conservative or reactionary sentiment. That is why the ways of reform are perilous and the careers of reformers short. But Pius IX surely saw that the reactions to the legacy of Gregory XVI had not made matters better—if anything, that form of repression had run its course. And so, Pio Nono began his turn at moderate change...at first. He appointed Pasquale Tommas Cardinal Gizzi as Secretary of State, and followed up with a commission on railroads—striking a very different pose from Gregory. The pope received plans for establishing gas lighting in the streets, creating a gas distillery, and supporting an agricultural institute. He enjoyed promoting scientific congresses in the Papal States, and was genuinely interested in school and prison reforms. By the end of the year, he had introduced tariff reform and established commercial ties with other Italian states, excused Jews from the onerous obligation of having to listen to weekly Christian sermons, reformed the criminal code and its courts, and supported the idea of guaranteeing the writ of habeas corpus. He even accepted a new law relaxing press censorship. It was an extraordinary performance by a pope.

Conservative Catholics, especially those in the Roman Curia, believed that the pope's spiritual power and autonomy were absolutely dependent on temporal control over a nation-state. Thus, the Papal States took on an importance that is now difficult to comprehend. The Papal States were in part a consequence of the long history of disunion that characterized Italy for centuries. That peninsula was a collection of independent republics, duchies and kingdoms that had resisted the centralizing monarchies that unified such disparate nations as Great Britain, France, Spain, Portugal, the Austro-Hungarian Empire, Sweden, and Czarist Russia, among others. Only Germany was as fragmented as Italy. The major components of what was Italy in 1846 were Piedmont with Sardinia and Savoy; Lombardo and Venetia; Parma; Tuscany; Modena; Lucca; San Marino; the Kingdom of the two Sicilies (the Naples region and Sicily); and in the geographic middle, the Papal States.[6]

Clearly, the new pope was a decent and amiable man, one who seemed to be a liberal at heart—but so did his predecessor, Gregory, who initially had come into office as a tolerant scholar and monk. The nature of the Papal States, however, required that the popes and their diplomats protect their temporal possessions, which were seen as essential to the integrity of the Church. The sovereignty over the Papal States was an outgrowth of the pope's spiritual primacy, even though he was also concerned with the policies of governments all over the world, especially in the areas of education, marriage regulations, and compulsory military service.

The Perils of Reforms

Ironically, the papacy and its enemies shared the same view about the necessary ties between politics and religion. Nearly a half century after the French Revolution, the Italian nationalist Giuseppe Mazzini would still view politics as a continuation of religious concerns. And Napoleon III, Camillo Cavour, and Otto von Bismarck may all have talked about the separation of church and state, but in fact they meant the subordination of the former to the latter. They even continued to flirt with control over clerical appointments and church pronouncements, closing convents, or even launching in 1871 a major attack on the Catholic Church in Germany called the *Kulturkampf*. Thus, it is not that the popes had an obsolete view of the desirability of the union of church and state, which was a mistaken retread of the glory of the past. The pontiffs understood all too well that many of the major secular states and their leaders also preferred dominance in the relationship, and they could not agree to that.

In those battles to preserve the assets of the Church, the papacy was rather flexible in furthering its objectives. As Pio Nono said, he was indifferent to "the forms of government." At times the papacy supported conservatives, but in France for example, the Holy See embraced the so-called Ultramontanists, who were anti-Gallican. The Ultramontanists (believing that the power of the papacy extended beyond the mountains past Northern Europe to Rome, thus the name) were generally liberal and opposed the Gallican, or nationalist, French church leaders who in turn supported the conservative authorities. [7]

Support for the Papal States was a part of a larger strategy which had religious as well as political implications. Criticisms of papal administration, however, had intensified over the years, even from the new pope, Pius IX, when he was bishop. Between the death of Pius VII in 1823 and the election of Pius IX in 1846, there were three other pontiffs: all of those men were preoccupied with the problems of papal restoration and the increasing difficulties in administering the Papal States. In 1831 the great powers of Europe formally asked the papacy to begin to liberalize some of its restraints in the States.[8]

In choosing the role he was to play, Pius IX was influenced, it was said, by the tome of Abbe Vincenzo Gioberti titled *Primacy* or *Ile primate morale e civile degli Italiani*. That priest from Turin saw the papacy as the center of what would be a new unified Italy, which would govern with the rulers of the Piedmontese monarchy. Under the presidency of the pope, the new state would embrace a federation of "consultative monarchies." In the end, the Risorgimento moved to accept that king, but abandoned the papacy as the nationalists embraced the revolutionary calls for unification, pushed by Mazzini, Cavour, and Giuseppe Garibaldi—the agitator, the diplomat, and the general, who finally created the new state.[9]

As noted, in the beginning, the pope was viewed as a liberal. In April, one witness saw a colorful procession with the approving citizens in Rome chanting *viva pio*, just one expression of his great popular support. The conservative statesmen were clearly uncomfortable with him, especially in Austria—a nation that had proven such a loyal son in protecting the papacy and its temporal claims over the years.

One of the major reforms announced in the Papal States was the introduction of some laymen into positions of authority. Obviously, the clergy were by their very nature and training more literate, and more worldly than many of the lay people, but there was increasingly a sentiment—especially among the Roman populace—that their problems would be dealt with more effectively if the role of churchmen was limited. In June 1847, the pope in response formed a Council of Ministers, but made no mention of lay Ministers of State, which some had hoped for.

However, in April 1847, he had invited lay representatives from the provinces to meet with him and to discuss the formation of a Consultative Assembly at Rome. The announcement was greeted with great enthusiasm in the streets of the city. Much later on October 14, the pope finally announced the formation of a council of twenty-four individuals to be elected indirectly. Although it was as the name implies only consultative, the Assembly could bring matters to the attention of the Council of Ministers. In addition, the prohibitions on a free press were lessened and a municipal government for Rome was established. The new Council of Ministers would have only one guaranteed position for a cleric—the Cardinal Secretary of State who would be responsible for foreign affairs. For all the other positions, lay people would be eligible to be ministers.[10]

The progress seemed remarkable, but what the populace did not realize was that in Pio Nono's view, these were the limits of his reform agenda. And he was clear on that point. He insisted on retaining the final power in the pope's hands, and on being the real head of the Papal States that he had inherited. Like many modern secular statesmen, he came to realize that the least traveled road is often the middle one—especially in explosive Italy in the late 1840s where the political universe was divided into two groups: committed reactionaries and revolutionary liberals.

Crowds that were marching and singing the pope's praises initially were also demonstrating against the Bourbons, or the Austrians, or whomever. Some of these individuals simply wished to participate in the great liberal reforms that were sweeping across the English-speaking world, some were still at heart liberal followers of the first Napoleon; others like the Italian Carbonari or the Mazzinians, wished for genuine revolution and the forcible union of the Italian states.

The conservative German Prime Minister Metternich continued to worry about the state of affairs in Italy, and on July 17, 1847, his forces moved into Romagna, Italy, without notifying his ally. The pope regarded that offensive as an insult and a hostile act directed both at him and at Italians in general. Then, rather remarkably, Pius appealed directly to the peoples of Europe against the outrage. When the Austrians would not yield, he threatened to break off diplomatic relations with them, to excommunicate Catholic Austrians, and to appeal to Italians to expel the invaders!

Suddenly it was the pope—the "Patriot Pope"—who was being hailed throughout the peninsula. Mazzini, who was anti-clerical and anti-papacy, wrote from England an obsequious open letter to Pius. "There is no man I will say in Italy, but in Europe, more powerful than you. You have, therefore, Most Blessed Father, immense duties: God measures them in accordance with the means which he gives to his creatures...humanity cannot live without heaven. The social idea is none other than a consequence of the religious idea. We shall, therefore, have sooner or later, religion in heaven." He then argued that the pope must believe in the nationalist cause and unify Italy in order to "achieve great, holy, and enduring things." Later, when the pope did not obey his prescriptions, he would unleash his effective, vitriolic rhetoric on the pontiff. In the end Mazzini would be hailed as a liberator of Italy, while Pius would become a prisoner in the Vatican.[11]

But for a time, Pio Nono seemed to encourage many in the Italian nationalist movement. On December 16, 1847, the Austrians left, and the pope emerged in triumph. Metternich, observing the situation, wrote to his ambassador in Paris, "Each day the pope shows himself more lacking in any practical sense. Born and brought up in a *liberal* family, he has been formed in a bad school; a good priest, he has never turned his mind toward matters of government. Warm of heart and weak of intellect, he has allowed himself to be taken and ensnared, since assuming the tiara, in a net from which he no longer knows how to disengage himself, and if matters follow their natural course, he will be driven out of Rome." As harsh as it seems, he was correct in his prophecy. Later Metternich was to say, "A *liberal* pope is not a possibility. A Gregory VII could become the master of the world, a Pius IX cannot become that. He can destroy, but he cannot build. What the pope has already destroyed by his liberalism is his own temporal power; what he is unable to destroy is his spiritual power; it is that power which will cancel the harm done by his worthless counselors. But to what dangerous conflicts have not these men exposed the man and the cause they wanted to serve." Later, Metternich said in a similar vein that the realities in 1848 had lifted the many veils that people had hidden behind, and of Italy, "The veil is liberalism; it will disappear in Italy, as in every other country, before radicalism and action."[12] To Metternich and his fellow believers, political revolution would lead to social revolution which in turn would result in immense catastrophe for all involved.

The pope came to accept the view that he could play a prominent role in a modest federation that could lead to a united Italy. In August 1847, he actually proposed a customs union similar to that in the German states. Major opposition to those initiations, however, came from King Charles Albert of Piedmont, who decided to wage a war against the Austrians, and thus unite at least northern Italy under his aegis.

In early January 1848, revolution broke out in Sicily, and soon Naples followed suit, and the pope was being cited as a supporter of liberation. In February, he issued a statement proclaiming the papacy as a rock of stability during those tempestuous times, and the next month he came forth with a constitution for Rome. The document established what was in effect a limited monarchy under the pope, and protected the rights of the Church and its officials.[13]

In March, Metternich was toppled from power in Vienna, and later the population of Milan rose up and drove the Austrians out of their city. King Charles Albert declared war on March 24, and the papal army moved toward the northern frontier to defend the state against any Austrian counter invasion. Pio Nono, however, stopped any aid to the Piedmontese, and insisted that his forces would not be involved in belligerent actions against the Austrians—a defensive policy traditionally held by many of his predecessors. He was the ecclesiastical head of a Church that embraced a variety of nationalities, and it was the position of the papacy that force could be used only for self-protection.

Although he had been proclaimed a blossoming revolutionary, Pio Nono was quick to distance himself from the radical ideas of Mazzini's adherents. He formally criticized the extremists in 1848, and dismissed any allegiance to what was becoming the Risorgimento. Consequently, he was seen not as a breath of fresh air, but as another reactionary pope. Now he had alienated the traditional protector of the papacy—Austria—and also disillusioned the liberals by refusing to go to war. Meanwhile, Charles Albert suffered defeat, and the dream of Piedmontese domination vanished, at least for the moment. To many it seemed that only the Mazzini radicals could deliver on the struggle for Italian unification.

After several false starts, the pope chose Count Pellegrino Rossi as premier for his new government—a one-time radical who was determined, however, to protect the Papal States. He believed in the pope's vision of a federal league with the pontiff as president. That policy ran headlong into the ambitions of the "Young Italy" partisans and Mazzini's revolutionary objectives. As for the pope, only a year after his much celebrated ascendancy, he was himself disillusioned and also disillusioning to the nationalist elements who saw him at first as a beacon of secular reform, and also as an ally in their anti-Austrian foreign policy. As Rossi sought to wind his way through the thickets of ambition, nationalism, and personal hatreds, he approached the Chamber in Rome on November 15.

Like Julius Caesar, he had been warned to stay away from the legislative body that day, and as he walked up the steps to the council chamber, he was murdered by Luigi Brunetti, the son of a Mazzini adherent. The rabble began to mingle with the carabinieri which led some to conclude that the beginnings of this revolt were carefully planned. Even the noble Garibaldi praised the act of treachery, comparing it to the assassination of Caesar by Marcus Brutus.[14] In the cause of revolution all can be forgiven.

The radicals subsequently sought to call a gigantic demonstration the next morning, and then to demand that the council declare war and establish also the separation of spiritual and temporal authority in the Papal States. But the pope stood in the way and instead quickly called the Chamber and the high council together and named a new prime minister. Soon the crowd forced the Swiss guards to disband and installed the Civic Guard in the Quirinal. The pope became a prisoner of the radical elements in his own Papal States.

The Bavarian ambassador, Charles Spaur, prepared to spirit Pio Nono away to Gaeta where a Spanish ship would take him to the Balearic Isles. Dressed in the garb of a simple priest and carrying the Sacred Host, the pope escaped through a secret passageway to a waiting carriage that traveled past the Lateran gate to a modest hotel in Gaeta, and then to a royal palace. There he remained, waiting for support from the Catholic monarchs and the Catholic populations in Europe.

The End of the Papal States
Meanwhile in Rome the nationalists voted to establish a republic and end the temporal power of the pope. On February 12, Mazzini, who was actually born in Genoa, was made a Roman citizen and his motto "for the name of God and the people" was promulgated. For a brief time, this revolutionary became one of the triumvirate chosen to rule the new state. Supporting the republic was the general of the armies, Guiseppe Garibaldi, one of the last of Europe's truly romantic figures, who arrived mounted on a white horse and dressed in a tattered red shirt, the symbol of his fighting men.

From November 24, 1848 until April 12, 1850, the pope took refuge in Gaeta in the Kingdom of Naples, when a French expeditionary force and European diplomacy finally prevailed against the revolution and the republic floundered. On February 18, 1849, the pope appealed directly to the Catholic regimes for assistance. The Spanish were ready, but Piedmont and Austria were opposed to Spanish intervention. Naples was also prepared to assist, as was Austria, but on its own terms. France, however under the duplicitous leadership of Bonaparte's nephew, Louis Napoleon (later Napoleon III) was not initially supportive. The Catholic regimes were more concerned about each other having an advantage in Italian affairs than in restoring the pope to his temporal authority. As noted, Charles Albert had abruptly sent his Piedmontese army into battle against the Austrians, but on March 23 his forces were decisively defeated at Novara. Eventually he would abdicate in favor of his son Victor Emmanuel, who ironically would become an ally of the pope initially, and then the first king of a unified and secular Italy.

But the consequence of Austria's victory was that France now feared the former's strength in Italy; thus the French government on April 20 dispatched a force of 9,000 men aimed at restoring the pope to power. The French troops, led by General Wichdas Oudinot, marched toward Civitavecchia and did battle with Garibaldi's legions, and later prevailed when they introduced more forces into combat after a series of deadlocks. The republic however continued, and soon outrages were reported against the clergy, along with sacrilegious treatment of Catholic rites and rituals. It seemed to some as if it were the French Revolution all over again. Even the British Queen Victoria sent the pope a note of sympathy, and the English, who loved Garibaldi and allowed Mazzini sanctuary in their land, now praised the so-called *liberal* pope.

The telling issue was the genuine sympathy of the French Catholics, many of them leftists, who pressed for a restoration of the Papal States. Consequently, the French moved to occupy Rome, staying until 1870. In the process of exile, restoration, and beyond, the pope seemed to turn more to the Jesuit order as the years passed. He manifested his allegiances by beatifying the Jesuits Peter Claver on July 16, 1850; John deBritto on May 18, 1852; Andrew Bobola on July 5, 1853; and Peter Canisius on August 2, 1864.[15]

By April 1850, the Italian Republic was routed and the pope was restored to his see in Rome, and also to his throne as the virtual monarch of the troubled Papal States. The pope returned as he left—through the Lateran Gate at 4:00 p.m. on April 12, 1850. His main advisor was a cardinal who had stood by him through his turmoil—the shrewd and calculating Neapolitan peasant-layman Giacomo Antonelli, who became his trusted Secretary of State.

Eight months had elapsed between the collapse of Mazzini's republic and the pope's triumphal return, and in the interval the state was run by three cardinals and the French army. After some difficult decisions were made and some punishments meted out, the pope came in and carried out modest reforms. He created a Council of State, pushed for elected provincial and municipal councils, introduced more laymen into the administration, and allowed only a small army to be maintained. Eventually the pope's ministers cut the public debt, pushed for railroad connections in the Italian peninsula, and held down taxes.[16]

Still, some of the causes of the turmoil remained. In the late 1840s and beyond, Italy and other parts of Europe faced grain shortages and hunger, price gouging, hoarding and speculation. In addition, the pope's difficulties were compounded by the beginning of a more aggressive administration in the Piedmont kingdom, with its new master, Camillo Cavour.

Through guile and duplicity Cavour would establish himself as a totally unscrupulous and extremely able diplomat who struggled to force another war in Europe so as to consolidate the hold of Victor Emmanuel's House of Savoy over all of northern Italy. Remarkably though, by 1860, he came to see that Garibaldi controlled southern Italy, and that the general could be persuaded to relinquish his dictatorial title and pledge his fealty to Victor Emmanuel as king. Thus, the stage was set for the control of virtually all of Italy, except for Venice and Rome. Soon the Papal States, with the exception of the Eternal City, fell to the Risorgimento. And by 1860, the pope was once again a prisoner in the Vatican—a king without a kingdom, a religious leader who insisted on calling down God's intercession on temporal politics. But that was all ahead of the pope as he returned to power in 1850, with a more guarded attitude toward liberalism, and what he saw as its inevitable allies—secularism and anarchy.[17]

During his extraordinarily and eventfully long reign, Pio Nono laid the groundwork for the modern papacy. His initial embrace of liberalism, his exile and triumphal return, his long battle against the forces of the Italian Risorgimento are all dramatic historical events, especially when played against the contrasting and colorful backgrounds of Mazzini, Garibaldi, Cavour, Napoleon III, Victor Emmanuel, and other nineteenth century historical giants. But Pio Nono was pope, and it is in his critically important ecclesiastical changes that his leadership is so apparent. His critics later said that Pio Nono learned his lesson and turned bitterly reactionary, both in politics and in his expressions of theology. But in fact, neither was true. As has been seen, the pope never posed as a friend of secular liberalism; as a reformer in temporal matters, he would only go so far, which is where he went during his first year in office. And this pope was a genuine Italian nationalist who shared many of the resentments about foreign occupation, especially against the

Austrians. Years later, he was to remark admiringly that he and Garibaldi were the only two people who had not gotten anything out of the Risorgimento. Unfortunately, Pius IX continued the repressive policies of his predecessors who re-took the Papal States after Napoleon's libertation. He even on one public occasion called the Jews "dogs." In 1858, the pope sided with the forces of the anti-Semitic Italian Inquisition, and refused to return Edgardo Mortara of Bologna who had been allegedly baptized in secret as an infant by his family's servant and was considered a Christian. Despite pleading from family and Jewish leaders across the world, the stubborn pontiff supported the child being raised a Catholic and later becoming a priest.[18]

Still, it must be admitted that he returned from exile far less likely to dally with the agendas of reform—progressive or moderate—than he was in the early months of his pontificate. His enemies, and later most historians, would see his condemnations of modern ideas and his support of the doctrine of papal infallibility as examples of a severe turn to the forces of reactionary politics. But to a large extent, those orientations were a long time in the making, both for this pope and for the Catholic Church. Like him or spurn him, Pio Nono was the father of the modern papacy, and not since the Council of Trent (1548–63) had the Church appeared more at peril and yet also more influential.

Even after his restoration and with all the spiritual reserves of authority he embraced, the pope's major undoing became the nearly irresistible urge of many of the educated populace for Italian unification. In this great battle he came especially into direct conflict with the designs and diplomatic skill of the Piedmontese prime minister. Camillo Cavour was born of Swiss, French, and Italian background, raised in an aristocratic family, and made wealthy by inheritance and his wise management of the family estates. At the age of thirty-eight, he became a political figure, and within five years he was named prime minister of the Piedmont-Sardinia kingdom called the House of Savoy. His overall objective was to extend Piedmont's control over most of northern and central Italy, and in fits and starts he used the strengths and the weaknesses of his state to encourage, instigate, and scheme for a major European war to destroy the Austrian empire. He would both meet clandestinely with Garibaldi and publicly attack Mazzini's radicalism in order to encourage Napoleon III to support the Piedmont cause as the more moderate and dependable way to guarantee France's influence in Italy.

As a young man, Cavour had indulged occasionally in revolutionary European rhetoric, but his real heroes were conservative English statesmen such as Robert Peel and especially William Pitt the Younger.

He attacked the Church relentlessly, and was excommunicated by the pope, but made sure that when he faced death he would have a sympathetic priest there to give him the last rites of the Church.

Over the years, Cavour argued that the Church controlled too much of the property and riches of the kingdom. There were 10,000 priests in Piedmont and almost as many monks and friars, one for every 200 people. In Sardinia the ratio was 1:127. There were 10,000 religious foundations, and the state contributed an additional one million lire a year for clerical incomes. Cavour's response was to end the subsidies, abolish any monastic orders not devoted to education or charity, end medicant orders that begged for their upkeep, and foster other anti-clerical measures.[19]

Key to his policy on unification was the need to court the fickle Napoleon III, the only hope Cavour had to break both Austrian and papal control over the upper part of the peninsula. He even convinced Victor Emmanuel to give his fifteen-year-old innocent daughter, Clotilde, to a profligate nephew of the emperor Napoleon. When an associate demanded to know how he could justify sending her to such a voluptuary, Cavour simply observed, "Oh, what scoundrels we would be, if we did for ourselves what we do in the name of Italy."

Still the king, Victor Emmanuel, retained a personal affection and regard for the pope, and his family respected the Holy Father and the tenets of the faith. But it was Cavour who would set the tone of the House of Savoy and its foreign policies from 1852 to his death in 1861. One of Pio Nono's major biographers, E. E. Y. Hales, concluded that the pope's hostility toward the onslaughts of the Piedmont regime and the broader Risorgimento laid the groundwork for his hostility toward what was defined as "progress," and resulted in his controversial encyclical, the *Syllabus of Errors*. Hales further argued that Pius' reign was a study of the relations of politics and religion, "The defeat of Mazzini's Roman Republic in 1849 was a check to the political aspiration of Mazzini and Garibaldi, but it was also a (temporary) victory for the papacy over Mazzini's religion of the people. Cavour's victory in closing the Piedmontese monasteries was the prelude to his assuming political sovereignty over the Papal States. Napoleon's planned withdrawal from defending Rome in 1864 provided the occasion for the issue of the notorious religious-political document—the *Syllabus of Errors*. The errors of that *Syllabus* were largely Cavour's, Mazzini's, and Napoleon's errors."[20]

Cavour's policies would result in both the end of the Papal States and belligerent attacks upon the prerogatives of the Church. It is easy to sympathize with his slogan of "a free church and a free state," but the premier more often advocated a campaign of anti-clericalism, ad hominem attacks on religious orders, and a genuine denigration of the spiritual worth of the ecclesiastical way of life. The pope saw the Papal States as a part of the heritage that he was sworn to uphold, and he was committed to protecting Church property. To him, it was "the robe of Jesus Christ," a part of the Passion of the Lord that he was pledged to guarantee. He wrote Napoleon III that he must defend "my sacred character, and the consideration which I owe to the dignity and to the rights of this Holy See, which are not the rights of a dynasty, but rather the rights of all Catholics."[21]

By 1860, Austria had lost its ability to influence greatly the situation in Italy, especially in the middle section of the peninsula, and Napoleon was not willing to challenge Piedmont and protect the Papal States any longer. In addition, the major Catholic powers as well as Spain, Portugal, Belgium, and Bavaria were reluctant to get involved. Protestant England summed up the new policy best—non-interventionism should prevail in Italy.

Still, the pope and his major advisors sought at first to place their wary confidence in Napoleon rather than create a large standing army of their own. But by 1860 they entertained the notion of a volunteer army of Catholics from all over Europe to protect the Papal States. In the south, Garibaldi had moved from Sicily across the straits toward Naples and was bringing his forces north, while the papacy faced an aggressive anti-clericalism coming down from Piedmont and elsewhere. Cavour insisted that he and the Piedmont regime were the real bulwarks against revolution—against Mazzini's radicalism—while in fact he was in contact with Garibaldi and with Mazzini partisans. Napoleon both counseled restraint publicly on the part of the Piedmont region and also let them know clandestinely that he would allow the dismantling of the Papal States.[22]

Cavour in turn had promised Napoleon Nice and Savoy in return for his cooperation. The French Emperor was growing unsympathetic toward the Church, fearing the strength of strong Catholic groups hoping for a Bourbon restoration in his own land. Napoleon genuinely believed that Cavour was a check upon Mazzinism as the premier had claimed. Thus the emperor would defend the pope's claims only around Rome as the old Carolingian kings had once defended the popes in their time, but he was not willing to intervene beyond that limited scope.

Both Napoleon and Cavour were counting on the death of the aging pope to ease the situation. Indeed, on Holy Thursday in the Sistine Chapel, the pope had collapsed and remained unconscious for several minutes. But he was to outlive by years Cavour who contracted an intestinal infection on May 29, 1861, and died several weeks later. The minister was received back into the Church, although his confessor was later berated for giving Cavour the last rites without him having exhibited much repentance for all the troubles he had caused the pope and the Church.

In a characteristic display of generosity, the pope remarked, "My God, be merciful with the soul of this unhappy man." And he then said Mass for his powerful foe. Later, in a rare moment of candor the pope seemed to observe admiringly, "Ah, how he loved his country, that Cavour, that Cavour. That man was truly Italian. God will assuredly have pardoned him as we pardon him."[23] Later, in the same spirit, the pope near his own end, graciously sent his confessor to minister to the dying Victor Emmanuel, who had so betrayed him and the cause.

The pope had to face the duplicity of Napoleon III who publicly had pledged his support of papal claims—to a large extent because of the power and influence of French Catholics who respected the pontiff and were concerned about his safety and welfare in the midst of the turbulence of the Risorgimento. Events were in the saddle, and outdistanced even Cavour's genius or Napoleon's duplicity. Garibaldi, the dictator of the Kingdom of the Two Sicilies, gave over control of that region to Victor Emmanuel, and Italy was coming into unification in a way few had thought possible. By January 1861, the whole peninsula, except for Venetia and the Patrimony of St. Peter, were a part of this new domain. Without Cavour, the king, however, lost a valuable ally in working with the uncertain Napoleon III. Indeed the latter wearily remarked, "Italy, with her unlimited pretensions, has ended by tiring even her friends."[24]

Napoleon decided to maintain the pope in Rome so as to satisfy Catholic concerns both at home and abroad and to continue some French influence in that region, especially after Garibaldi began his celebrated march to Rome in August 1862. Through his advisors, the pope insisted that the Papal States had to be fully restored, but that bargaining position was gone forever. Pio Nono had come to recognize that he could not put his faith in the French or the emperor, but only in God. As for the lame suggestion that the emperor wanted him to reach some agreement with the new Italian government, the pope responded that he did not need foreigners to intervene on that score, "When all is said and done, we are Italian!"[25] Indeed, the pope exhibited throughout much of his adult life many of the attitudes that Italians of his class and era had concerning Italy and the pernicious influence of foreign elements.

The papacy with its weak-standing army was dependent on foreigners—on France, Austria, Spain, and Bavaria over the decades.

The temporal state required the pope and his agents to treat, bargain, and cajole other states to protect the papal territories. Those territories were central in the battle over a unified state. The pope insisted that the Papal States must be maintained for the good of the spiritual mission of the Church, but for the Italian nationalists the maintenance of a separate state in the central region would destroy the dream of one Italy. And the romantic vision of a pope heading a united Italian confederacy was an early casualty of intrigue, anti-clericalism, and of the pope's own reservations.

Looking at the loss of the Papal States territories, it is easy to judge that somehow Pius IX made grave judgments that led to disaster. But if one examines his real options, that conclusion is somewhat flawed. He could have pursued the reactionary policies of Gregory XVI, made minor adjustments in the administration of his regions, and hugged closer Metternich's Austria. But Gregory had done just that, and there is little dispute that that path, though well-worn, had not solved any of the papacy's problems. Besides, Metternich himself would be cast out of power in 1848, despite his preeminence in the world that followed the Congress of Vienna.

The pope could have embraced the Risorgimento more vigorously, but could he really have become any ally with such a violent, secular, anti-clerical movement and still claim spiritual leadership? He could have tried the diplomatic approach, but no diplomats were more subtle and able at playing the European court games than the Vatican secretaries of state in this period—and still they could not accomplish their one major objective, which was to hold their wavering ally, Napoleon III, as guarantor of the Papal States. The only option for the pope was to create a large powerful army, and then he would have had to become a very different sort of religious leader—a Julius II, a priest warrior during the Renaissance. Consequently, he would have lost some of the valuable support of the Catholic princes and also had to raise taxes in a territory already honeycombed with agitators and traitors, thus accelerating the level of complaints that were already high for a variety of reasons. It just may be that in life one can fail just because the circumstances and odds are overwhelming.

Attacking the Errors of the World
By December 1864, the pope decided to turn his focus on the whole catalog of the world's problems, some of which he had experienced in the most personal and intense ways. In that mood, if not in that spirit, he issued a syllabus of modern errors of thought and opinion and an encyclical *Quanta Cura*, which were sweeping and harsh denunciations

of the times. The *Syllabus of Errors* and the accompanying statements cast the pope, the papacy, and the Roman Catholic Church in the popular eye as totally reactionary institutions, opposed to reason, freedom, and progress across the world. The pope's statements became grave embarrassments to the Church, especially in democratic states, and set the tone for the Curia and for the promoters of orthodoxy that lasted until Vatican II and in part throughout the twentieth century. In one sad sense, the *Syllabus* did what Napoleon I and Cavour were never able to do—it helped to severely undermine the intellectual credibility of the Church.

Pius' secretary of state, Cardinal Antonelli, sent the document out with the introduction that "the bishops may have before their eyes all the errors and pernicious doctrines which he has reprobated and condemned."[26] Apologists then and now have said it was a technical theological document, but it was also a catalogue of eighty propositions that attacked such assorted errors as: pantheism, naturalism, moderate rationalism, indifferentism, latitudinarianism, socialism, communism, secret societies, Bible societies, and liberal societies. It dealt with the rights of the Church, the limits on civil society, natural and Christian ethics, matrimony, the pontiffs "civil princedom," and the relationship of certain errors to contemporary liberalism.

In a much quoted sentence, it attacked the expression that "the Roman Pontiff can and should reconcile and harmonize himself with progress, with liberalism, and with recent civilization." It has been said the *Syllabus* was a specific attack on the Piedmont regime's definition of progress and civilization, but to many it was an assault upon the nineteenth century's liberal tradition. As noted earlier, the biographer Hales has seen the specifics of the *Syllabus* coming from the Italian situation with Mazzini and Cavour, with its new nationalist, atheist and pantheistic propaganda; thus, "progress, liberalism, and recent civilization," really meant the closing of monasteries and convents in Italy and the imposition of secular education in the new state.

Perhaps, but it also reached beyond those experiences to call into question the Church's position on the democratic American state, the toleration practiced in Great Britain, and the acceptance by many French of the revolutionary changes of 1789. What the *Syllabus* called the "pest of indifferentism" was actually called elsewhere religious toleration and personal respect; what the *Syllabus* denounced as "the corruption of manners and morals," others saw as freedom of speech, press and assembly.[27] Almost immediately, progressive clerics sought to explain away what the pope had said, and the Bishop of Orleans, Monsignor Felix Dupanloup, in fact wrote a widely circulated pamphlet (which had the approval of the pope) that sought to tone down the encyclical by explaining away what the effects of the tenets would be in the real world.

But clearly to liberal Catholics, especially those living in pluralistic societies, it became a terrible burden. It gave credence to the view that the pope believed that there was no salvation outside the Church, and that errors should not be allowed to be spread among Catholic peoples. For the pope, it was perhaps a revenge for the ill treatment he had received after being forced into exile, after the violent death of his prime minister, after the duplicity of Napoleon III and Cavour, after the aggressiveness of the Italian nationalist movement, and after the overall betrayals of the world. But for the Church in Europe, it gave its enemies more ammunition in their anti-clerical crusades.

Pio Nono seemed even more extreme than his predecessors, more prone to a siege mentality, and to a defensiveness that moved beyond the logical safeguards to simple intransigence. Added to that impression was the very real fact that his problems increased as Rome was occupied, and as the pope declared himself to be a virtual prisoner in the Vatican, as the anti-clerical campaign intensified during Victor Emmanuel's reign, and as Bismarck in the German Reich began in his *Kulturkampf*—the blunt and vicious attack on Catholicism.[28]

When the increasing assault against the papacy began, Pio Nono turned to a bold reassertion of papal authority within the Church where he could count on his authority to prevail. On a personal level, the clergy and some of the faithful celebrated with enthusiasm his anniversaries as priest (1869), pope (1871 and 1876), and bishop (1873). Despite the intrusion of secular events, Pius IX was characterized as the "pope of prayer," as a patriarch who encouraged audiences to meet with him, who favored extensive missionary work in Africa, Asia, and America, and who restored the Catholic hierarchies in Protestant England and Holland.

Like many modern popes, he developed a strong attachment to the Blessed Virgin Mary, and was instrumental in furthering what some critics called the cult of the virgin. Of all the mainstream Christian religions, Catholicism has been more committed to such a veneration of Jesus' mother than any of the others. Some have charted the Church's devotion to a conscious or subconscious affection for the earth mother or old pagan fertility goddesses. Mary is the linear descendant of those female guideposts in that simplistic anthropology. Others argue that a church run by celibate men seems fascinated by female beauty and virtue, by their charms, and by the need of all men to replace mother with another woman. It is love and passion by another name.

Perhaps there are such manifestations in the cult of the virgin, but it is more likely that orthodox Christianity remains bewildered and fascinated by its central theological tenet—that God could become man to save humankind. And so the vessel of this remarkable occurrence is even more revered than one's mother. For centuries the exact relationship of Mary to God and to the common man had been debated, discussed, theorized and proclaimed. By the reign of Pio Nono, there was some demand, which he eagerly recognized, to define the dogma of the Immaculate Conception of Mary.

As all knew, the pope had a special high regard for the Mother of God, and on June 1, 1848, he appointed a commission of twenty theologians to deal with the issue. The final dogmatic statement was that the Virgin Mary, from the moment of her conception, was exempted from original sin. The Bible really did not deal with the issue except in the Angel Gabriel's salute, "Hail Mary, full of grace." But the Church fathers had speculated that God could not have been conceived and carried in a mortal body with such a taint—as all of us have. In the Church Council of Ephesus in 431, the participants recognized her special sanctity, and later councils had acknowledged a concept of Immaculate Conception. In any case, the pope asked for comments on the draft concerning the dogma, and nine-tenths of those responding were supporters with only several opposing any such definition. Pio Nono released the proclamation and ordered a column erected at the Piazza de Spagna that celebrated the Virgin's appearance to Catherine Labouré at Paris. Most importantly, the pope issued the proclamation on his own authority, not jointly with the bishops. In 1950, Pius XII would in a similar way proclaim the dogma of the Assumption of the Blessed Virgin, body and soul, into heaven.[29]

Even with his secular troubles, his contemporaries again and again commented on his winning personality, kind wit, and patience during his troubles. Most significantly, he decided in 1867 to call a general council of the Church for the end of 1869 to deal with the climate of adversity that the papacy and the Church found itself in. It was expected by some that the council would focus on reasserting the temporal power of the papacy, and that it would make the *Syllabus of Errors* church doctrine.

In fact, the council and its document *Die filius* emphasized doctrines of accepted faith concerning God and revelation and did not deal with some of the major parts of the *Syllabus of Errors*, such as political liberty and freedom of expression. But its most important claim to history is that Vatican I is best known as the council that defined the dogma of papal infallibility.

Establishing Infallibility
The history of that dogma is a complicated one. Some historians (including several Catholic ones) have argued that some of the early

popes promulgated what were later and are still regarded as heretical positions. How then can there be papal infallibility as a guarantee of the purity of the faith deposited in Rome by St. Peter himself? Others maintain that it is the Church council or the congregation of bishops that should have the final say on what constitutes articles of faith. Still others hold that the Church itself is not spared the opportunity to be in error even on basic dogmas, but that the ecclesia (the Church) is infused with the spirit of the Holy Ghost which in turn guarantees that *overall* the Church persists in the truth of Jesus Christ.

What Pius IX and his ardent followers wanted was a very strong definition that when the pope speaks *ex cathedra* on matters of faith and morals he is infallible, that is, unable to be in error. There is no requirement that he has to speak in accord with a council or with the bishops, but rather that he is granted this very specific divine guarantee. Although papal infallibility has had some articulate critics during and after council, most notably Lord Acton in England, and some clergymen in Germany and especially in France, it is clear that the overwhelming majority of the hierarchy supported the assertion. Even if one admits that the pope had appointed a good many of these men to their bishoprics, and that there was enormous social pressure to move along with the authority in the Church, papal infallibility was a tacit assumption on the part of many clergy in very many ways.

It has been charged that Vatican I was in a sense hoodwinked by the Jesuits or the Roman Curia, and that the pope was not above campaigning before some groups such as the American clergy in Rome. Actually, some of the Curialists such as the Secretary of State Antonelli were concerned about the summoning of a council in the first place. They feared it would bring to Rome dissident German and French theologians who would challenge Rome's authority, and there was also a worry that Napoleon III would be displeased by any such council. He was, after all, the protector of what was left of the pope's temporal realm. Indeed, Garibaldi had not given up on his final quest of that region, and his forces were crying, "Rome or death" on their marches. By late 1866, the last of the French troops had left the city, although Garibaldi, who had continued his invasions in October, suffered a major defeat at Mentana in November 1867 when French troops were reintroduced.[30]

Added to the triumph of the papal cause was the public image of the pope himself. He was not a great Vatican diplomat or a fine intellect or a distinguished theologian as some other popes were and have most recently been, but he seemed to be a man of deep sensitivity, genuine spirituality, and usually personal kindness. His critics have charged that he was mean-spirited, prone to shade the truth, subject to mental lapses, and manipulative of bishops. In that view, the council was a choreographed dance that was not free to discuss dogma. Pius's reign of thirty-one years was the longest in modern history, and in his appointments he had reached out to create a large number of non-Italian cardinals, thus underscoring the Church's claim to universality. Still, some of the Church fathers felt that it was inopportune to define papal infallibility at that time. Napoleon actually sent a very blunt warning that the council should not dare make the *Syllabus of Errors* council dogma—probably a position due to the urging of some of the French hierarchy. As for the pope, he faced the beginning of the council philosophically observing, "The council always passes through three phases. First, there is that of the devil; then comes that of men, finally that of God." After the defeat of Garibaldi in 1867, the Italian government was reluctant to antagonize Napoleon, and there was a lessening of pressure on the papal government in Rome. Thus, in December 1869, on the Feast of the Immaculate Conception of Mary, Pio Nono finally opened the Vatican Council with about 700 bishops from all over the world in attendance. Critics of the council claimed that deliberations were crudely stacked and influenced by the pope. Pius IX's attempt to find suitable lodgings and provide some subsistence for bishops from poor dioceses or with little means was cast as another way to gather supporters.[31]

Some have asserted that the pope named the presidents of the special congregations or commissions, and in the general congregations the right to speak could be denied. In the public sessions, discussions were to be excluded and members could vote only *placet* or *nonplacet*. The rule of unanimity that had previously prevailed where dogma was concerned was not honored, and a simple majority was all that was required. The acoustics were poor, so people could not often hear each other, and the propositions were distributed singularly and in piecemeal fashion so that participants could not see the full range of what was being discussed and in what context.

Very quickly a proposition on papal infallibility was presented and advanced. The pope's position on the issue was clear to the bishops, and he promised them in turn more control over the lower clergy. When there was a reference to the ancient tradition of the Church, Pio Nono was supposed to have answered imperiously, "I am the tradition." The debate on infallibility lasted from June 15 to July 4, and it was maintained that speakers in opposition were interrupted and subjected to expressions of displeasure. However, of the 635 bishops who voted on the issue, only two voted no. Thus, papal infallibility was finally recognized.[32]

It is true that the pope abandoned his earlier public position of neutrality on the subject and made it clear that he believed in the dogma, and also that he was frustrated with the attempts of some members of the liberal minority to use their governments to influence the deliberations of the council. Pius also privately sought to manipulate opinion through the press and other media outlets. He charged that that the minority did not believe that the "council is governed by the Holy Spirit." And as the argument on infallibility progressed, the majority was indeed getting more and more impatient. Still it is obvious that the proposition had the overwhelming support of the bishops, even without the pope's views being expressed so firmly. In the general congregation, there was endless debate with constant repetitions on the issue, but as with most deliberative bodies, few votes were changed by speeches.[33]

After the voting a great storm swept across the region, and darkness enveloped the Basilica. The pope stood by a large candle, moved through the ceremony, and then blessed those before him. Most importantly, on July 15, Napoleon III declared war on Germany, and the Franco-Prussian conflict began—a precursor, and some believe a contributing cause to the more awesome conflagrations in the twentieth century. Preoccupied with this struggle, Napoleon moved his remaining troops out of Rome for the last time and gave up any semblance of protecting the papacy once and for all. On September 20, the forces of Victor Emmanuel entered Rome, and the council was adjourned *sine die*. Victor Emmanuel who had made mendacity into a regal style wrote the pope as a son, a Catholic, and an Italian, he said, to announce that he felt responsible for keeping law and order on the Italian peninsula.

Pio Nono called his masters "white sepulchers and vipers" and ordered only token resistance to the king's forces. He insisted that a white flag fly high from the cupola of St. Peter's, and then almost whimsically the aged pope began to compose a riddle on the verb "tremare"—to tremble. Later the annexation of the Patrimony of St. Peter's to the kingdom was approved on October 2, by a vote of 133,681 to 1,507. The pope then withdrew into the Vatican and became by his own will a prisoner. In November 1870, the government issued a "Law of Guarantees," as the unilateral agreement was called, which would regulate the rights of the papacy until the Lateran Treaty under Mussolini in 1929. The law recognized the pope's sovereignty, held him immune from arrest, and protected him under the treason laws. The pope could establish diplomatic relations with other governments, could keep his personal guard, and was given exclusive use but not ownership of the Vatican, the Lateran, and Castle Gandolfo. The papacy was also to receive an annual sum of 3,225,000 lire for the lost territories, but Pio Nono ignored the law and waived aside the subsidy. Still, when the pope criticized Bismarck for his campaign against the Catholic Church in Germany, the chancellor sought to apply pressure on the Italian government to curb the pontiff. That government refused to act, thus upholding its guarantees to the papacy.

Bismarck's *Kulturkampf* began as an attack upon the religious orders in 1871 and sought to subject the training of priests to the directions of the state. Later, as opposition mounted to the chancellor's high-handed policies, he backed down beginning in 1879. The key to Bismarck was his cold calculation of strength and his ability to know when to compromise. Still, his actions encouraged anti-clerical campaigns in other German states, Austria, Switzerland, and even Italy. Despite the guarantees to the pope, the government in Italy later pushed for a "Clerical Abuses Bill," which would subject clergy to special penalties for criticizing the state. The ministry insisted also on interfering in the rights of bishops; thus, the rhetoric of a free church and a free state was stripped bare.[34]

Matters Spiritual
Still the pope continued on—preaching and living a life of prayer and devotion. He urged greater dedication to the Sacred Heart of Jesus and to the special recognition of the Blessed Virgin Mary. On February 7, 1876, he died, and the papal chamberlain who would be his successor tapped him on the forehead with a silver hammer three times. Appropriately enough, the chamberlain called him by his baptismal name. The lengthy reign of Pius IX was over. Three years later his coffin was carried to his final resting place at San Lorenzo Fuore le Mure. Even at night, a crowd surrounded the coffin and chants and jeers were heard, and then mud was thrown at the remains of the longest reigning pope in modern history.

The papacy of Pius IX has been seen by its friends and by its critics as the beginning of the modern papacy. Clearly, the Ultramontanist position with its cult of papal personality, its strong Roman Curial bureaucracy, and its monopoly over dogmatic teachings had arrived. The pope was now even outside the traditional constraints of the councils of bishops and the ecumenical council with his assertion of authority and control.

Pio Nono had been a participant and a victim in the great movements of revolution and nationalism. Even his staunchest supporters had to recognize that he left papal relationships with most of the great states in shambles, and that his insistence on proclaiming the doctrine of infallibility and non-cooperation with many secular states left Catholics isolated and vulnerable to their enemies. He had commanded an army, supervised sophisticated and often cynical diplomats, and enacted a program of moderate reform. But the Papal States were central to the unification of Italy, both in terms of location and history. And so the temporal power of the pope fell as did the collections of duchies and small kingdoms that once marked medieval Italy and later Germany. Those two states both became like the rest of Europe—unified regimes. In one sense the loss of the Papal States was as logical as the loss of the power of the Duke of York or the barons of France. It just happened in the 1860s and the 1870s, not earlier, as in Britain under the Tudors, the French under the Bourbons, and the Spanish under Ferdinand and Isabella.

But he left the legacy of the modern papacy in a spiritual sense also. The pope, through incredible courage and Herculean effort, refused to be consumed by those monumental temporal events. He encouraged religious devotions, endorsed Scholasticism, and advocated papal infallibility as a guard against impurities creeping into the faith. In the end he was neither a typical reactionary pope, nor a successful liberal reformer. He was essentially a pastor in thought and practice—blessed with wit, perception, and at times a generous spirit. It was his unfortunate destiny to be alive during unfavorable and yet momentous political and social events.

CHAPTER SEVEN
LEO XIII, (1877–1903)

In September, 1877, Joachim Cardinal Pecci, Bishop of Perugia, was named by the Vatican to be the camerlengo (papal chamberlain) in the household of the aging Pius IX. When the pontiff died, Pecci, according to the rite of the Roman Catholic Church, tapped Pius' forehead thrice with a silver hammer and said his name each time, proclaiming, "The pope is really dead." He then took the Fisherman's Ring off Pius' finger and had it smashed, a symbol of the end of his authority. In the interim between the death of a pope and the selection of a new one, the papal chamberlain controls the temporal power of the papacy—whatever is left of it. The Sacred College of Cardinals represents the spiritual power of the Church.

Two days after Pius' temporary interment and three days before the conclave would begin to choose a successor, important political happenings were occurring. Henry Cardinal Manning of England, and Alessandro Cardinal Franchi, Pius IX's prefect for the Propagation of the Faith, met with some other cardinals to discuss the critical question of choosing a new pope who could reconcile the Church and the Italian government on the so-called "Roman Question." Apparently, they decided on the aged Pecci as their choice. Pecci had been a cardinal since 1853, but he had never been a part of the inner circle because of his early disagreements with the policies of Pius' Cardinal Secretary of State, Giacomo Antonelli. Now nearly sixty-eight, it was expected that his papacy would be a short, transitional one. Instead, it lasted more than twenty five years, and has been judged to be one of the most significant reigns in the long history of the Church. On the third ballot Pecci was elected and chose the name Leo.[1]

The Cardinal of Arts and Letters
Joachim (or Gioacchino) Vincenzo Pecci was born on March 2, 1810, not far from Rome in the mountainous village of Carpineto in the then

Papal States. His father and mother both came from illustrious families, although they were not wealthy. He was the sixth of seven children and studied at the Jesuit College in Viterbo and at the Roman College. He was interested in the sciences, theology and law, received doctorates in both civil and canon law, and was later recognized by Gregory XVI for his courage during a cholera epidemic in 1837. He was named governor of Benevento in 1838 where he vigorously sought to control banditry in the region and to curtail the excesses of liberalism—two favorite causes of Gregory, who prized order and theological stability. He was later transferred to Perugia in 1841, and proved to be a good administrator with a concern for economic improvements and who established a savings bank for farmers.

In 1843, at the age of thirty-three he was sent to Belgium as papal nuncio and made Archbishop of Damiette. But unfamiliar with the subtle arts of diplomacy, and not knowing French, he seemed to some ill-prepared. His letters to his family show that he was less concerned with serving the Church and its spiritual mission, than in bringing more distinction to the Pecci family. He wrote to his brother that he would "rise in the hierarchical branches of the prelacy, and thus ensure the just respect which our family enjoys in the land." He scrupulously sent every certificate of appointment and every other document that singled him out to the family archives. And after he was made an archbishop, he had a life-sized portrait of himself commissioned and sent home to be hung between the two portraits of his parents in their salon.[2]

It is interesting to record some of the observations made about him at different stages in his long career. In Brussels, the Austrian Ambassador Count Dietrichstein said Pecci was "the best of good fellows, but young, passive, without initiative, without authority and altogether lacking in that adaptability which was necessary to keep the affairs of his office in order." Later, the wife of Italian Premier Urbano Rattazzi said of Archbishop Pecci, "I have seen few such expressive heads as his, on which firmness, resolution, and strength are so clearly stamped. He inspires alike fear, esteem, and sympathy; but fear is the predominant feeling. One would like to love him, but one is afraid to. One thing is certain—he is no ordinary person. His voice is sonorous and full. He has not the princely bearing of Pius IX, but he is equally imposing. His demeanor is majestic and full of dignity; the chief impression one gets is that of asceticism and sternness, but this is softened by a certain benevolence, especially when he unbends to children. In a word, Cardinal Pecci of Perugia is a grand and impressive figure, and...he may one day be our pope." The biographer Rene Fülöp-Miller observed, "He was a slight, nervous figure with long, slender hands, that infinitely clever head crowned with locks, the white locks, the dark piercing eyes, the massive nose, and a broad, strong-willed mouth."

Prince Bernhard von Bülow gave another vivid picture of the man, this time shortly before Leo's death, "Everything about him had a spiritual aspect. He was very amiable, but in accordance with Italian *gentilezza* without too much emphasis on officiousness. His poise was perfect, particularly in the sense that no impression from without could shake his equilibrium, let alone endanger it. He had wonderfully fine eyes in which there shone the unassailable faith of the earthly representative of Christ...he appeared to have transcended matter and, so to speak, to have reabsorbed it into himself."[3]

In Belgium, Pecci for the first time experienced the merciless ravishings of the new industrial society and the wreckage of workers and their families. With no protection from the state or unions, men, women and children labored long hours, often endured hunger, and lived in hovels. Gone were the placidness and fresh air of peasant life; gone were the communities that nourished rich and poor alike.

At first, Pecci got along well with King Leopold and even received the Grand Cordon of St. Leopold. He met Queen Victoria in London and King Louis Philippe in Paris, thus being exposed to two important monarchs and two great capital cities. But in a critical dispute, he supported the Belgian bishops and Catholic politicians who opposed Prime Minister Jean Baptiste Nothomb's proposal to have the government name members of "University Juries."

The king ordered the nuncio recalled by the Vatican because of his interference in local political matters. The Church had done fairly well under the liberal administration in Belgium, and the Vatican did not wish to get involved so directly in an academic controversy. In a sharp personal rebuff, Pecci was sent back home to Perugia where he was to be banished in a sense for the next 30 years. His high-level career in the Curia bureaucracy was over, and it surely must have taken a toll on the bright and ambitious cleric. There in Perugia he stayed and ran a well-organized and caring diocese. In 1853, Pius IX rewarded his quiet successes with a cardinal's hat.[4]

Unlike the pope and much of his inner circle, Pecci was above all an intellectual—a man who loved and lived for ideas. What had set him off from the dozens of pastorally oriented clergy in the Italian peninsula was his deep commitment to learning, his fearless respect for intellectual curiosity, and his high regard for the medieval theologian St. Thomas Aquinas. Together with his Jesuit brother, Joseph, he opened the Academy of St. Thomas and promulgated what would become the ascendancy of Neoscholasticism. Added to his interest, Pecci was a fine classicist himself, possessing a beautiful Latin style. At the local diocesan seminary, he reversed the prohibition against reading Dante's *Divine Comedy*, a classic he admired and knew somewhat by heart. In addition to his initiatives in seminary and university training, he founded evening schools for the sons of working men and opened institutes that advanced money on corn.[5]

The Bishop and then Cardinal of Perugia stayed away from Curial politics and achieved a record as a social liberal who supported the conservative Pius IX. Blocked by the powerful Antonelli, Pecci remained an illustrious provincial leader, but not a major figure in the papal court hierarchy. Later when he was pope, Leo observed that to talk of Antonelli still distressed him too much. He concluded, "I think if it had not been for him, the Pope today would not find himself in such a difficult position."[6] At the Vatican Council, he was an adherent of Pio Nono's views, but he left no real contribution to that short and turbulent time. Across the continent, the Church was swept up in the tides of anti-clericalism, especially the *Kulturkampf* in Germany, tense relationships with the state in France, and the unsettled Roman Question, which led to the self-imposed captivity of the papacy. In addition to those political and ecclesiastical disputes, the rise of industrial capitalism was bringing forth a new ideological movement—socialism in all of its varieties.

Then as if touched by the hand of destiny, the obscure Cardinal of Perugia seemed to come out of his library and published a series of well-regarded pastoral letters on the Church and modern society. Unlike Pius IX, Pecci fought the ideas of nationalism and socialism, not just with authority, but with other ideas. In a famed Lenten message in 1877, he reminded his adherents that the Church and civilization were not enemies, but in fact were allies. It was the Church that had for so many centuries held back the forces of barbarism and darkness. He maintained that the Church wished that mankind should have a better material life on earth, and he went on to quote not the Bible or St. Augustine, but the French philosopher Baron de Montesquieu that the "Christian religion, which seems to have no other end but to secure our happiness in a future life, also ensures our felicity on earth."[7]

Pecci placed the Church on the side of decent working conditions, beneficial science, and true progress, but he still argued that the basic question before mankind was not politics or economics, but the relationship of men to nature, knowledge, and the Church itself. The cardinal thus turned the *Syllabus of Errors* upside down and made it not a defensive doctrine, but a powerful critique of man's inhumanity to man. Something very different was going on in these responses, and Pecci soon acquired fame and prominence. In November 1876, he was called to Rome after Antonelli's death, and in September of the following year named the new papal chamberlain, taking up residence in the historic Falconieri palace. The Pecci family had acquired a contemporary luster to its old, but worn nobility. Six months later, on February 28, 1878, he became pope.[8]

Thin and aesthetic-looking, the sixty-eight-year-old cardinal complained at his election that he was a feeble, old man, who could not handle the burdens of the papacy. He was to live twenty-five more years, burying his friends and foes alike—proving that in life only God can set the measure of things, and that on a baser level longevity is the best revenge! Despite his initial inclination, he did not give his first blessing from the outside gallery of St. Peter's that overlooks the piazza—thus honoring the Curia's insistence that the pope must remain a prisoner in the Vatican. On March 28, Leo XIII professed his faith and took an oath to observe the Apostolic Constitutions, which included protecting the Church's lost territories.

Diplomatic Overtures

The Roman Question and the establishment of an Italian state would bedevil Leo throughout his papacy. Although he would depart at times from the traditional wisdom on many issues, he backed away from repudiating Pius IX's legacy on the need for a separate state. Still, many Italian political leaders and even some Freemasons applauded at first his elevation as pope.[9]

Although Pecci's only foreign diplomatic assignment had ended in less than success, it was diplomacy that would lead to some of the major achievements of his papacy. Immediately after his coronation, he instructed the Deputy Secretary of State, Mgr. Vincenzo Vannutelli, to send out letters to the sovereigns and heads of states. The letters were remarkable for their general reconciling tone. To the emperors of Germany and Russia, he underscored the importance of liberty of conscience for their Catholic subjects, and also reassured them of his co-religionists submission to imperial authority and of their "scrupulous obedience." He wrote to each that while there was no official diplomatic relations between the Holy See and their nation, "We appeal to the magnanimity of your heart to ensure that peace and tranquility of conscience may be granted anew to so large a portion of your subjects..." Later in his encyclical on civil sovereignty, the pope said, "The Church of Christ *cannot* be either suspect to princes or disliked by peoples."

To the president of the United States, Queen Victoria, the kings of Holland, Sweden and Norway, and the emperor of Austria, he thanked them for what each had done to benefit their Catholic citizens or subjects. On the issue of Switzerland, he acknowledged the estranged relations over the last two years and urged that "suitable and effective remedies would be found for those evils without delay." There was some complaint from the Curia that the pope had not consulted with its members on those overtures, but he simply moved along. It was time to reach out to the international order and to increase Catholic influence in those circles, he seemed to indicate. Even Pius IX had recognized the changing realities. Before his death, he observed, "Everything around me has changed: my system and my policy have had their day, but I am too old to revise my orientation. That will be the work of my successor."[10]

Later, critics were to say Leo was autocratic, despotic, greedy for power, but to the larger world, the aged pontiff seemed to be pushing early in tentative but distinct ways toward some reconciliation with the contemporary world. He would later be called the pope of the working class, but he loved to grant his benedictions from the regal gestatorial chair above the crowds of nobles and commoners alike. He enjoyed the liturgical pomp, but lived a personal life of frugality. Leo read extensively, approved of the introduction of modern electricity and communications, was usually affable, but did not have the easy humor of his predecessor. He was the first pontiff to be recorded on cinema, and the first to allow electricity into St. Peter's Basilica. He had a deputy in the Secretary of State's office prepare daily digests of newspaper articles across the globe, and was well-read in the sciences as well as in theology and literature. Shrewdly he once concluded, "I want to see the church so far forward that my successor will not be able to turn back." And he observed, "It is for me to sow, for others to reap."[11]

At first, Leo seemed to strike several different poses though. He reaffirmed Pius' insistence that the spiritual power of the Church required a temporal state, condemned "enemies of the public order," and opposed Catholic associations participating in national elections in Italy. On the other hand, he reissued his earlier letter on the compatibility of the Church and modern civilization, and mixed easily with intellectuals. The pope expressed an interest in anthropology and archaeology—tossing aside the fears of some that science of all sorts was a synonym for atheism. This new pope, an old man, was harder to categorize than his predecessors. He seemed committed to his papal prerogatives and to his predecessors' policies; yet he enjoyed ideas and was deeply concerned about the savagings by the new industrial order.

Kulturkampf

Immediately Leo sought to face the difficulties called the *Kulturkampf.* As has been seen, the Church had conflicts in Prussia with its chancellor,

Otto von Bismarck, which then had spread to other German states, Austria, and Switzerland. Rudolf Virchow, a Prussian atheist and scientist, in the Prussian Landtag had called the disputes the *Kulturkampf*—or a struggle between different cultural value systems. Thus the *Kulturkampf*'s original points of contention had been over religious mixed marriages, increasing intolerance of Protestant rulers, growing Catholic demands for civil liberties, and a fear of papal power, especially after the Vatican Council's declaration of infallibility. In addition, since the Revolution of 1848, German liberals had become more hostile towards Catholicism, and they had advocated eliminating all religious influences from public and private life.

To add to suspicions, Catholics favored the inclusion of Catholic Austria in the new Germany—a proposal Bismarck opposed, since it would threaten Prussian ambitions to becoming the leading state in the new Reich. In 1870, Catholics also took the initiative in forming the Center political party which became one of the major sources of opposition to the Chancellor in Germany.

Bismarck, an astute and crafty politician, genuinely disliked Catholicism and also misunderstood its traditions and sources of power. He grew increasingly belligerent as Catholics tended to favor a more federal union, not a Prussian-run Reich, and when Catholic clergy in Silesia supported the use of Polish in religiously-run schools, Bismarck argued that the Center party with its advocacy of papal sovereignty in Italy was really a state within a state, more concerned with fostering Catholicism's power than with loyalty to the empire he was building. On July 8, 1871, the government ominously abolished the Catholic Bureau in the Prussian Ministry of Education and Public Worship. The *Kulturkampf* had begun.[12]

The chancellor then ordered all normal schools and school inspections in the Alsace-Lorraine region removed from the control of the Catholic clergy where it had been housed previously. He also pushed for the Pulpit Law, enacted on November 28, 1871, which provided for severe penalties for those who used the pulpit to criticize the state. Tensions increased when Pius IX refused to accept Gustav Cardinal Hohenlohe as his nation's first ambassador to the Vatican, in part because the cardinal had opposed the council's declaration on infallibility. Bismarck then publicly attacked the Church and proclaimed defiantly, "We shall not go to Canossa"—a reference to the humiliation of German Emperor Henry IV, who waited in the snow before Pope Gregory VII's door for forgiveness in the year 1077.

First the Prussian Minister of Education and Public Worship, Adalbert Falk, prepared a law for the Prussian Landtag to subject all schools to state inspection. Then in June, religious orders were prohibited from participating in public education in Prussia. The German Reichstag ordered all Jesuits dismissed from the empire within six months, and in December 1872, Bismarck severed diplomatic relations with the Vatican after the pope protested his government's actions. In 1873, four other religious orders were also expelled. Then in the same year the Prussia Landtag passed the so-called "May Laws" that placed seminary training under the auspices of the state and required students for the priesthood to go to a German university for three years and to submit to examinations in literature, history and philosophy. The state also established restrictions on the Church's powers of excommunication and discipline and made episcopal decisions subject to an appeal before a civil tribunal.

The reaction was swift and strong among Catholics as they became more of a unified force after several influential bishops were arrested. In 1874, bishops and priests who opposed the laws were subject to exile, and nine out of twelve bishoprics in Prussia were vacant. Later in February 1875, Pius IX declared the May Laws null and void. In July 1874, a Catholic had attempted to assassinate Bismarck, and the chancellor used that attack to add fuel to his fires. In February 1875, civil marriage was made obligatory in Prussia, and soon other German states followed that lead. In April, the state suspended financial grants to dioceses where the laws were not being obeyed, and in June, all church property was confiscated. Later a determined Pope Leo was to observe of the chancellor, "I shall have to continue to battle foot-to-foot against the man of iron."

Elsewhere in Germany, other states emulated Prussia's policies. Baden had actually preceded Prussia in enacting restraints on the Church in 1860, controlling clerical appointments, and aiding those "Old Catholics" who had opposed the Vatican Council. In Austria, the government, using the papal infallibility decree as a pretext, broke the Concordat of 1855. In 1874, the parliament restricted the rights of religious orders, curtailed Church control over its own finances, and sought to interfere with ecclesiastical appointments. Even in usually mild Switzerland, the monasteries had been closed earlier, and bishops who supported the Vatican Council were harassed. Religious orders were expelled in 1874, the papal nuncio was asked to leave, and diplomatic relations were severed until 1884. Civil marriage was required, and schools became interdenominational. This was the situation that Leo faced in the rest of the German-speaking world as he assumed the chair of St. Peter.[13]

In Italy, Leo continued his predecessor's policy of Catholic non-involvement in Italian government and political life, the so-called edict of *non expedit*—it is not expedient to participate. Leo was wise enough, however, to admit that such a declaration would eliminate the moderating influence of Catholic laymen and parish priests in the civic life of the new state, and consequently increase the power of radicals, anti-clericals, socialists and Freemasons, but still he would not change.

Continuing Disputes
When in April 1880, the Chamber of Deputies in Italy was dissolved, prominent Catholics begged the pope to reconsider. He then convened a committee of cardinals to examine the issue, but they urged a continuation of the ban. The prospect for liberalization of the ban suffered another setback when in July 1881 a crowd attacked the casket containing the remains of Pius IX as it was being transferred to his final resting place. Horror was expressed by those outside the faith, and even by opponents of the Vatican. Deeply upset, Leo began to consider removing the papacy from Rome altogether.

Later, in 1886, loyal Catholics again pushed to end the ban. This time even the Italian government quietly asked the papacy to lift the prohibition, citing its own fear that a more radical and anti-clerical element would end up controlling the Chamber of Deputies to the disadvantage of both the Church and the state. But again the Holy See reiterated that prohibition and actually even tightened it. Leo concluded almost with a tone of resignation, "As long as I live, the *non expedit* will be maintained; my successor will see what is best to do afterwards." By 1900, the complete bankruptcy of the policy was obvious to all, yet the pope let it continue.[14]

In his diplomatic efforts, Leo XIII struggled to use the diplomatic leverage of the Vatican to persuade Italy to restore some of the Church's temporal power. The pope and his secretary of state tried for a decade to have Germany and Austro-Hungarian Empire convince Italy to make some accommodation on the issue. France was now run by republicans who would not lend their services to protecting the Church. As Leo moved toward bettering relations with Bismarck, he tried to get him to pursue that policy toward Italy as well. Relations with the German Reich did improve, even to the extent that Bismarck urged that the pope serve as an international mediator in the dispute between Germany and Spain over possession of the Caroline Islands in the Pacific. He also quietly asked the Vatican to persuade the Catholic Center party to support a military appropriations bill—which it did. Later Leo offered to make Bismarck a Knight of the Order of Christ and gave him the insignia of that order!

But on the divisive Roman Question, the "Iron Chancellor" did not wish to interfere in Italian policies, especially after 1882 when that nation became a German and Austro-Hungarian ally. Austrian Emperor Franz Joseph also welcomed some bettering of ties between Germany and the papacy, but he too did not choose to provide any help on the Italian problem. While Leo remained optimistic, his new secretary of state, Mariano Cardinal Rampolla, saw no real use in further cultivating the Reich and the Austro-Hungarian Empire, and turned his attentions back to France. As anti-clericalism and Freemasonry increased their hold on Italians, Leo faced even greater opposition in Rome and was looking for allies. The new Italian prime minister, Francesco Crispi, had made a career out of fiery, anti-clerical rhetoric, and let it be known that if Leo left Rome as a protest, he would not be allowed to return. He even encouraged the unveiling of a statue of Giordano Bruno in the Campo di Fiori on June 9, 1889. Bruno was a philosopher who was burned by the Church on that very spot as a heretic in 1600, and now he became a hero to Italian anti-clerical elements. Leo in turn often expressed his fears of the Freemasons and tried unsuccessfully to foster counter revolutionary activity.[15]

The pope did decide to stay in Rome, but the Vatican's foreign policy turned toward its traditional protector, France, which by now, though, was unsupportive of the papacy. Years later, a rapprochement was begun with Italy under Pope Benedict XV, and a settlement on the Roman Question was reached under Pius XI, when the dictator Benito Mussolini agreed to the Lateran Accords of 1929. Those agreements codified much of what Leo had advocated decades before.

The English Church
Leo had easier times with the English-speaking world. In 1850, the Roman Catholic hierarchy was re-established in England, and the first cardinal archbishop of Westminster was named, Nicholas Wiseman. He was followed by Henry Edward Manning who was instrumental in Leo's election, and who blazed the path for greater concern for the worker in the Church. Almost immediately after his coronation, the pope honored former Anglican clergyman and Catholic philosopher John Henry Newman with a cardinal's hat, re-established the Scottish hierarchy, and urged Irish Catholics to curtail their opposition to Her Majesty's government. As nuncio to Belgium, he had once dined with Queen Victoria and had met the prince consort, Lord Palmerston, and foreign minister Lord Aberdeen, and he retained a respect for British achievements.[16]

On December 9, 1886, Leo conferred honors on fifty English martyrs who had been murdered for their faith under the regimes of Henry VIII and his daughter, Elizabeth I. Two of the most famous of those figures were Sir Thomas More, Chancellor of England, and Bishop John Fisher of Rochester, both symbols of Catholic courage and resilience, who were eventually canonized by Pius XI in 1935. Later, the pope was to name the ancient British ecclesiastical historian, Venerable Bede, (673?–735) as a doctor of the universal church, and on April 2, 1895, the intellectual pope also approved Catholics attending the universities at Oxford and Cambridge.[17]

With the renaissance of the church in England, Leo had to face two very difficult problems: the relations of the clergy with their hierarchy and the validity of Anglican orders in the eyes of the Roman Catholic Church. The absence of a hierarchy for so long resulted in an uncertain relationship between the lower orders of the clergy, who were used to doing things their own way, and their newly consecrated bishops. Added to that ambiguity were the conflicts between the hierarchy and the Jesuits in England. Under pressure from that hierarchy, especially Cardinal Manning, Leo agreed to deal with the basic issues under contention.

One of the principals in the dispute, Bishop Herbert Vaughan of Salford, argued that the Jesuits "attach great importance to this case because it will regulate America. And it is better to settle the case with the English Bishops than with the American Bishops, who are Irish and more violent."[18] Although Leo was under considerable pressure from a variety of quarters, he kept his own counsel and moved at his own pace. In the end, he sided with the hierarchy—as one would have expected—and enforced the authority of the Church over its own. It was after all a matter of discipline. The second issue was the controversy over whether Rome would accept the validity of Anglican clerical orders, that is, after all the centuries of divisions, was there still a clear line of succession from the Apostles down to the present? Could the Roman Catholic Church recognize as valid an Anglican priesthood similar to its own?

As so often happens, the episode began with a chance meeting, this time between Abbé Fernand Portal and Lord Halifax. Halifax argued that his views and those of many other Anglicans were theologically close to the Roman Church, and that many wished for a reunion of the two. Halifax, like Cardinal Newman, had been deeply influenced by the Anglican High Church spirit in the Oxford Movement, which emphasized ties to traditional Catholicism despite problems with a strong papacy.

The Abbé spread his views about the allienation of both churches in a well-received pamphlet published under a pseudonym, and argued that Anglican orders "may be regarded as valid." In 1894, the Abbé Portal went to England and saw for himself the elements of at least the High

Church that incorporated the vestiges of the Roman ways: vestments, Stations of the Cross, solemn Masses, Holy Souls chapels, Catholic literature, the Lady altars, and the like. He then met Secretary of State Cardinal Rampolla, and later the pope himself. One report of the meeting claimed that the pope was enthusiastic, and foresaw the beginning of a reunion after centuries of estrangement. Recognizing the incredible opportunity for him and the Church, he surely saw it as a fitting capstone to his career—"You know I am 85 years old," he kept on adding, recognizing how little time he thought he had left. He even considered writing directly to the archbishops of Canterbury and York on the possibilities of such a reunion. The Catholic hierarchy in England obviously was dismayed, and its representatives hurried to Rome to meet with the pope and the secretary of state to talk about the "wild ideas in Rome."

The pope then ordered a scholarly examination of the validity of Anglican Orders, and the archives included background material on Pope Paul IV's bull, *Praeclara Charissimi*. Issued on June 20, 1555, the bull dismissed the validity of those orders and was cited in the current dispute. Leo again temporized and held his own counsel while the arguments were being made. Obviously, the issue of a possible reunion meant more than dealing with the problem of Anglican orders. The real roadblock was and remains the right of the pope to teach and govern the Church—the assertion of papal supremacy worldwide. A commission of six theologians was established to examine the question, and clearly Leo was excited and preoccupied with the possibilities. His own secretary of state supported the Anglican claims, and Leo was aligned with him.

But the pope finally received the argument against the claims, and on September 13, he issued his own bull, *Apostolicae Curae*, which concluded that the orders were null and void because of defects in form and intention. Among other issues, serious questions were raised about whether the Church of England itself had recognized the apostolic succession of the priesthood and the sanctity of the sacraments. Leo the scholar recognized the force of tradition, and Leo the pope kept the faith. But he still was human, and he was a proud Pecci. Leo probably deeply desired to be remembered in history as the pope who brought back the Anglican Church—or at least the High Church element—into the fold of Christ. In their own ways, in their own times, old popes, like young men, can feel the tides of excitement, the sense of wild achievement, the flush of possible triumph that adds pinnacles of emotion above the flatness of life and duty. But in the end, duty and orthodoxy prevailed.[19]

On the Matter of France

In France, Leo seemed to face complex problems that rivaled those he had with Germany. There the turmoil continued as the Franco-Prussian War (1870–71) led to the destruction of the Second Empire and the ascendancy of the German Reich under Prussian aegis. As Napoleon III's armies went down to defeat, a self-appointed committee of Republicans established a Government of National Defense that sought to keep up the fight. But Paris fell and a new Assembly was necessary in order to meet and come to terms with the victorious Germans. A plebiscite to elect the Assembly led to a majority of Monarchists and not Bonapartists being elected. But Paris was taken over by a proletariat group with some republican bourgeoisie that created the Commune of Paris—a government separate from the rest of the nation. After a bitter battle and a repressive aftermath, the Commune was defeated by the armies supported by the new Assembly. Later, other uprisings took place in Marseilles and Lyons under the auspices of French anarchists opposed to the centralization of power in France, but to no avail. Now the world was to hear the name of the greatest socialist theorist and apologist, Karl Marx, who praised what he called the civil war in France.

During all of this turmoil, the French Church continued to favor the restoration of the monarchy, but those who wished to reinstitute the royal line were divided in their allegiances. The Bonapartists were discredited by the war, but the Assembly still had factions divided between the Legitimatists who wanted the Bourbons restored, and the Orleanists favoring the descendant of Louis Philippe. Compromise was ruled out when the Bourbon heir, the Count of Chambord, stubbornly refused to accede to power unless the state used his white flag, instead of the tricolor which commanded the allegiance of many Frenchmen. The Monarchists' cause seemed to lose some of its luster as these disputes dragged on.[20]

The clergy's views ran counter to the Republican positions on education, marriage and religious orders, even though they received financial support from the state. Leo at first tried to avoid taking sides, hoping that the French would somehow help him recover Rome, just as twice in his lifetime popes had had their temporal power restored to them after European upheavals. Somehow the legacy of Pius IX still governed the church. But by 1875, it was clear that popular sentiment in France had shifted to the Republicans, and Leo continued to contemplate the problem during the early years of his pontificate and beyond. Added to those dynamics, the pope named a new secretary of state, Lorenzo Cardinal Nina, following Cardinal Franchi's death five months after Leo's ascension. Nina had been the nuncio in Paris and understood the liability of continuing intransigence and following the Ultramontanist sentiment.

The influential cardinal archbishop of Algiers, Charles Lavigerie, also warned Leo XIII of the consequences of Frenchmen continuing to support the lost monarchical cause. On October 22, 1880, the pope wrote to the archbishop of Paris and reminded Catholics that the Church rejected no specific form of government per se, that citizens should obey those who govern, and that order is the foundation of public security.[21]

In late August 1883, the Count of Chambord, or "King Henri V," as his followers wistfully called him, died. Who then was the legitimate heir to the throne for the Royalists, which included a good part of the Catholic clergy? Leo responded with a letter to the hierarchy of France in which he tactfully recalled the glory of their nation's church, and then rejected the desire of some to change the form of the established government in their divided nation. The pope in turn criticized the attacks on the Church, especially in the area of education, the institution of civil marriage and military service for the clergy. The message to the Catholic hierarchy and to the populace was clear—they were not to be fellow travelers anymore in the monarchial cause.

In his encyclical, *Immortale dei*, the pope also laid out general principles on the Church/state issue. The Church, he maintained, lived in the world, but was not of it, and it could endure in a variety of nations with very different forms of government. He opposed popular revolution and treason against legitimate authority. Quoting the famous words attributed to Jesus, "Render to Caesar what is Caesar's and to God what is God's," he authoritatively supported such a policy of accommodation. Leo, however, opposed those who thought that liberty could survive without being allied with virtue and truth. But still, he separated himself from the view that any person should be forced to embrace Catholicism, quoting St. Augustine who insisted, "Man cannot believe otherwise than of his own will."

But the anti-Republican sentiment continued its aggressive campaigns in French life, and Leo clearly feared the consequences for Catholics and his Church. On November 12, 1890, Cardinal Lavigerie gave a luncheon for the staff of the French Mediterranean Squadron and other distinguished guests. At the toast, a calculating Cardinal saluted the legitimate authorities in France and urged national unity. He then had the White Fathers' band play the national anthem, the "Marseillaise."

The pope who probably had encouraged the general overture remained quiet as the monarchist Catholics reacted bitterly. Tensions increased, and even after a decade of effort, Leo still was not successful in normalizing the relationships between the aggrieved Church and the difficult French state. The Vatican continued to apply pressure on the

French clergy to reach some accommodations with the Republic, and the French cardinals reaffirmed that the nation "has need of governmental stability and religious liberty."

On February 16, 1892, the pope in a letter to the French people proclaimed that Catholics were to support the republic. Privately, Leo assumed that Catholic political strength would prevail and that consequently the Constitution would be changed. He noted that the French could later establish a monarchy and revealed, "I am a Monarchist myself." There was strong rightist opposition, but the pope's authority ended for some at least the legitimacy of fighting the fruits of the Revolution. Leo insisted that French Catholics faced the inevitable triumph of the events of 1789, although many refused to comply. By then, the great ideological challenge to Catholicism was not coming from the remnants of the revolution, but from secular socialism which was growing in the fertile fields of discontent in France.[22]

The Holy See refused to get involved in the Dreyfus Affair, despite appeals from the international Jewish community. While the pope made considerable progress in opening up avenues of dialogue and accommodation with Germany and France, he continued to be wedded to the policies of Pius IX with regard to the Italian situation. Although he seemed at times to grope for some new ways of dealing with the so-called "Roman Question," Leo was, on that issue, too much of a traditional cleric at heart and too much of a traditional pope in practice to accept closure on that controversial issue. In that rigidity he was surely influenced by the long, nasty, and threatening influence of anti-clericalism that engulfed so many of the members of the Italian ruling class. They were still the heirs of Cavour, Mazzini, and Garibaldi, who defined the nationalist struggle, somewhat correctly, as opposition to the temporal and religious power of the Roman Catholic Church. Only when that generation of revolutionaries passed away, and conservative Italians began to fear the advent of socialism did the quarrel begin to become more mute during the reign of Pius X.

As for Leo, this anti-clericalism was also fueled by the forces of Freemasonry—an international brotherhood that was bound together by secret rights, rituals, and its own hierarchy. It is in fact hard to overestimate the genuine fear and dislike that the normally open-minded Leo XIII had for that order. In part he was correct—it was an element of an international vanguard aimed at destroying the influence of the Church and the papacy, and it had many adherents in Italy, a romantic land given to extremes of sentiment.

In his first allocution or formal address delivered on March 28, 1878, Leo had already dealt with the Roman Question. He supported, as all expected, the righteousness of Pius IX's position, but did so in remarkably mild terms. "The papacy and the church needed its temporal state in order to exercise its special mission," he argued. A month later, he reiterated that view and explained that a temporal government was necessary for "the security and well being of the entire human family is also in jeopardy." He pressed the Church's claims, and yet seemed to try to strike some sort of an accommodation.[23]

A year later, after his election, he explained that the Holy See needed only as much territory as would make it completely free. The new pope indicated that he was willing to renounce the former States of the Church and would accept something that approximated the "Leonine City" or the papal enclaves in the heart of Rome, with a passage to the sea. Actually the Church generally enjoyed the complete use of those areas and edifices already, but what was being asked for was the juridical separation of the "Leonine City" from the Kingdom of Italy. Even Pius IX had come to accept that formulation toward the end of his life. Unfortunately for the Church, that modest solution came to fruition only some fifty-one years later.

There were other diplomatic endeavors in which Leo was involved: he urged the abolition of the African slave trade; restrained the King of Portugal's right to control the Goa area of India; established or re-established the hierarchies in India (1886), North Africa (1884), and Japan (1891); and reorganized the missions in China. In addition, he had some hopes of reunion with the Oriental and Slavic churches and recalled the famous historic apostolic missions of Sts. Cyril and Methodius. The Eucharistic Congress in Jerusalem in 1893 and his apostolic letter on November 30, 1894 were meant to encourage a reunion with the east which did not materialize. He did though reach some accommodations on Church/state relations with Belgium in 1884 and Russia in 1894. And although Leo was seen as a political pope, he established 248 sees, 48 vicariates or prefectures, and 2 patriarchates, and he devoted 11 of his encyclicals to topic of the Blessed Virgin Mary. After a vision at Mass he added a prayer at the end to St. Michael. He also urged a respect for the rosary, established a feast of the Holy Family, and consecrated the human race to the Sacred Heart of Jesus during his jubilee in 1900.[24]

Leo and Americanism

For the other great English-speaking nation, the United States of America, Leo had a real fondness for the confusing pluralistic democracy which had recently gone through its own terrible Civil War. He regarded it as one of the most promising missionary lands, a huge country with enormous possibilities and one that permitted full civil liberty. The growth of Catholicism, however, in the United States was due less to the conversion of Protestants or nonbelievers than to the massive migrations of Irish, German, and later Italian and Slavic peoples. The hierarchy was basically Irish-born or first generation Irish-American, and there was little in the way of ecclesiastical laws, especially as the new Church reached out into the hinterlands. In 1878 there was still no official representative of the pope in the United States, and the American government had no minister accredited to the Holy See. Some American bishops had been especially vocal about the inopportuneness of the infallibility declaration at the Vatican Council, although, in the end, they fell into line. Still, the Curia had several concerns about the American church, especially on the need for Catholic education for the children of immigrants and the organization of proper discipline between the bishops and the far-flung clergy.[25]

From the founding of the United States in 1789 to 1878, the number of Catholics had gone from 30,000 to nearly six million. The number of bishops had climbed from one, John Carroll of Baltimore, to one cardinal, twelve archbishops, 51 bishops, and over 5,000 priests organized into sixty-three dioceses or vicariates. The Catholic population included not just the immigrant masses coming after the Civil War and the old Anglo-Americans in the seaboard states, but also Spanish, Indian, and French missions dating back often to the sixteenth century.[26]

In 1875, the Curia moved to impose traditional canon law on the American Church. Some of the bishops in the western states also had advocated a Plenary Council in the United States to discuss the problems that they were facing, and in 1884 one was held. The year before, the pope and the Curia sought to impose a series of broad-based rules covering seminaries, cathedral chapels, irrevocable pastorships, ecclesiastical garb, participation of Catholics in non-Catholic organizations, Catholic education, the care of immigrants, and Negro and Indian missions among other items. Several of these proposals were opposed by the Americans, and there were some compromises. After the plenary council, however, canon law was effectively imposed on the American Church and later a resident delegate was sent to the United States.

The Vatican though retained some real reservations about the American Church, which were fueled in part by internal squabblings among the American clergy over issues of foreign language churches and the so-called heresy, "Americanism." Unlike many Europeans, the American prelates were resounding patriots who celebrated the constitutional separation of church and state. They regarded such a development not as a pragmatic necessity as in Europe, but as a matter of principle that resulted in pluralism, toleration, and the sectarian peace imposed by the Constitution. While Pius IX and Leo were fighting their wearisome battles against nineteenth century liberalism, nationalism, and anti-clericalism, the American Catholics were exempt from much of that particular bitterness.

Like the early Catholic Church, the Americans recognized that there was a difference between society and the state. In Europe, the two had become thoroughly fused from the Middle Ages on into the nineteenth century, and Leo accepted the separation of church and state really to protect the Catholic faith from its enemies. If he had his choice, he probably would have liked to have seen church and state joined if his Church could prevail. It is not that he was an intolerant man; he believed that freedom had to be grounded in protection for truth and morality which was the very essence of the Church's code of conduct. The new European philosophies came to celebrate instead the triumph of sentiment, of man freed from law or constraint. Their definition of heroism was grounded in individualism, which was personal and particularistic to time and place. Leo lived in history, in an ancient network of natural laws and natural rights that were meant to both protect and to civilize people. And central to the advance of civilization was the influence of the Catholic Church.[27]

The Americans had their own problems with anti-Catholicism, which was linked in part to anti-foreign nativism and usually anti-Irish feelings. But the wars of religious ideology, the inquisitions committed by both Catholics and Protestants on each other and on themselves, the personal attacks on the papacy with its exiles, its humiliations, its reactions were residues of a past that did not wash up on their shores. It is not that Americans lived in a pristine, utopic state. It was that Europe was a long way away both geographically and intellectually. Besides, most American Catholics outside of the clergy could care less about theology, papal pronouncements, and Curial politics.[27]

The non-Irish parishes and congregations resented the power, influence and arrogance of their counterparts in the Church. Opposition built up especially in the Midwest among the Germans, and in 1886 a petition went to Rome from a group of German priests asking for redress. In 1891, a German merchant, Peter Paul Cahensly, and others renewed that petition for foreign representation in the American hierarchy and for special protection of foreign language immigrants. The American Catholic establishment, led by Archbishop John Ireland of St. Paul and James Cardinal Gibbons of Baltimore, vigorously protested in part because of their preference for the assimilation of Catholics so as to underscore their allegiances to the new nationality being created. The pope ended up supporting his hierarchy.[29] Ireland in particular had been criticized for his support of a proposed law in neighboring Wisconsin requiring the use of English in all public schools and for his ingenious proposal where schools supported by the state of Minnesota could have instruction done by Catholic teachers. In one sense, he was evading the Church's requirement that a separate (and expensive) Catholic parochial school system be set-up. Later, he had to defend himself both against Protestants in the United States who saw his proposal as another nefarious Catholic attempt to break down the wall of separation of church and state, and also from traditional Catholics who accused him of abandoning the Vatican's directives.[30]

In 1891, Ireland went to Rome, this time to defend himself. Before in 1886, he traveled to the Vatican to push for the establishment of the Catholic University of America, a proposal that the new senior prelate, Cardinal Gibbons, had reservations about at first. The pope, though, loved learning and quickly agreed to the new institution. Leo had apparently asked Ireland, who spoke fluent French, to visit Paris and urge the Catholics to support his controversial encyclical of February 1892 calling on French Catholics to cooperate with the Third Republic. Ireland agreed, and was well received there, although resistance continued. Later Leo sent Vatican-held documents on the explorer Christopher Columbus for the Columbian Exposition in Chicago in 1893, and he authorized Francesco Satolli, the Archbishop of Lepanto, to be his representative to the Fair. Satolli soon was named by the pope as the apostolic delegate to the United States—to the reservations of some Catholic prelates. He was to be the major source of information for Leo on that very confusing and yet bustling continent, and he generally supported the progressive hierarchy.

But all was not well for the progressives. There was a World Parliament of Religions in the Exposition which treated each faith in an ecumenical and equal way. Gibbons, Ireland, and other clergy participated in this friendly celebration, and consequently left themselves open to bitter, conservative criticism for not recognizing the special validity of Catholicism. In another altercation, they had stopped Leo from attacking the Knights of Labor in America, as he had done at the instigation of the Canadian hierarchy in their country. In that maneuver, Gibbons enlisted the powerful support of Cardinal Manning in England, who convinced the pope that the labor organization was not an anti-Catholic secret society. Later, Gibbons was not as successful when the Holy Office insisted on banning Catholic membership in the Odd Fellows, the Sons of Temperance, and the Knights of Pythias—generally benign secret organizations that probably reminded the Vatican of the hated Freemasons.

In September 1895, Leo in his encyclical *Loginqua Oceani* praised American Catholics and admitted that their progress was due to the toleration embedded in the federal Constitution and in the laws. Still he argued that separation was not the ideal formulation for the relationship of church and state everywhere. He also criticized divorce and civil disobedience in his letter and proscribed membership in societies dedicated to violence. In response to the critics of the Parliament of Religions, the pope mandated that Catholics had to hold their own congresses or meetings apart from others. The second rebuke came on the issue of Americanism.

In 1891, a complimentary biography by Walter Elliott of Isaac Hecker, a convert to Catholicism and founder of the Paulist Fathers was published. The volume was translated into French where it became a major literary event. Hecker was portrayed as a role model for priests, as a man who sought to reconcile the church and democracy. The French Catholic conservatives, however, bitterly attacked the volume, and the controversy went to the Vatican. Gibbons again asked for a delay before any condemnation of what was being called "Americanism." And Ireland again went to Rome, but arrived too late to stop the pope's letter.[31]

On January 22, 1899, in a papal letter to Cardinal Gibbons, titled *Testem Benevolentiae* Leo criticized certain doctrines that had arisen on the occasion of the Hecker biography. Very gingerly the pope made it clear that he was not talking about those "characteristic qualities which reflect honor on the people of America." Instead, he was referring to the view that the Church should modify her doctrines to suit modern civilization so as to attract those outside the faith. He went on to enumerate some specific errors: "that the Holy Spirit bestows more charisma in the present day than in earlier ages; that direct inspiration obviates the need for spiritual direction; that natural virtues are preferable to supernatural, because the former prepare the Christian better for action in the world; that, therefore, active virtues are preferred to passive ones like humility, meekness, and obedience; that the vows taken by members of religious orders inhibit liberty and are out of step with the imperatives of the present order; and that new methods, more in harmony with contemporary reality, should be employed to convert non-Catholic Christians."[32]

Ireland simply indicated that he did not hold such views; Cardinal Gibbons also agreed that no educated American Catholic had such opinions, and other American Catholics blithely referred to it as a "phantom heresy." Clearly, Gibbons and other progressives were trying to sidestep the controversy, but the pope's admonition gave considerable strength to the conservative wing of the Catholic Church. Later, Leo was supposed to have insisted that the letter was meant to stop the controversy in Europe, and that Americans need not worry. But he was being disingenuous if he had said that, for the letter was sent to Gibbons for a real purpose. It is doubtful if many of the faithful from the United States even knew of the controversy, but it surely led to a very cautious and timid hierarchy for generations to come. Later Catholic clergy avoided theology and church history—except in the most celebratory modes. And as for their hierarchy, those men became preoccupied with building parishes, cathedrals, churches, schools, and colleges, but rarely would they be what Leo had been as a bishop—a man of ideas. After the appointment of William O'Connell as Bishop of Portland, the pontiff told him that a bishop cannot afford to be a "near mystic," but had to be a "man of action."[33]

Indeed, Leo XIII was one of the few popes who could easily be called both an intellectual and a man of action. He not only read and respected the works of St. Thomas Aquinas, but in his *Aeterni Patris*, he proclaimed Aquinas' theological system in effect the Church's official philosophy. To many it was an aged pope simply returning to the medievalism of the past. Indeed Leo added to that impression by building a splendid mausoleum in St. John Lateran in 1891 for the remains of Pope Innocent III (1198–1216), the epitome of powerful popes in the early Middle Ages.

But in fact, Leo was a broader scholar than that. In 1893, he urged Catholic experts to come to the defense of the Scriptures by studying Oriental languages and the techniques of biblical criticism. Against the opposition of the Curia, he opened up the secret archives of the Vatican to the year 1831 and commented, "We have nothing to fear from the publication of the documents." He showed a deep interest in the Vatican Library and in the Vatican Observatory, established a school of paleography and comparative history, funded or assisted in the establishment of national colleges in Rome, and pushed for a seminary in Ceylon for the training of priests.

He encouraged, subsidized, and approved of a variety of intellectual ventures, saying at one point, "Every newly discovered truth may serve to further the knowledge or the praise of God." He established the Thomist Academy in Rome and at his own expense gave it 300,000 lire for an edition of the works of St. Thomas Aquinas; arranged for another 150,000 lire to go to the University of Louvain to help fund a chair focusing on scholastic philosophy and its relationship to the natural sciences, and he helped set up academic chairs at the Universities of

Fribourg and Lille, and in Washington. In his advanced years, Leo returned to an early love—he supported a public subscription for a statue of Dante in Ravenna and advocated a special chair in Dante studies at the Roman Institute. Yet at the end of his pontificate, his attitudes seemed to harden as he curtailed scholarship on the Scriptures (1893), set standards for censorship (1897), created another Index of Forbidden Books (1900), and agreed to set up a permanent Biblical Commission (1902).[34]

From Justice to the Social Gospel
If the above were a summary of his papacy, he would be seen as a pope who concentrated much of his considerable efforts on diplomatic maneuvers to protect the Church and educational endeavors to enhance her teaching mission. He would be a substantial figure in the papacy, one who tried skillfully to repair some of the damage caused or at least manifested during Pius IX's long reign. But in fact these activities are overshadowed by the most famous encyclical ever issued by a modern pontiff—*Rerum Novarum,* the papal letter on the condition of labor.

The Industrial Revolution had started in the textile mills of Great Britain at the end of the eighteenth century and moved onto the European continent and into the United States, especially after the Civil War. Great fortunes were made by the industrial leaders who created this new world. The very landscape changed, and so did the patterns of immigration as families left their farms and rural estates and went into the burgeoning cities. Railroads became increasingly important as arteries that moved material and production, not just in Europe, but in the United States. In the United States for example, the number of rail miles jumped from 70,000 in 1873 to 193,000 by 1900. Added to that was the rapid growth in population. In Europe, the figures went from 140 million in 1740 to 188 million in 1800 to 266 million in 1850 and then increased by another 130 million by the turn of the century. The reach of education and the sharp decline of illiteracy also followed in most of the northern and western European countries. And so, concomitantly did the rise of newspapers and journals of opinion and the presence of broad-based democratic enfranchisement for many adult males.

The conditions of poverty grew more burdensome however, and in the cities more visible. Factories and slums lived side by side and men and their families worked twelve to fifteen hours a day for low wages. It was said that a whole generation of urban children rarely saw the sun rise or set.

The Catholic Church began to become more critical of the new industrial state and more sensitive to the so-called social question. In the past, the Church of Rome, of course, had been committed in many ways to a more regulated guild-oriented commercialism, one ready to accept constraints on the use of property, on the exploitation of people, and on the need for religious holidays, vacations, and regulated workdays. In part, the roots of the medieval Roman Church allowed it to realize that capitalism was not the only economic order in the history of mankind—a balanced view not as prominent in some Protestant countries.

The major secular response to the social question came with the rapid growth of Socialist or Worker parties, many of them committed to the doctrines of Karl Marx. Socialist parties grew up in Germany by 1875, in Austria and Switzerland by 1888, in Sweden and Holland by 1889, and in Italy, Poland, and Finland by 1892. The Church then not only had to wage war against nationalism and the anti-clerical impulse, but also against disciplined Socialist parties and a compelling ideology that addressed the great social issues arising in the West. By 1880, the working class in France—the eldest daughter of Catholicism, as it was called—was lost to the Church.

In England, however, Cardinal Manning, who had been converted from the safe haven of Anglicanism and become a Catholic and later a prelate, brought his adopted Church into the battle for better working conditions. In December 1872 he appeared at a rally to support the cause of farmers. He urged Prime Minister William Gladstone to advocate legislation to end early childhood labor and regulate housing conditions. In 1874, he delivered an electrifying address on "the rights and dignity of labour" in which he supported the right of unions to organize and demanded legislation to regulate hours and control child labor. Serving on a royal commission on housing, he pushed for community-oriented town planning. In 1889, Manning supported the use of arbitration in the London dock strikes, and he was to be a major inspiration for Leo's encyclical.[35]

Rerum Novarum had two purposes: to thwart the advances of socialism and to lay out a social policy on the abuses directed against workers under the new industrial order. Thus, by the end of the mid and late nineteenth century, the greatest ideological challenge to Catholicism was coming from a counter ideology, not nationalism or Freemasonry, or a variety of hybrids of romantic individualism, but the attractive philosophies of socialist theorists, reformers, and utopians. There were many variations in the age-old beliefs in economic equality and common ownership. But none exercised greater attraction than Marxism, which maintained that in the dialectic or movement of history there would be an inexorable triumph in Lenin's words of the tough disciplined dictatorship of the proletariat.

Karl Marx's ideology would meld or mix the humanitarian and

utopian dreams of equality and brotherhood, the acceptance of conflict, turmoil, and violence for the greater socialist good, and the alliance of idealism and the power impulse that so fascinates elites and intellectuals. Much of nineteenth century socialism was aligned to the Romanticism of Jean Jacques Rousseau, the cult of violence, the celebration of naked reason, and the promulgation of atheism—a brew that was bound to capture the condemnation of Roman pontiffs.[36]

But to Leo, it was more than another heresy—it was a new coalition that would be distinctly anti-Catholic. Soon conservative politicians and the upper classes came to understand the powerful appeal of socialism and the organizational strength of Marxist cadres and agitators. The pope's encyclical started off with a deeply moving analysis of the vast expansion of industry and science and the enormous fortunes of the few who cared little about the utter poverty of the masses and the prevailing moral degeneracy that resulted from such power and abuse.

Gone were the ancient workingmen's guilds that had been in operation up to the last century, and since then no other protective organization had taken their place. "Working men have been surrendered, isolated, and helpless [left to] the hard heartedness of employers and the greed of unchecked competition," the pope declared. A small number of very rich have "been able to lay upon the teeming masses of the laboring poor a yoke little better than that of slavery itself." The encyclical read as if it were written by Rousseau or Marx.[37]

Then Leo proceeded to make five basic points: first, he attacked socialism for its refusal to recognize the right of people to own private property, which promoted man's sense of intelligence and independence and protected his family. Second, the pope outlined the important role of the Church in social affairs, noting its indispensable presence in a well-ordered society. Third, Leo talked of the importance of charity and justice to alleviate grinding poverty. Fourth, the pope departed from the fashionable argument for a *laissez faire* state and presented a positive view that stressed not just the government's role in promoting public safety, but also the need to regulate conditions of work, the guarantee of a just wage, and the encouragement of a wide distribution of private property. Then lastly, he emphasized the importance of voluntary organizations like trade unions and Catholic social action groups.

Today those ideas are rather modest and dated, the language a bit archaic, but in 1891 it was an extraordinary document to come from the Vatican. Leo and other high-ranking clergy in Germany, the United States, the United Kingdom, and Ireland had explored for some time a recognition of the problems of labor and farmers. But this encyclical became a rallying cry for what was to be called "Social Catholicism."

After Leo's death, it was heralded as papal approval for the development of Christian Democratic parties in Europe—movements that checked socialist and communist governments, even though Leo was not generally sympathetic to political parties.[38]

Leo thus had transformed the Church in many ways that his colleagues had never imagined. He was seen at times as imperious and to some a bit too intellectual, but he had lived a long time and had seen much foolishness and turmoil. He mixed very conservative theology at times with canny diplomacy and a strange curiosity toward new ideas. Whereas his predecessor fought the enemies of the Church with his willpower and courage, Leo tried to avoid confrontation with states and regimes. Sometimes against the admonitions of the Curia, he insisted on recognizing the realities of those states, and did so occasionally with calculated abandon.

Above all, he sent his orthodoxy into battle against the ideas of secular ideologues, and in the great social challenges of his time he was not found wanting. In other pronouncements, Leo vigorously denounced the remnants of slavery, pressed for peaceful solutions of international disputes, and embraced in tentative ways the avant-garde views of a social gospel. In the first cause he sought to make the historic Archepiscopal See in Carthage a center for the anti-slavery campaign.

Still, he was a prisoner in the Vatican as was his predecessor. Leo would walk the Vatican gardens, sit and read under the old oaks, and occasionally welcome pilgrimages of working men. Concerning the developments of biblical scholarship at the end of his life he once wistfully remarked, "I would like to have ten years to resolve this question in harmony with the words of the church and the exigencies of science."[39]

On July 3, 1903, at the age of 93, he became very ill, and as he approached death, he asked about the page proofs of one of his Latin poems. He then recalled his own role as papal chamberlain and warned that he should not be tapped too hard on the forehead for he might wake up! Later two figures were carved on the either side of his tomb, one a mourning woman representing the Church, and the other a tradesman with his tools and characteristic dress, marking the passing of a prelate called the pope of the working man.

In his quarter century reign, Leo remained true to many of the dogmatic statements and public pronouncements of his immediate predecessor. One of his biographers has argued that as a cardinal in Perugia, he had actually encouraged Pio Nono to issue the *Syllabus of Errors*, push the Vatican Council to advance the infallibility decree, and promulgate the dogma on the Immaculate Conception. Thus, by all predictions, Leo should have been a keeper of Pio Nono's flame.[40]

But from the very first, Leo XIII charted a different path in two significant areas—the relationship with sovereigns and states and the perils of industrial capitalism. On the first issue, he simply abandoned Pius' orientations and diplomatic style—seeking to make the Church more protected from the adversities of the world by somewhat making peace with it, except on the Italian or Roman question. As has been seen, before Leo, the Church was constantly on the defensive, especially among the educated elites and their ruling classes. After Leo, the Church seemed to become intellectually respectable once again. Shorn of its temporal possessions, the Vatican and the pope were able to assume more of an intellectual and moral force than in generations before.

After their first dismay over the labor encyclical, conservatives praised Leo as a major impediment in the way of secular socialism sweeping across Western Europe. There is some truth to the observation that the Catholic Church became a great fortress against Marxism, in the same way that the United States of America became the foot soldiers stopping the advance of Communism—the most virulent form of Marxist ideology.

But Leo and his advisors saw the labor encyclical as a genuine response to the evils of industrialization and the dehumanization of workers and their families. It is something quite remarkable to witness an eighty-one-year-old, sheltered, religious prelate electrifying the Western world with a denunciation of exploitation and a call for justice and comity. No encyclical in modern times has had such a positive impact on people, and none has so added to the intellectual and teaching powers of the Roman Church.

Leo had his pastoral side, his personal commitment to piety and the religious customs of folk Catholicism. But at the core, he was a man who recognized the play of the intellect, although he occasionally embraced forms of censorship and doctrinal admonitions. But in his long papacy, there was a remarkable confidence that the Church had the ability and resilience to face the advances of science and the critiques of philosophy, and still prevail in fair debate and discussion. Leo at age sixty-eight seemed to have learned the limits of authority and the need to persuade, cajole, and encourage the recalcitrants, the skeptics, and the unscrupulous. Some observers of his time said that as the pontiff aged, he began to look more and more like the French atheist and philosopher Voltaire. But appearances are deceiving. Leo drew strength from his beliefs, hope from his faith, and a sense of irony earned from the lessons that life on earth is but a trial and not the totality of human fate.

CHAPTER EIGHT
BENEDICT XV, (1914–1922)

As the young and the romantic celebrated the beginning of the Great War, the old man in St. Peter's, Pius X, pleaded for peace. But peace would not come. The conflict started in the miscalculation of diplomats, the timetables of military strategists, the purveying of nationalistic hatreds. In the end, in the trenches of France, on the frozen tundra of Russia, and in a million hearts that lost the dreams of a single young man, the lessons of war were soon learned. When the war was relegated to the annals of history, it left four major empires destroyed and set in place the beginnings of the terrible totalitarian states that led to a second, and even more destructive war.

When the conclave met in 1914 to choose a successor to Pius X, the cardinals wanted a man who would combine personal piety with strong diplomatic experience. Some seemed to accept intuitively that his pontificate would be defined by the Church's reactions to the war that was just beginning. Still others realized that the preoccupations of Pius X with internal Church matters may not have served the faithful in that period of strife. They were correct. After that conflict was done, a disillusioned John Maynard Keynes was to conclude, "Never in the lifetime of man now living has the universal element in the soul of man burned so dimly."

The formal "veto" of certain Catholic states over candidates for the papacy was ended by Pius X right after his election, but the French ambassadors in London and in Madrid were still instructed by their government to use their influence in this conclave to form a united bloc of English, French, Belgium, and Spanish cardinals so as to get a candidate who would be sympathetic to the Entente. The favorite of France was Domenico Cardinal Ferrata, a former papal nuncio to that nation who was seen as friendly to its interests.

In the conclave the ultra-conservative zealots supported the young and brilliant Domenico Cardinal Serafini, a Benedictine monk, assessor to the Holy Office, and former Apostolic Delegate to Mexico. Opponents rallied around Pietro Cardinal Maffi, the popular and patriotic Archbishop of Pisa. Later, the supporters of both Maffi and Ferrata were to throw their support to a compromise candidate. When all was said and done, the cardinals again chose one of their own—a conservative Italian, a reliable product of the Curia, a protégé of Secretary of State Rampolla, and the Archbishop of Genoa, Giacomo Della Chiesa, or "James of the Church" as it could be translated.[1]

The Making of a Diplomat
A small, quiet person, he walked with a slight limp, spoke in a high-pitched voice, and seemed an unlikely successor to the strong-willed Pio Nono, the regal Leo, and the forceful saint, Pius X. As a youth Giacomo had heeded his father's advice and gone to a public institution, graduating with a doctorate of civil law from the University of Genoa, and he was associated with the Catholic Action movement. Having completed those studies, he was then free to follow the religious vocation that he felt in his heart and become a seminarian in Rome. After ordination and further study, he received a doctorate in sacred theology from Capranica College and another doctorate in canon law from the Gregorian University.

Della Chiesa boarded at the Accademia dei Nobili Ecclesiastici—a special training school for the diplomatic corps of the Church, which included such distinguished alumni as the legendary Ercole Consalvi, Leo XIII, Rampolla, Merry del Val, and later Pius XII. There he was called to the attention of the rising Monsignor Rampolla who had been in turn promoted by Leo XIII to become his nuncio in the difficult arena of Spain. Rampolla was permitted to bring a personal secretary with him, and he took the well-recommended student, Della Chiesa.

It was Mariano Rampolla's responsibility as papal nuncio to unite the Spanish Catholics and implement Leo's encyclical *Quam Multa* addressed to the nation's hierarchy. Rampolla was to prove rather adept diplomatically and rather charming personally. When a cholera epidemic swept through the nation in 1885, he and his secretary tended to the sick and dying. In the best charitable traditions of Christianity, they organized the relief effort, cleaned soiled beds, prepared food and medicine, and seemed heroic and immune to the disease's ravishes. On March 14, 1887, Monsignor Rampolla was made a cardinal, and two months later he was chosen by Leo XIII to succeed Cardinal Iacobini as secretary of state.

Rampolla promptly recalled Della Chiesa to Rome to become his "minutante" (personal assistant) and later made him undersecretary in the Secretariat of State where he remained for some fourteen years. His contemporaries generally found him to be an unprepossessing and courteous colleague with a lively sense of humor, an incredible capacity for work, and a marvelous memory. One Italian observer paid him in 1887 the highest compliment: Monsignor [later Cardinal] Agliardi observed he was " a new Consalvi," secretary of state in the 19th century. The quiet undersecretary lived in Rome with his parents in rooms in the Arcione, and later the Palazzo Brascha.[2]

During that period, his career would parallel the handsome and brilliant Rafael Merry del Val who would become for a time a sort of rival. Indeed Merry del Val was everything Della Chiesa was not, he was impressive, witty, engaging, and carried himself with a domineering presence that both inspired and pleased. Della Chiesa on the other hand was diffident, slight, and so small that he was nicknamed by some "Il piccoletto"—the dwarf. He said of himself, "I am but an ugly gargoyle on the beauties of Rome."[3]

When Leo died, Rampolla was cast out of power, and it was Merry del Val who assumed ascendancy as the thirty-eight-year-old secretary of state under the new Pius X. Rampolla's protége had lost his patron, and it seemed that he was no longer the charmed staff person advancing in the Curia. Still for four difficult years, he remained in the Secretariat of State, while loyally visiting his old friend who was tucked away in the ecclesiastical corners of the sacred city.

Under Rampolla's guidance, he had been promoted in 1901 to the office of deputy secretary of state and given the title Secretary of the Cypher. There he acquired a profound understanding of Church diplomacy, the subtle workings of the Curia, and the intricacies of dogma and canon law, and in the process took the measure of the personalities who had moved past his desk, and who would later become important during his reign.

Pope Leo, a shrewd judge of character, had actually considered him for the Archbishopric of Florence in 1902, but apparently Leo informed him that Rampolla objected, fearing he would lose his most valued aide. Later, when Della Chiesa's mother complained to the cardinal secretary of state that her son deserved a higher position in the Church hierarchy, Rampolla countered, "Have patience, Lady Marchioness, your son will make a few steps forward, but they will be great ones."[4]

When Pius became pope, he replaced Rampolla as was the custom, but by 1907, he decided to advance Rampolla's protégé to archbishop of Bologna, although he did not name him a cardinal as many expected. Apparently, a wary Merry del Val had stopped Pius from making Della Chiesa the papal nuncio to Spain, seeking to end Rampolla's influence and diplomatic legacy there permanently. On the other hand, the pope claimed that God had inspired him to send Della Chiesa to Bologna rather than Madrid, and so it was done. It was only in May 1914 that

Della Chiesa was named to the College of Cardinals, and that honor lasted for only three months, since he was soon elected pope in his own right. Della Chiesa knew well the men with whom he was dealing. He had, for example, close contact with Pius X, and early in his reign in 1903 had observed sardonically, "The new Pontiff is a sweet delicacy. If it were possible to sin by an excess of charity and amiability, then I think the new pope would be guilty of that fault."[5]

As for Della Chiesa himself, the observations of his contemporaries were often diverse. In 1913, one person wrote, "He has a high, pale forehead, crowned by the blackest hair; his eyes are black, vivid and penetrating; he has a large mouth with thin, drawn lips, but full of expression. He reminded me of Leopardi, and, in fact, his face and figure belong undoubtedly to the same type as those of the great poet."[6]

With his fastidiousness, his deep ties to his widowed mother, his tendency at times to be prissy and even surly, Della Chiesa seemed to be forbidding to some, even though he lacked the pretentiousness so often apparent in Roman clergy, especially those on the rise. Above all, he was in demeanor and bearing a natural aristocrat. Although Della Chiesa was strongly in accord with Pius' attacks on the Modernist heresy—indeed was called the pope's right hand in the cause—he appears to have disagreed with the controversial methods of Monsignor Umberto Benigni's *Sodalitium Pianum*. Although it was not generally known, apparently that group was investigating him at that time as well, probably because of his seeming approval of quasi-secular Catholic journalism.

Those "integral" or pure Catholics, as they like to call themselves, were obsessed with any signs of doctrinal deviation from their traditional views, and even casual friends of their critics were suspect. Cardinal Rampolla, then in retirement and living at the Palazzino di Santa Maria behind St. Peter's, denounced what he called the "sad impression that they made with their excessive zealism." Later his protégé, early in his pontificate, would criticize those who would split the Church into groups because of their mistaken zeal.[7]

Della Chiesa, safely tended to his archdiocese from 1908 to 1912, and did not visit Rome at all. In 1913, he led a major Italian pilgrimage to Lourdes; in December of that year he received news of the death of his great patron, Rampolla. The gossip was that the pope and Cardinal Merry del Val had removed Della Chiesa from power in Rome in order to guarantee a clear break with the progressive policies of Leo and his last secretary of state. Now that challenge and that presence were gone. By not granting a cardinal's hat to a see that had traditionally been headed by one, the message was clear about the reservations that some in the Vatican, including the pope, apparently had about its current incumbent.

Even the Bolognese were dismayed, and one group finally went to see the pope, and bluntly declared that if Della Chiesa was not worthy to be a cardinal, then he was not worthy to continue to be archbishop of Bologna, and should either receive the honor or be transferred.[8] Even saints can be petty at times and not above politics in their dealings with mere mortals it seems. After Rampolla's death, the archbishop of Bologna received the honor.

The major and unintended consequence, of course, was that Pius had cleared the path for the emergence of a successor who would look back with favor on the progressive policies of Leo and on his diplomacy. At the conclave, the cardinals listened intently to the opening sermon of Monsignor Aurelius Galli who warned that the Church in the midst of war must choose a man of superior intelligence, savoir-faire, and genuine holiness, and one who was especially imbued with Christian charity. Then in secret the cardinals voted; it has been speculated that Della Chiesa received only the minimal two-thirds vote necessary to be elected. Apparently, there was even a challenge, based on the rumor that he had voted for himself—which was not permitted—an accusation which proved to be groundless. Impassively, he accepted the office and then to the surprise of his fellow cardinals, chose Benedict as his new name in honor of both the great monastic saint and Church reformer, and also out of respect to the last bishop of Bologna to succeed to the papacy, the cultured Prospero Lambertini (1740-58), Benedict XIV.

It was said that in greeting one particular individual at the ceremony, the new pope quipped, "And We assure you the Holy Father is not a Modernist." Within earshot of Cardinal Merry del Val, the pope was also supposed to have remarked, "The stone which the builders rejected is made the headstone in the corner." The cardinal diplomatically responded, "It is the Lord's doing, and it is marvelous in our eyes." It was a tactful rejoinder, but Merry del Val's days were numbered, and he was given forty-eight hours to vacate the secretary of state's apartments. Thus, Benedict XV, the Church bureaucrat and the Curial spectator, inherited the manifold duties and the lengthy title of his office: Vicar of Christ, Bishop of Rome, Successor of St. Peter, Supreme Pontiff of the Universal Church, Patriarch of the West, Primate of Italy, Archbishop and Metropolitan of the Province of Rome, and Supreme Steward of the Temporal Possessions of the Holy Roman Church.[9]

In his first actions as pope, he seemed to be a traditional figure returning to the clerical court he knew so well. Indeed, Benedict moved easily and comfortably through the familiar Vatican corridors where he was no stranger. He restored the custom that the pope would eat alone, permitted the faithful to kiss his slipper, and was crowned not in St.

Peter's Square, but as Leo had been in the Sistine Chapel. He replaced Merry del Val as secretary of state, choosing Cardinal Ferrata who soon died of appendicitis, and then appointed Pietro Cardinal Gasparri—the son of a sheep raiser from the Umbria region. Gasparri was also a Rampolla protégé, and a talented person who seemed a bit disorganized as he surrounded himself with parrots who shrieked in his office while he did the Church's business.[10]

Without having close ties to his extended family as Pius had, Benedict withdrew into himself more—even avoiding the members of the Apostolic College. He made no special provision for his sister to visit him, although he did travel through the Vatican Gardens with his partially paralyzed brother. He rarely held public audiences, in part because of the restrictions on foreign travel for the faithful during the war, and he was punctual and businesslike in his dealings with subordinates. Appropriately, the new pope seemed to have a fetish for watches and for avoiding lost time.[11]

The great and consuming issue before Benedict was the immensely gruesome and costly war. Soon, Europeans were to know that what some had mistakenly predicted would be a pleasant little engagement was reaching into still another year of terrible battles and untold tragedies. Later, the pope was rightly to condemn the war as simply "useless slaughter,"[12] and the "surrender of civilized Europe." In late 1914, the pope issued his first encyclical, *Ad Beatissimi Apostolorum Principis*, which was roundly criticized as a disjointed and saccharine exposition on the importance of love and charity in the midst of the horrors of mechanized warfare.

But if one reads the papal letter, it is difficult to comprehend the vehemence of the criticism. There is no question that Benedict incorporated into *Ad Beatissimi* some brief observations, especially at the end, on Modernism, the need for an independent papacy, the role of bishops, and the desirability of unity among Catholics. It is clear that his lamentations over the war set the real tone of the letter and indeed for most of his pontificate. It has been speculated that Benedict had in general an instinctive repulsion toward violence, which may have been connected with his physically weak condition, and that the repeated slaughters of the war moved him even more than most observers of the human condition.

He eloquently denounced the ruin, slaughter, and bloodshed, the increase in the number of widows and orphans, the disruption of economic life, and the general misery of the poor, "All are in distress," he judged. It is true that Benedict did not give a sophisticated summary of the causes of the war, for he was not a historian, but a moral critic.

Still, he focused on the absence of mutual love among mankind, the disrespect for authority, the injustice in relationships between economic classes, and the inordinate striving for material goods. Later chroniclers of the conflict would cite the importance of imperialism, nationalist envy, the overconfidence of the military, and a score of other "causes," which surely supplemented Benedict's initial diagnosis.[13]

The Causes of the Great War
Indeed several generations of historians and countless other citizens across the globe have struggled then and now with the question of what caused the First World War. It is as if they sensed that it was too gruesome and far reaching to have come about by accident or as a consequence of the murder of the Austrian Archduke Ferdinand and his wife on June 28, 1914. Authorities on the war still disagree, but in general there are probably four underlying causes that can be identified.

The most important was the development of a web of entangling alliances in the period following the Franco-Prussian War in 1871. As a result of that war, Germany annexed Alsace-Lorraine, and Otto von Bismarck, the Reich chancellor, created a series of alliances in order to isolate France and prevent retaliation from that humiliating loss. A second destabilizing factor was the rapid growth of huge national armies and armaments. The success of the Prussian armies made a profound impression throughout Europe, and those developments led to an increase in standing military forces. A third factor that led to the outbreak of war was the long-term consequences of imperialism as a way of thinking and as a way of life. The great powers coveted colonies for their cheap raw materials and markets for manufactured goods over which they could have a monopoly. And fourth, added to these dynamics was the spread of nationalism among various ethnic groups, especially in the Balkans.

In December 1912, a secret memo of the German general staff predicted that in the coming war with France, it "would be necessary to violate the neutrality of Belgium." By early 1914, the Russians were meeting secretly to plan for action in the straits near Constantinople, and laid out plans for a military offensive in the West. In general, the European chiefs of staff expected a short war, one that would favor the first nation to strike. Their model was the German wars of unification; a more appropriate lesson would have been the long bloody civil war of attrition in the United States. Grant and Sherman would have been better reference points for the military strategists of this time than the European generals Karl von Clausewitz or Helmuth von Moltke.

When Archduke Franz Ferdinand, the heir to the Austro-Hungarian or Hapsburg throne, went to the capital of Bosnia, he was aware of the threat of assassination in that region. At the alleged instigation of the head of the intelligence division of the Serbian chief of staff, several Bosnian men volunteered to kill the archduke. To the Hapsburgs, the assassinations of the archduke and his wife lent themselves to a reckoning with Serbia and, with the support of Germany, they prepared for a localized war. The Austro-Hungarian regime issued a series of ultimata, nearly all of which the Serbians surprisingly agreed to. But the Austrians wanted war and severed diplomatic relations with Serbia as a prelude to military engagement. Concerned about these happenings and preoccupied with the fate of Constantinople and the Bosphorus Straits, Russia supported the Serbians. As tensions increased, the British foreign minister, Sir Edward Grey, proposed a peace conference and a mediation of the dispute. To avoid any such mediation, the Austrians declared war on Serbia on July 28 and bombarded Belgrade the next day. Meanwhile, the Russian military had also been preparing for war, and on July 29, it mobilized against the Austrians. Soon France and Britain followed Russia and the war began.

Germany's success in the war depended on rapid action, while Russia, because of her vast areas and poor transportation, needed more time for mobilization. Now the system of entangling alliances fueled the fires of war. Great Britain insisted that the neutrality of Belgium and Luxembourg must be respected, but the Germans needed to defeat France quickly, and the corridor through those small countries was the fastest way to accomplish that objective. This "brutal" invasion of Belgium was used by some British leaders who wanted war to defend their empire's interests. British public opinion was treated to detailed statements on "the rape of Belgium" by the Huns. In fact, British foreign policy had been historically committed to protecting the narrow seas across from the channel and to stopping any one nation from gaining hegemony on the continent. Partially for those reasons, the British had gone to war in the past, against Louis XIV and Napoleon I, and would go to war again. The Germans protested that "necessity knows no law," and expressed shock that Great Britain would go to war over "a scrap of paper"—its treaty obligations with Belgium. But by August, even Japan and Turkey were in the conflict, and it had indeed become a worldwide conflagration. In his own way, British Foreign Minister Grey correctly summarized what was happening when he grimly prophesied, "The lamps are going out all over Europe. We shall not see them lit again in our lifetimes."

Europe had known war before, but never with the mechanized barbarity that this total war brought. The casualties were so high that their count even today numbs the mind. The official statements indicated that Russian casualties reached 1.7 million men—the true total, though, is probably double that; Germany lost 1.8 million, surely another underestimation; France, 1.3 million; the United Kingdom, 744,702 and the British Empire, 202,000; the Austro-Hungary Empire, 1.2 million; Italy, 460,000; Turkey, 325,000 plus many more unaccounted for; and for the late-arriving United States, the count was 115,660 casualties.

Even more stark were the casualties of the major battles of the war. A few will suffice to give a frightening sense of the carnage. On the eastern front in September 1914, the Austrian chief of staff Conrad von Hotzendorf lost 350,000 of the 900,000 men in his army near the Galicia region. At Tannenberg, the German generals Paul von Hindenberg and Erich Ludendorff in August 1914 defeated Aleksandr Samsonov's Russian armies and took 120,000 prisoners and decimated that fighting force. In September, they defeated the Russian First Army, inflicting 125,000 casualties alone in the battle of Masurian Lakes.

In the west, the first battle of Ypres resulted in the loss of 58,000 British officers and enlisted men—the virtual destruction of its regular volunteer army corps and led to conscription to fill the new ranks. On the German side, the battle would be called by some "the slaughter of the children," a lament over the demise of so many young men of promise. In May 1915, at the battle of Ambers Ridge, the French suffered 100,000 casualties and the British lost 27,000 with the military results negligble. In ten days in September, the French lost another 145,000 men, achieving no military objectives at all. By March 1916, the Germans suffered the loss of 81,000 and the French 89,000 at the battle of Verdun. After ten months, the total on both sides reached an incredible 700,000 killed and wounded. After four months at the battle of the Somme even more carnage resulted—415,000 British Empire casualties, 195,000 French casualties, and German losses at least equal to the total of the Allied nations they opposed.

In the Balkans, the Serbian army, with thousands of old men, women, and children following, retreated through the mountain snows. Only one quarter of the 400,000 people survived the march. After eighteen months of war, Serbia had lost over one-sixth of its total population. In June 1916, the Russian general Aleksey Brusilov attacked the Austrians in Galicia, taking 400,000 prisoners. Later in his last desperate offenses, Ludendorff's plans for victory cost the Germans over 350,000 men. And on it continued—staggering casualties for literally meters of disputed territory, incalculable civilian losses, new weapons of frightening efficiency, and the early introduction of gas warfare.[14] Following on the heels of the terrible war was a frightening influenza epidemic that in 1918 killed more people than the armed conflict itself. It has been estimated that the influenza took more lives than any epidemic since the Black Plague that decimated Europe.

Thus, it was in this frightening context that Benedict would live and react during nearly all of his papacy. Initially, the British and the French press especially criticized his first encyclical. One author, Robert Dell, characterized it thus, "It is really difficult to believe that this was actually written in the year 1914; it sounds like the utterance of an elderly gentlewoman of about the year 1830."[15] There also was the assumption that because the pope did not condemn the Central Powers by name, he was in effect showing his sympathy for Germany and the Austro-Hungarian Empire. The pope simply responded, "The Holy See has not been, nor wishes to be, *neutral* in the European War. It has, in turn, the right and duty to be *impartial*." Privately, he observed, "My appeals not only have gone unheeded, but have been scandalously msinterpreted."[16]

He regarded the attacks on him so early in his pontificate as a concerted campaign to prevent him from speaking out, and Benedict insisted, "They want to silence me, but they shall not succeed in sealing my lips; nobody shall prevent me from calling to my own children, peace, peace, peace." In fact, there is some substantiation for Benedict's speculation. The Italian government, especially Foreign Minister Sidney Sonnino, had insisted that the Treaty of London, which was signed on April 26, 1915, contain a clause, number 15, which would require that members of the Entente bar the pope from participating in the crafting of a final peace treaty. That agreement only became public at the end of 1917 when the renegade Bolshevik government in Russia published it. Resorting to its anti-clerical tradition, the Italian government had forced the article on the reluctant British and French governments who were anxious to have another ally at any cost.[17]

The Wages of Neutrality
During the war, Benedict would be accused of both remaining silent and of favoring one side or the other—usually of tilting toward the Central Powers, who were supposed to be closer in attitude to the historic authoritarianism of the papacy. In an interview with *La Liberte,* on June 22, 1915, the reporter Louis Latapi gave the distorted impression that Benedict was indeed an authoritarian prince with an aristocratic demeanor who seemed somewhat flippant about the German invasion of Belgium. Benedict was also supposed to have criticized the Italian government for its censorship of mail that was going to the Vatican, which in turn brought forth the predictable anti-clerical Italian barrage and hindered the pope's ability to deal with the Roman Question.

His secretary of state, Cardinal Gasparri, had to return from vacation quickly and conducted a press conference to control the damage, but the critics of the Vatican's diplomacy continued their work. Actually, Gasparri, in the name of the pope, had condemned the violation of Belgium neutrality on July 6, 1915, a public criticism that other neutral nations including the United States, had not levied. When questioned about whether he was taking sides, he remarked quite correctly that even the German Chancellor admitted the invasion was contrary to international law.[18]

In May 1915, three weeks after the torpedoing of the *Lusitania*, Benedict deplored "methods of attack both by land and sea, contrary to the laws of humanity and international law," but he refused to condemn German submarine warfare specifically.[19] Benedict insisted in that year that the pontiff "must embrace all the combatants in one sentiment of charity," and yet he censured without modification "every injustice by whatever side it may have been committed."[20] By May, Italy had joined the Entente against the pope's entreaties, and German and Austrian nationals were told to leave that nation.[21] For the Vatican and its basically Italian Curia, the war took on a new urgency and reality.

On January 10 of the same year the pope asked for a day of peace, and he even composed his own prayer to be said until the war was over. In Italy some people denounced the peace prayer, and a Socialist journalist by the name of Benito Mussolini criticized the invocation when it was circulated among the fighting men.[22] In France, the police actually seized newspapers that published the prayer and then released them the next day. Events were not going well for the Western powers, and the war leaders were not able to either bring victory or to stop the fighting. Benedict's appeals thus were a problem for them, for his repeated insistence on peace was seen as a hindrance to waging total war and promoting high morale for the cause. Indeed he even refused to let chaplains appear in military uniform in St. Peter's, citing again the need to be impartial.

To add to the pope's difficulties in trying to stay impartial, he was presented with evidence of treason against the Italian state by one of his own high-ranking officials. In August 1916, the warship *Leonardo da Vinci* was blown up off the harbor of Taranto. The papal chamberlain and keeper of the wardrobe, Monsignor Rudolf Gerlach, was heard to say that that was the price Italy paid for her treachery toward Germany. What was suspect was that Gerlach made this observation several hours *before* the news had reached Rome about the explosion!

Gerlach had previously received permission from the pope to stay in the Vatican even after the Italian government had expelled all German and Austrian nationals, and he apparently led a life of luxury, including buying an expensive Lancia automobile. The pope at first defended his chamberlain, but it was soon clear that Gerlach had indeed received money from agents of the Central Powers and had been subsidizing pro-German newspapers. Benedict had no option but to confront him with the charges and then dismiss him. The Vatican simply recorded of Gerlach, "He did not respond as he should have done," and the monsignor was led by Italian officials to the Italian-Swiss border at Lugano. Quixotically, Benedict observed, "He was always so jolly and seemed so frank and loyal." Later Gerlach was tried in absentia and sentenced to life in prison at hard labor. But by then he was gone. The whole episode reflected poorly on the pope's judgment, and surely did not help in his desire to settle the vexatious Roman Question.[23]

One of the most sensitive issues during the war was the relationship between the Holy See and Italy as the latter moved toward entering the fighting in August 1914. At first, Italy had stayed neutral in the conflict, since Germany and Austria entered the war without consulting her as was required by the pact of the Triple Alliance, which all three states had signed. But some of the Italian leaders feared that their nation might be punished if her previous allies were victorious and she had deserted them, while others expressed concern, that Italy might miss out on the fruits of victory if she ignored the entreaties of the Western Allies. Businessmen in the banking community generally favored neutrality, as did the Socialists and some of the clerically-oriented Italian Catholics. But the strong Nationalist element saw the war as the final chapter in the Risorgimento, and pushed for an adjustment of Italy's northeast boundaries with Austria.

In fact Benedict had privately encouraged Emperor Charles of Austria to discuss the question of Trieste with Italy. At first Charles agreed, but after the Austrian and German victories in the Julian Alps, he refused to make any concessions. Still others, including the Freemasons, viewed the Western nations as advocates of democracy and liberty, and the Central Powers as oppressors and autocrats. To them, the war was another chapter in trying to establish a society "without altars and without thrones."[24]

The Law of Guarantees mandated Vatican independence, but it never really dealt with the complexities of Italy going to war and the Vatican remaining neutral. What was the status of diplomats accredited to the Vatican by the Central Powers, for example? Italy decided that while it would guarantee the diplomatic immunity of such ministers, the Vatican had to censor their correspondence. When the pope refused, the diplomats voluntarily retired to Lugano making the question moot. Later, the Lateran Treaty of 1929 allowed such representatives to stay on Italian soil, even if Italy had severed relations with their nations during war.

There were discussions that the pope should remove himself from Italy during the conflict, and the Spanish government offered the Escorial several times as a papal residence, but Benedict XV, remembering the tribulations of some of his predecessors in exile, refused. As might be expected, there were some real tensions during the war years between the Vatican and Italy, such as when the Italian government seized the residence of the Austrian ambassador to the Vatican in late August 1916, after an air raid on the Palazzo Venezia. But generally the two sides were remarkably circumspect and correct.

And while the pope remained impartial as he so often said, Benedict and most of the Curia were still men of Italy in their sympathies. When there was some newspaper speculation that the Vatican expected to recover its Temporal States if Germany won the war, the Holy See was clear and to the point. Cardinal Gasparri indicated that the Holy Father regretted Italy's intervention in the war and had hoped for some Austrian concessions on the disputed border territories. However, with regard to the Roman Question, the pope did not desire to seek its solution through foreign intervention and arms. He expected that that controversy would be dealt with fairly by Italians as a sentiment of justice advanced. It was a fine and somewhat patriotic response.[25]

During the war and after it, the pope's record was continually denigrated by the accusatory question—why did Benedict remain silent? It would be asked later in a more inflammatory way of Pius XII's performance during World War II. In Britain a pamphlet was published titled "The Silence of Benedict XV," containing a sweeping indictment of organized Christianity for its impotence and timidity, and especially focused on what it called the most organized and universal organization, the Roman Catholic Church. The pamphlet claimed the pope "wields the greatest power in the world, for how do the greatest empires compare with the Roman domination over the hearts and minds of 240 millions of the human race?" The author concluded that Benedict could be "a trumpet call of hope and inspiration to the hearts of millions," but instead, he had exhibited a sphinx-like quiet because of fear or reasons of Vatican policy, thus exhibiting both silence and moral cowardice.[26]

The indictment focused on several general charges: 1) the pope had not spoken out to stop the war; 2) during the war he and his Church had done nothing; 3) he had not protested against the violation of the moral law; 4) he had taken up an attitude of neutrality which was cowardly and indefensible; and 5) by his silence, he had compromised not only his own Church, but Christianity in general. These charges were not unique to this one pamphlet. In fact, they were the general stuff that was repeated again and again in some of the anti-clerical and even the mainstream presses. From a historical perspective it is remarkable to realize the number of adherents who held those views, and to re-read the intense censure that was directed at Benedict. Obviously, the pope should not have been immune from legitimate criticism, but the grounds of that criticism were generally baseless, which was obvious even at that time. Looking back, it seems as if some of the frustrations and anger over the bloodletting settled on the fragile pope—as if even non-Catholics seemed to feel betrayed by his inability to bring an end to this war. Ironically, some of the anti-clerical elements and their allies who worked so energetically to cripple and destroy the papacy complained that the Holy Father lacked the moral power and authority to end the carnage. As Pius X observed early in the war, the days when the pope could force a truce or a settlement were long since over.

Later, when even the French hierarchy raised the issue of the pope's alleged pro-German sympathies, the cardinal secretary of state again responded. Gasparri laid out Benedict's views: Belgian independence, maintenance of the Austro-Hungary empire; establishment of Poland within limits; guarantee of the traditional integrity of France and her role as a first-class power; and a settlement of the Balkan question which would exclude Russia from Constantinople and the Straits—a provision meant to protect Catholic interests in the Middle East. Those policy objectives were remarkably close to Britain's public statements.[27]

At this point in time, the pope did not put forth a peace proposal publicly, but was waiting for President Woodrow Wilson to take the lead. The Vatican instructed Cardinal Gibbons to present to the president and to Secretary of State Robert Lansing the Vatican's views, but the American government did not feel that it could pursue an offer of mediation since the belligerents had not requested such a step. Thus, Benedict in this period concentrated on quiet, but rather effective humanitarian efforts.

The pope in fact became a remarkable model of appropriate behavior in his salutary efforts at humanitarianism, which exceeded even those of the Red Cross and neutral states such as Spain, and initially the United States. Benedict had learned the lessons of diplomacy well in the school of Leo and Rampolla, and he was not lacking in subtlety, in tact, or in understanding the true nature of the international conflict. Indeed, out of his pontificate came the great Church diplomats who would end up as his successors—Pius XI, Pius XII, and indirectly John XXIII and Paul VI. They were men who were either schooled by him or by his associates and who helped shape the twentieth century world and the Church in which they lived.

In December 1916, the kaiser and the leaders of the other Central Powers, which included Germany, Austria, Belgium, and Turkey, suggested to the Entente, which then included Great Britain, France, Russia and Italy, that peace negotiations should begin. The Vatican did not comment on the proposal despite the pope's often repeated desire for an end to hostilities. Only later did it come to light that British leaders indicated to the pope that any intervention on his part would be poorly received by both their nation and France, and so Benedict did not abandon his posture of impartiality. In Britain, David Lloyd George summarily dismissed the Central Powers proposal and committed himself to total victory; across the Channel, the French leader Aristide Briand simply called the proposal a "trap."[28] And so the war continued.

During all of this, the pope did not remain idle. Benedict decided to reach into the ranks of the Curia and appoint the young Eugenio Pacelli as his nuncio to Bavaria, so that he could have a listening post there and in the kaiser's court. Pacelli was quickly consecrated archbishop, then sent to Bavaria, and on May 26, 1917 he presented his credentials to King Ludwig III. Later he visited the chancellor of the German Reich, Theobald von Bethmann-Hollweg, and discussed four points as a basis for a possible settlement: the general limitations on armaments; establishment of international courts to handle disputes; restoration of the independence of Belgium; and the settlement of territorial disputes such as Alsace-Lorraine by the agreement of those concerned.

The chancellor maintained that Germany was willing to restore Belgium if that nation did not fall under British and French domination, and indicated that he was willing to reconsider a readjustment of Germany's western frontier. On July 19, the Reichstag overwhelmingly passed a resolution embracing moderate peace terms introduced by Deputy Matthias Erzberger of the Catholic Centre Party. The German Socialists were also moving toward supporting a Swedish proposal for an international Socialist conference in Stockholm aimed at achieving a peace "without annexation, and without indemnities." Some Catholics proposed that the pope issue a peace proposal to upstage the Socialist plans before the Stockholm meeting. In the meantime, Pacelli had also met with Kaiser Wilhelm II, who, among other matters, insisted that the pope should have used his papal infallibility to denounce the Entente![29]

Unfortunately, for the peace efforts, in August 1916 the kaiser appointed Paul von Hindenberg as field marshal, and Eric von Ludendorff as quartermaster, which consequently made the military increasingly autonomous from the civilian government. When Chancellor Bethmann-Hollweg pushed for a conciliatory peace plan, they insisted that he be removed, and he was replaced with George Michaelis on July 14. Michaelis at first seemed to support the Vatican's overtures, but quietly and effectively with the support of the new military leadership, he strangled them in the cradle.

Not knowing Michaelis' true intention, Benedict was encouraged by the German response, and he contacted the British minister to the Holy See, Count John De Salis, asking him to present his peace proposal to His Majesty's government, France, Italy, and the United States. The papal note of August 1, 1917 began by reiterating his general policy of absolute impartiality, respect for people regardless of their backgrounds, and a firm commitment to end the war. Benedict then laid before the powers a very specific peace proposal revolving around the following principles: 1) the substitution of "the moral force of right" for the law of material force; 2) a simultaneous and reciprocal decrease of armaments; 3) international arbitration as a substitute for armed force; 4) true liberty and community of the sea; 5) reciprocal renunciation of war indemnities; 6) evacuation and restoration of all occupied territories; and 7) an examination "in a conciliatory spirit" of rival territorial claims.

The British reply formulated by its Minister of Foreign Affairs, Anthony James Balfour, refused to accept or reject the note, but indicated that Germany had never pledged that it would restore Belgium independence. Meanwhile, there was some argument between Britain and France as to how to respond jointly to the pope's overture. Their dilemma was solved when on August 27, 1917, Secretary of State Robert Lansing, writing for President Woodrow Wilson, chastised the pope, concluding that in their judgment the war was a crusade to free peoples by stopping the vast military establishment that sought to dominate the world. Wilson thus refused to endorse the papal note.

To add to the pope's problems, the kaiser, under prodding from his new chancellor and his military, began to insist on the importance of having some presence on the coast of Flanders after all. The chancellor wrote to the pope that his government would support every effort to bring about peace if it were consistent with the interests of the German people; Ludendorf later complained that in his judgment the pope's plan was too favorable to the Entente. As for the Entente, France insisted that it really did not wish to pursue such peace efforts. Radical French Socialist deputy and later Premier Georges Clemenceau termed it a "German Peace Plan." Italy chose not to respond, although the Socialists favored the pope's plan, while the Nationalists and the Liberals generally did not. Emperor Charles of Austro-Hungary supported the proposal, as did Ferdinand of Bulgaria, and the Sultan of Turkey, Mohammed V, expressed his approval of "the lofty thoughts of His Holiness."[30]

As the deliberations continued, Chancellor Michaelis refused to provide a conclusive answer on the critical Belgium question, thus giving the Entente both a reason and an excuse not to pursue the pope's note seriously. A bitterly disappointed Benedict watched as his plan unraveled, and as he was once again subject to suspicious attacks from both sides. Later, on January 8, 1918, Woodrow Wilson presented to Congress his Fourteen Points, which contained propositions similar to parts of Benedict's proposals.

Unlike his recent predecessors, Benedict, a seasoned diplomat, chose to abandon the defensive postures of the past and to get the Vatican directly involved in the most difficult arena of international politics—the attempt to end the war and guarantee peace. There have been different explanations offered for his failure. It was said that Michaelis was influenced by his ties to the anti-Catholic German Evangelical Alliance, which in general opposed working with the papacy. The secret Treaty of London, which prohibited the pope's participation, clearly presented another obstacle for the Vatican's attempt at peacemaking. When it became public, the British government tried to explain away the provisions by citing the Italian government's insistence on having such a veto. In Rome, Baron Sonnino, attempting to cover up his role in the prohibition, actually charged that the Bolsheviks had forged the text.[3]

Those factors severely limited Benedict's ability to command a sympathetic audience, but they did not sidetrack an ongoing process. The war continued because neither side could imagine that it would not win. When czarist Russia collapsed in February/March 1917, it seemed that a war nearly totally waged on the Western front would spell victory for Germany and her allies. When the United States entered on behalf of the Entente on April 16, 1917, that influx of supplies and fresh troops would eventually lend credence to the view that victory would belong to the other alliance.

Thus it appears that both sides fought on and on for their own honor, self-interest, patriotism, and folly. And following that intransigence, the upheavals in Russia and the United States' new military presence in Western Europe changed previous calculations of the war. People knew suffering at home, but not the true condition of their armies out of sight. When Germany surrendered, a substantial portion of both the armed forces and the populace felt betrayed by its civilian leadership, charging that it had stabbed the military in the back. They thought all was going well on the war fronts at least, despite their personal calamities.

Sadly, the pope addressed his cardinals on Christmas Eve 1917, and lamented, "We do not deny that when we saw the effects of once flourishing nations given over to the paroxysm of mutual destruction, and feared the hourly near-approach of the suicide of civilized Europe...We sadly asked: When and how will this savage tragedy ever end?"[32]

While it is always dangerous to play the speculative game of "what if" history, one can still wonder what would have occurred if the pope's peace plan had been accepted. We do know that the war brought not only incredible destruction, but it ended four stabilizing empires: Austria-Hungary, czarist Russia, the Ottoman empire, and the German Reich. In its place came fragmented nation-states, Communism, and eventually Nazism and Fascism. If the belligerents had reached an armistice when Benedict proposed it, the United States would not have deployed troops in Europe and would not have emerged as a world power that soon, for the forces of isolationism were strong and traditional in that nation.

France would not have been given the whole of the Alsace-Lorraine region and may not have so strongly antagonized the German people such that a Hitler could rise to power. An independent Belgium would have been restored, and Italy would have claimed only those modest gains and territories where populations truly desired her rule. Poland would have been smaller, and perhaps less desirable as a target to both Russia and Germany. And maybe even the moderate provisional government in Russia would have staved off the Bolshevik coup d' etat. Wilson in fact had warned Benedict that the pope's initial proposal would lead Russia to intrigue and counter-revolution. He was wrong, the crushing burdens of war led to Communism and to its later tragedies.

The Austro-Hungarian Empire might have been realigned eventually and might have remained a much-needed mild authoritarianism in a region that seems sadly to require such a form of government to avert age-old nationalistic hatreds and genocide. And perhaps the peace plan would have allowed the Ottomans to maintain some organized control over most of its areas, with the exception of Armenia.[33]

This is all speculation, of course, but it is a speculation informed by the judgment that the world the war conceived and helped to deliver could not be any worse than what resulted. Opponents of the German Reich at the time argued that a negotiated settlement would allow the autocratic Wilhemite regime to continue—that it would not have learned any lesson from its aggressions. So it was taught that lesson, and the consequences were a worse regime with even a more disastrous war and a long protracted non-peace lasting until the 1980s. One may not learn from history, but its muse is surely a terrible and harsh witness to human follies.

The Humanitarian Agenda

In the end, the pope could not bring peace. Instead Benedict had turned to important and good works during the war. He had facilitated the exchange of prisoners, helped more than 50,000 of the sick and wounded to get to Switzerland, repatriated those captured soldiers with tuberculosis, and proposed Sunday as a day of rest for prisoners. He intervened to see that the dead at the Dardanelles were cared for, photographed, and identified. His private donations were truly remarkable, as he gave away a considerable amount of the liquid assets of the Vatican and steered contributions in the direction of genuine need.[34]

The pope was instrumental in getting over $250,000 to Belgium to assist in the relief efforts, and he sent the archbishop of Paris 40,000 lire, 10,000 lire to Luxemberg, 10,000 lire to Eastern Prussia, 25,000 lire to German captives in Russia, 10,000 lire to Poland, and then 145,000 lire to the same cause under various guises, 10,000 lire to the Lithuanians, 10,000 to the Ruthenians, the same sum to the Serbs, and 10,000 crowns to the Montenegrins. Benedict also authorized vast amounts of clothing, food, and books to concentration camp prisoners, and he earmarked another 140,000 lire for the war orphans of Italy. He gave other smaller sums to Italian captives at Sennelager, who had sent him a postcard appeal, and money to refugees and orphans affected by attacks on Italy. On occasions, the pope directly solicited more donations for specific causes, and even clemency for particular individuals as well.[35]

Then reaching back into the vocabulary of the Middle Ages, he tried to resurrect the *Treuga Dei* or the prohibition of hostilities on certain days. He pushed for a Christmas truce in 1914, but France's general staff refused, saying the Germans could not be trusted to observe it. Another complexity in that disintegrating world was that Russia and Serbia, under the Julian calendar, did not observe the same day for Christmas as did the Western powers. There was still some criticism that the pope should have issued a statement blaming the war on one side or the other. Yet, as noted, he was the only head of state who had protested the violation of Belgian neutrality by Germany. Even Woodrow Wilson at that time stayed silent, as did Switzerland.[36]

In addition, Benedict fostered the "Save the Children Fund" to alleviate the sufferings of the youngest and most vulnerable, and the Vatican also established an "Office of Prisoners"—volunteers who took care of thousands of letters of inquiry and appeals. Eventually hundreds of thousands of such questions about prisoners were processed and researched, and repatriation was facilitated, although the office was eventually closed after critics persisted in calling it a facade for espionage.[37]

These actions were not one-time occurrences, but long-standing, systematic humanitarian efforts undertaken by one man in a tiny "city-state." These efforts and other direct gifts to beleaguered peoples, children, and cultural institutions, including the Louvain University Library, reached striking totals. Benedict's successor, Pius XI, was startled to read the summary of figures of how depleted the Vatican treasury was that he inherited; there was only 10,000 pounds left. The Vatican had to actually borrow money to bury Benedict and undertake the conclave in 1922.[38]

At the end of the war, the pontiff had moved from being an easy target of anti-Catholic and anti-clerical abuse as a German or as a French sympathizer, or as a temporizer who feared making a moral choice in the war. He became instead "the pope of peace"—a voice of reason in the midst of incredible carnage. In the process of seeking that peace, he extended the Holy See's sway diplomatically as no pope, including Leo XIII, had done in recent memory.

In January 1919, the pope and President Woodrow Wilson met at the Vatican. Wilson had abruptly turned down Benedict's original peace proposal, and in his personal life was never an admirer of things Catholic. However, Cardinal Gibbons had previously told the president of the pope's high regard for him which surely helped set the right tone. After his conversations, as the pontiff solemnly blessed Wilson's efforts, the president seemed genuinely touched by his kindness. Barred from being a part of the peace conference himself, Benedict seemed to put some confidence in the U.S. president. The pope asked for the president's assistance in protecting the Church's missionary efforts in German-controlled colonies, and Wilson agreed to be of assistance. The pope later sent Monsignor Bonaventura Cerretti to Paris to watch over Vatican interests at the peace conference and to protect the missionaries' freedom and the right of the Church to hold private property in those lands.

The pope later sent a letter of thanks to Wilson and also asked the president to speak out against any proposed trial of the kaiser and his military chieftains. Using research from a legal expert at the University of Bologna, the pope argued against war crimes trials. Wilson wrote back concurring, and Italy and then Japan and the United States dropped their support for any such efforts.

To those who criticized Benedict's alleged pro-German leanings, the pope quietly reminded them that Kaiser Wilhelm II had never been a friend of the Church; later, General von Ludendorff, who had benefitted from the pope's direct intercession on the war trial issue, attacked the pontiff after his death for his alleged sympathies toward France.

Gratitude is rarely a virtue for serious men of affairs. At the peace conference, Wilson again presented his Fourteen Points, which incorporated themes similar to the pope's peace note, and Benedict was on record favoring the idea of a league of nations and international arbitration, although he had serious reservations about what he saw as a harsh peace treaty and the role the new league would play in enforcing it.[39]

Postwar Diplomacy
There were, of course, other events happening besides the Great War during Benedict's pontificate. Although he was a protégé of Leo XIII and his secretary of state Rampolla, Benedict did not return to their rigidity on the Roman Question. In January 1919, he allowed the Sicilian priest Luigi Sturzo to organize a political party—Partito Popolare Italiano—although Benedict himself insisted on staying out of partisan politics. The People's Party, as it was termed, would support religious, civic, and social liberty, labor legislation, educational changes, agrarian reform, and even women's suffrage. In November of that year, the party won over 100 seats in the Italian Parliament. Thus, the *non expedit* was quietly abandoned.[40]

In addition, Benedict directed that his secretary of state, Cardinal Gasparri, meet with Benito Mussolini, the one-time Socialist editor and new leader of the Fascist party. The first steps toward a settlement on the Roman Question were being taken. Deep in his heart, Benedict was an Italian patriot, truly distressed by the havoc and wreckage that the war brought to his homeland, and he actually wept when Italy was defeated at the Battle of Caporetto in December 1917, and 300,000 of its troops captured. Reports were transmitted that the retreating Italians had cried out, "Long live peace, long live the pope, long live Giolitti" [an anti-war politician]. And some of the Italian military staff were supposed to have proposed that the pope should be hanged for his pacifist sentiments.[41]

For the first time a pope referred respectfully in his correspondence to "the King of Italy," then Victor Emmanuel III. In the past, the Vatican had refused to acknowledge the legitimacy of the House of Savoy and also refused to see Catholic princes who had visited the King of Italy, or receive any head of state who visited the King of Italy first. The situation was an embarrassment to all involved, as was obvious in the episode involving Merry del Val's response toward the president of France during Pius X's reign. Benedict simply dropped the whole policy, citing "the changing conditions of the times and the dangerous trend of events." In fact, Cardinal Merry del Val wrote a protest criticizing the way Cardinal Gasparri was working so closely with the Italian government.[42]

Benedict also moved toward repairing ties with the French government, saying to his secretary of state, "If France gives me only her little finger, I will hold out both my arms." In that spirit, the pope decided to canonize that nation's legendary heroine, Joan of Arc, and expressions of admiration were made between the Vatican and the French hierarchy. In 1919, the French government proposed a resumption of diplomatic relations with the Holy See—a major accomplishment for the pope.[443]

In dealing with Catholic Poland, the pope recognized the newfound independence of that state, which had freed itself from the crushing sway of czarist Russia and the threats of German and Austrian interference. He accepted a surprise nomination from his secretary of state for the apostolic visitor position there—Monsignor Achille Ratti, a fine scholar and well-known Vatican librarian. Benedict's odd choice proved to be remarkably astute. As papal nuncio, Ratti was generally well-regarded and hardworking. He also used his post to establish some tentative contacts with Bolshevik Russia and to give the Vatican a better understanding of that new harsh regime.

However, when Ratti wrote a letter in German and Polish asking both nations to understand each other's point of view and to remember that they were Catholics first, he was bitterly denounced by both Germans and Poles and his recall was pressed. Benedict, the subject of much bitter abuse himself, initially rejected the demand. But Ratti was also involved in some very difficult territorial questions while serving on the Inter-Allied Commissions for the plebiscite areas in Upper Silesia, and his position as papal nuncio became untenable. He was eventually transferred and then consecrated cardinal archbishop of Milan; four months later he became Pius XI, Benedict's successor.[44]

Although Benedict had often stressed his impartiality during war, he clearly favored the Polish forces over the Bolshevik Russians who were moving west and threatening not only Poland but Germany and the rest of Western Europe. On August 15, 1920, Marshall Jozef Pilsudski stopped the Soviets at the gates of Warsaw. Not since 1683 when the Polish King Jan III Sobieski destroyed the Turkish armies of Grand Vizier Kara Mustafa in the battle of Vienna had that nation played such a role in world history. The pope clearly celebrated the victory in a most substantial way. On May 18, Pilsudski was received in triumph in Warsaw, and on the very same day in the much smaller town of Wadowice, a baby was born named Karol Jozef Wojtyla, who would become the first non-Italian pope in nearly a half a millennium, John Paul II.[45]

Benedict, the trained civil and canon lawyer, was also able to celebrate the completion of the codification of the Canon Law and to acknowledge graciously Pius X's initiative. He also encouraged interest in the Scriptures and in the widespread dissemination of the Gospels, underscoring once again his intense commitment to missionary efforts and to closer relationships with Eastern Orthodox Christianity. It was also during his pontificate that the apparitions at Fatima began. On May 13, 1917, three children in Portugal claimed to have seen the Virgin Mary in what would turn out to be one of the most persistent and powerful expressions of the folk religion tradition of modern Catholicism. As for the pope, he referred to Mary in his letter *Inter Sodalicia*, as "the co-redemptrix", and he also paid homage to Thérèse of Lisieux, the so-called "Little Flower," another popular religious figure of the time. On April 24, 1920, a reasonably healthy pope called for his old rival Cardinal Merry del Val, the Archpresbyter of St. Peter's, to accompany him while he visited the crypt of the tomb of Pius X. There, near that spot, he indicated he wished to be buried, a little over a year later, he predicted a new conclave soon,[46] In January 1922, Benedict apparently caught cold, and he died of complications at the relatively young age of sixty-eight.

In his time, Benedict proved himself to be an expert diplomat, one who carefully advanced the interests of the Church and encouraged monumental humanitarian gestures during the war. At times he was criticized for not clearly denouncing the war guilt of the one side or the other. But it must be remembered that the final burden of such guilt was not as clear as it seems today. First, we tend now to link the blame of causing World War I with German responsibility for World War II, which is now obvious, seeing it thus as a historical continuum. And then too, it was only in the 1950s that the Italian historian Luigi Albertini presented a definitive analysis that clearly established the heavy weight of German and Austrian responsibility in creating the conditions that led to the World War I. Neither side was exemplary, of course, but it is now clearer to us than to Benedict and his counterparts that the military staffs and the diplomats of the Reich and the Austro-Hungarian Empire were the major architects of the First World War.

In his attempt to broker a peace, Benedict maintained an impartial position and was denounced by both sides for his alleged sympathies to the other. It was said he tilted toward France, was anti-Italy, was pro-German, that he leaned toward his native Italy, or was ready to welcome a German victory so as to restore the Papal States and stop Orthodox Russia. Many times, his detractors cited the same incidents and examples to support their very divergent cases. Actually, his peace plan was scuttled by a West that wished victory, by an anti-Catholic German chancellor, and by an Italian government feeding off anti-clerical feasts. Still, his humanitarian record was simply unparalleled by anyone of his era, including the Red Cross, neutral Spain and Switzerland, and even rivaled the fine U.S. relief administrator, Herbert Hoover.

The intensity of criticism directed at Benedict was in part a legacy of the anti-clericalism that plagued his predecessors. But the widespread denunciations of the pope also came from a sense of futility and despair—that somehow Benedict should have been able to stop the carnage and the killings, and restore civility to the European community. The successors of the very forces that had cut the papacy down in the previous century, weakened its sway and range, now seemed at times to denounce the very successes that they had celebrated. In life it often seems that we come to regret the very world that we ourselves labor to create.

The war was a terrible conflagration, and it seems historically to overshadow Benedict and his pontificate. Indeed, except for John Paul I who was in office for only thirty three days before he died, no pope in the twentieth century had vanished so quickly into obscurity. Just before his death, there was a fine statue done in 1919 by the Italian sculptor Quattrini that memorializes the pope in his tiara and cope, standing in front of his throne and reaching out as if trying to help those in desperate need. In his left hand is a document, a list of names, and on his face are the etched marks of a tired man motivated by human sympathy.

The statue was not erected in the native Italy he so loved, or by the efforts of Catholics he labored for, or at the instigation of the Church he so protected all his adult life. Instead, it lies in Muslim Turkey meant to remember one man's charity, and at its base is the inscription:

> To the Great Pope of the World's Tragic Hour
> BENEDICT XV
> Benefactor of the People
> Without Discrimination of Nationality or Religion
> A Token of Gratitude from the Orient.[47]

CHAPTER NINE
JOHN XXIII, (1958–1963)

After Pius XII died in 1958, it was said that his influence would last for over a century. In fact, it ran its course in two years. The austere, intellectual, regal Pacelli would be replaced by a homely, overweight seventy-six-year-old, nondescript cardinal who caught the international public imagination and left his positive impression on the Church in a very short period of time. No pope in this century had proven to be so popular so quickly. Other popes, including the crafty Leo XIII, have been dedicated and committed men who were insistent on keeping society somewhat at arm's length away from the Catholic Church. They were in one sense traitors to the world—to its values, its élan, its sense of secular progress. That distance is the strength of the Roman Catholic Church, and that is its profound weakness. Pope John was an exception to that approach, for he embraced with love and vitality the world and its diverse peoples. With that receptivity, he created enormous enthusiasm and goodwill, and also unwittingly undercut in some ways the traditions and authority of the church for which he lived his life.

The Apostle of Good Will
As the cardinals arrived for the conclave, they were faced with an embarrassing spectacle. The new embalming techniques done by the pontifical physician, Dr. Riccardo Galeazzi-Lisì, on Pius' body were deficient. The odor of his remains and the eerie popping sounds from his casket conveyed a sense of immediate decomposition and decay that nauseated the papal guards near it. Some bitter critics said it was a fitting metaphor for the last years of a declining pontificate.[1]

The very organization of the Roman Curia had been neglected in many ways. There was no cardinal chamberlain, and there had been no secretary of state since 1944; the number of cardinals was at a low point of 55, and nearly half of the cardinals (nineteen members) were seventy-eight years of age or over. Pius was both an authoritarian and a mystic, a centralizer and a person who cut himself off from the congregational chieftains in Rome who populated the Curia.

Because of the advanced age of the College of Cardinals, the conclave faced a real problem with succession. There was a strong minority movement which advocated reforming the Church; some of those changes in liturgy and biblical scholarship had been initiated by Pius himself.[2] In fact, it was speculated that the late pope avoided dealing with the Curia because even he found it too conservative! The hero of some of the progressives was Giovanni Battista Montini, the archbishop of Milan, but he was deliberately not made a cardinal by Pius, and the tradition of choosing from those ranks was too powerful to be ignored by the conclave.[3]

The Pacelli wing of the College of Cardinals through various appointments and interlocking relationships controlled the major departments, congregations, and agencies of the Roman Curia. They had no intention of losing those positions of privilege and power, which they identified with the traditions of Catholicism that had hardened since the Council of Trent which ended four centuries before. They too wished reform, but the reform they desired was more power to curtail the experiments, the dissenting views, and the unorthodox opinions of the national episcopates and their theologians, especially in the non-Latin countries of continental Europe. Their major candidate at first was Guiseppi Siri, the cardinal from Genoa, who at fifty-two was deemed by some too young for the papacy.

Thus there was a generational problem—the younger candidates did not have large followings or much experience, and so behind closed doors the conclave turned to a man some viewed as a transitional figure—Angelo Giuseppe Roncalli, the Patriarch Cardinal of Venice. Roncalli was an amiable, seemingly simple, pious churchman—one who had performed well in diplomatic positions and who conveyed a sincere impression of good humor and general toleration. He reminded people of a benevolent uncle, an easygoing duffer, the classic European country priest. Smarter than he seemed, Roncalli confidentially told one French colleague that he would be chosen pope if the conclave were looking for a man with "common sense."[4]

When his diary, *The Journey of a Soul*, was published after his pontificate, it was criticized for its lack of critical introspection, its seemingly naive expressions of faith, and its remarkable confidence in the strange ways of God. When he was considered for canonization in 2014, that very diary was hailed as a pious statement of faith. All his life Roncalli placed his career and his good fortune in the hands of the Almighty. He said he wished to be above all a good and obedient priest.

He wrote in his diary, "I intend to use joviality, pleasantness and happiness with all persons, but to act in seriousness and modesty, especially with those who have mistreated me." It seems difficult in the twenty-first century to understand such a man, but it was such people who had built and maintained the Catholic Church through heresies, revolutions, plagues, and its own insolence.[5]

The Journey of a Saint
Angelo Roncalli was born on November 25, 1881 in a small village near Bergamo, to a humble and religious family. After his election to the Chair of St. Peter, it seemed remarkable to reporters that his relatives were still tilling the fields as they had done for generations.[6] What else should they do, this was their living. There were thirteen children from the Roncalli marriage, and they lived the life of simple sharecroppers with half of their produce going to pay their landlords. Angelo once quipped, "There are three ways of ruining yourself —women, gambling, and agriculture. My father chose the dullest."[7]

His was really an extended family that at times expanded to 30 people. The family was poor, hardworking, and undemonstrable emotionally, and Roncalli was to say that his elders were "a bit surly but truly good and worthy folk."[8] Later as pope, he would somewhat defensively explain to his family why he did not grant them titles, saying he did not wish to lift them out of their "respected and contented poverty." On another occasion, he observed that he owed his priestly vocation to his family "which was not as poor as some like to make out, but was above all rich in heavenly gifts." In his youth, Angelo was especially close to his pious great uncle, Zaverio, and at the age of ten he entered the neighboring junior seminary. It seemed that he never desired to be anything but a priest.[9]

Six months after his ordination in 1904, Roncalli became the secretary to Monsignor Giacomo Radini-Tedeschi, the Canon of St. Peter's and an ally of Mariano Cardinal Rampolla, the Secretary of State of Leo XIII. Years later, Roncalli as pope, recalled that his patron was "my spiritual father...the Pole Star of my priesthood." Radini-Tedeschi who became bishop of Bergamo, called then "the most Catholic of cities," proved to be a powerful church reformer in that small ecclesiastical universe, and a strong supporter of laboring people and unions.[10] In 1905 Roncalli also became acquainted with Carlo Andrea Cardinal Ferrari, the powerful archbishop of Milan who was deeply distrusted by Pius X. Soon Roncalli developed an interest in one of Ferrari's predecessors, the Council of Trent reformer Saint Charles Borromeo, who had been a cardinal of Milan in the sixteenth century.[11]

Historian Hannah Arendt argued that many of his contemporaries thought Roncalli a bit "stupid, not simple, but simple-minded." But in fact he wedded his own commitment to obedience with the pride of a self-made man and the self-confidence of a person who is content to do God's will here on earth.[12] Like many leaders, he had a clear view of himself, a good sense of timing, and an almost innate feel for the right gesture or the inspiring phrase.

Despite the fact that Roncalli was a cautious and pious priest, he nearly got caught up in the web of Modernist denunciations so approved by Pius X. Such accusations could have ruined a career of much promise, and Roncalli quickly scurried away from powerful forces that dealt in guilt by association. Some have concluded in retrospect that Roncalli was easily cowed by that near mishap, but such is the problem of living in a closed ecclesiastical society. It is probably for this reason that John XXIII was remarkably permissive in dealing with unorthodox and dissident theologians during his term as pope. Years later as pope, he asked to see the Curia file on himself, and to his chagrin he saw a reference to his alleged Modernist associations. In the file, he angrily penned, "I, John XXIII, Pope, declare that I was never a Modernist."[13]

On the surface he would seem to have had much in common with Pius X—being poor, humble, devout, and later fascinated by the appeal of Venice. But Roncalli retained a critical eye toward his sainted predecessor even during his own papacy. He judged Pius X "certainly holy, but not fully perfect in that he let himself be overwhelmed by anxiety and showed himself so anguished." Probably that is as close as one pontiff comes to criticizing another one in modern times. His friend Cardinal Ferrari was even more blunt concerning Pius' excesses, "He will have to give an account before God of the way he let his bishops down when they were attacked." Benedict XV, himself under scrutiny earlier during the Modernist hysteria, ended the attacks by simply observing, "There is no need to add epithets to the profession of Catholicism. It is enough to say, 'Christian is my name, and Catholic is my family name.'"[14]

In 1911, Roncalli quietly became a member of the diocesan congregation of the Priests of the Sacred Heart, making him a diocesan religious committed to perpetual vows of obedience and promising to live in deep commitment to the ways of the Spirit. When the war came to Italy in 1915, Don Roncalli was called up for active military service and became a hospital orderly stationed in Bergamo, and later a chaplain. In 1918 he was employed as a warden of a student hostel. In all these jobs he performed credibly, but they were not exactly stepping-stones to higher glory.

In 1920, he was called to Rome to be the National Director for the Propagation of the Faith as part of Benedict's continuing preoccupation with the missions. How a little known provincial priest was chosen for the position is unclear. Some say it was due to Benedict's friendship with Radini-Tedeschi; others say it was Roncalli's organizing efforts at the Italian Eucharistic Congress in Bergamo.

When he met with the pope, Benedict simply told him, "You will be God's traveler." From that position he came to know both Italy and also the intricacies of the imposing Roman Curia better. His viewpoints broadened, and in 1921 he was named a monsignor; the revenues of his agency more than doubled in two years, and Roncalli became a recognized figure in ecclesiastical circles. For the first time he met another accomplished Curialist bureaucrat—Giovanni Battista Montini, whom he later raised to the cardinalate and who became his successor, Paul VI.

Ambassador to the East
On February 17, 1925, Roncalli was summoned to see Secretary of State Pietro Cardinal Gasparri, who informed him that he was the new apostolic visitor to Bulgaria, the first one in over 500 years. After his term in "purgatory," as the reassignment was called, he was promised a post in more hospitable Argentina which then had a large Italian Catholic population. Roncalli protested that he knew nothing about Bulgaria, but Pius XI had already for some reason concluded that Roncalli had been chosen by Providence for the position.[15] Remembering his own years in Poland, the pope insisted that Roncalli needed a more prestigious title, and so Pius XI made him an archbishop in the bargain. The pope also gave Roncalli a copy of *Scintillae Ignatiana*—a collection of maxims of St. Ignasius Loyola, meant to tide him over like the good soldier that both Roncalli and the author were in the service of the papacy.[16]

Bulgaria was a confusing country for the Vatican. It had over 60,000 Catholics of various rites who survived in a hostile Orthodox religious environment. In 1924, Bulgaria had experienced some 200 political assassinations, and the government of King Boris III responded with many arrests and widespread executions.[17] It was in such a world that the mild-mannered diplomat found himself. Roncalli's new flock embraced about 48,000 Latin rite Catholics living mainly in urban areas and 14,000 in the Uniatie Slavic rite, mainly in the rural areas. By cart, horseback, and mule, the new apostolic visitor with his interpreter crisscrossed Bulgaria. Soon the stranger was being called, "Diadu," or "the good father." He modestly assumed that their praise was due to their love for the pope rather than the esteem they felt for him. More importantly during this time, he came to understand the practical importance of getting along with other religious denominations—an early lesson in what would be called later ecumenism. And he encouraged that prayers be said in Bulgarian, rather than in the French taught by the missionaries.[18]

Roncalli's stay was supposed to be a short one. Instead, he was assigned for ten years to the diplomatic backwaters of Bulgaria. At times he worried about his lackluster dead end career, but once again he trusted in God's ways. He noted in his diary that many of his trials were not caused by the Bulgarians, but by the Roman Curia to whom he reported. He lamented over the petty meanness of the Vatican, saying "everybody is busy talking and maneuvering for a career." Part of his problem was that he had to deal with three different Vatican departments, often having diverse views of how matters should be handled—the Secretariat of State, Propaganda Fide, and the Oriental Congregation.[19]

Even the pope who appointed him was quick to criticize. Pius was markedly unhappy when Roncalli allowed the Bulgarian Orthodox patriarch, Stefan Gheorghiev, to send his secretary to reciprocate a visit from Roncalli. The pope found that demeaning to the prestige of the Holy See; Roncalli blandly responded that it was not so intended, the patriarch was a very busy man. Pius XI simply stared at his delegate and inscrutably pronounced, "One sows and the other reaps." Later when Roncalli wrote a critical letter to the Curia, the pontiff also read it and characterized it, "Behold the wrath of the lamb."[20]

Unfortunately for Roncalli, King Boris III of Bulgaria, originally from the House of Bourbon-Parma, was raised a Catholic, but had to convert to Orthodox Christianity in order to assume the throne of that nation. When he decided to marry, he chose to ask for the hand of King Victor Emmanuel III's daughter, Princess Giovanna. A dispensation was granted by the Vatican, and the marriage was performed according to the Catholic rite at Assisi on October 25, 1930. The royal couple had agreed that their children would be raised Roman Catholic. Then a week later, on October 31, the couple was married again, this time according to the Orthodox rite in the Cathedral of St. Alexander Nevsky in Sofia. Pius XI was furious and publicly denounced the royal couple on Christmas Eve, and Roncalli consequently took some of the blame both from the pope and from the king for the dispute.

The archbishop was subsequently banned for a year from the Bulgarian court. And when he visited Rome right after the Orthodox baptism of the couple's son, Prince Simeon, the pope acted in a rather boorish manner. He kept Roncalli kneeling before him for 45 minutes as a penance. Years later, he extended his regrets to Roncalli—saying he apologized as Achille Ratti, but not as Pius XI, calmly adding "I give you my hand in friendship." Roncalli later said only his pride was hurt, and he graciously dedicated one of his volumes on Borromeo to that pontiff. The usual view in the Curia at that time was that Roncalli was in general a naive diplomat, one given to such foolish hoodwinking by smarter men, but Roncalli was rather clear as to what the limitations were that he faced. In an Orthodox country where the Catholic Church was barely tolerated, he felt it was better to exhibit what he called "unbroken and non-judgmental silence."[21]

At times even the ebullient Roncalli grew weary and depressed. In 1929, on the twenty-fifth anniversary of his ordination, he had an intense sense of being forgotten and frustrated over the lack of progress in his career.[22] The years passed by—ten in all—and then in late 1934, the Vatican informed Roncalli that he had been transferred to be Apostolic Delegate to Turkey and Greece. Istanbul was, of course, the major city in Turkey, and it was the descendant of the great capital called until 1930 Constantinople—the famed center of eastern Christianity. Roncalli arrived and soon visited the Cathedral of the Holy Spirit; there in its courtyard was a statue dedicated to Benedict XV, the Pope of Peace who was called "the protector of the East."[23]

The dictator of Turkey, Mustafa Kemal, or Ataturk, as he preferred, was waging a vigorous and often aggressive campaign to modernize his state, ruthlessly suppressing national customs and traditional Islam. He went on to ban the old Arabic alphabet and non-Western dress, including clerical garb. So Nuncio Roncalli wore a business suit and a bowler hat, looking like a hefty Italian banker, it was said! Philosophically he was to observe "It will become apparent that clothes do not make the monk."[24]

On the ecclesiastical front, as early as 1936 Roncalli had tried to introduce some words of Turkish into the liturgy, a step that was won the praise even of Ataturk. He was however soon denounced to Rome; in frustration, Roncalli called some of the reactions of his superiors "my only real cross." In addition to his immediate difficulties was the Italian invasion of Ethiopia which added to tensions with the Turkish regime due in part to the fact that Roncalli was still an Italian citizen. He had also been given the responsibility by the Vatican for relations with Greece, since the government there wanted no special Vatican representative named. He proceeded very cautiously, and in a surprising and warm gesture he visited some of the 1000 year-old Greek Orthodox monasteries at Mount Athos that were still operating in that peninsula. Then in 1939, Pius XI died, and the next war soon came. With Italy in the conflict, Roncalli's position became even more difficult, especially in Greece which had strong ties with Britain.[25]

The German ambassador to Turkey during this period was Franz von Pappen, who originally had been a supporter of Hitler, arguing that he could be controlled by the right sort of conservative influences. Now as the war began, von Papen insisted to Roncalli that the conflict would be over by November 1940, and that Catholicism could end up being "the formative principle" of the new German social order. Roncalli was unimpressed, and sharply demanded on one occasion, "And what shall I tell the Holy Father about the thousands of Jews who had died in Germany and Poland at the hands of your countrymen?"[26]

Roncalli dutifully reported von Papen's offer to the Vatican without any endorsement on his part, but Monsignor Tardini at the Secretariat of State's office bluntly concluded of the archbishop, "This fellow has understood nothing." He among others felt Roncalli was simply naive and gullible, and two decades later, even as Pope John's Secretary of State, he exhibited at times the same disdain for Roncalli's capabilities.[27]

Caught up in the vortex of war, occupying a diplomatic post in a sensitive city with fairly open borders, Angelo Roncalli became a source of invaluable information for the Vatican and also a strong ally in the underground to save the Jews on the run. Pius XII was buffeted by immense forces on the question of how far to go in attacking the Nazi and Fascist tyrannies. Roncalli was a witness and a participant in a small but meaningful way in that struggle. Later when he became John XXIII and quickly an international folk hero, there was much praise for his work in Turkey in helping an estimated 24,000 Jews. Some even contrasted his caring attitude with the alleged silence and indifference of Pius XII, but Roncalli himself acknowledged freely he acted under specific instructions from that pope.

Through his activities and the assistance of King Boris, thousands of Jews from Slovakia who had been sent to Hungary and then Bulgaria, and who were destined for concentration camps, received transit visas for Palestine. Roncalli signed the visas and von Papen, representing a very different and more humane strain of German life than Hitler, was credited with overlooking the archbishop's activities. Later Roncalli would testify in writing to von Papen's complicity—a letter that probably saved him from the death penalty at the Nuremberg trials.[28]

Roncalli listened to the Grand Rabbi of Jerusalem plead for 55,000 Jews in the Transnistrian region, but by June 1944, he reported the arrival of only 730 passengers from that area. Legend has it that Roncalli issued thousands of fraudulent Catholic baptismal certificates to Jews. The true story is that he forwarded to Vatican diplomats in Hungary and Romania "Immigration Certificates" issued by the Palestine Jewish agency. At times though, both the Vatican and Roncalli insensitively expressed concern that the Holy Land was being flooded with Jewish immigrants, as if they had so many other offers of asylum from which to choose.[29]

On to Paris

Then in December 1944, Roncalli was shocked to receive a telegram from Monsignor Tardini informing him that he had been appointed Papal Nuncio to France. French General Charles de Gaulle had insisted to the pope that the current nuncio, Monsignor Valerio Valeri, had been pro-Vichy and had to go. Pius refused at first, but he recognized that Valeri's position was untenable under the new regime after the liberation of France. Some critics of Roncalli claimed that Pius sent him to Paris as a calculated rebuke to the haughty general—the implication being that Roncalli was a naive bumpkin. In fact, Pius clearly wanted Roncalli in that position, overruled Tardini's objections, and informed his nuncio that he was the pope's choice for that position. "It was I, Monsignor, who thought of you myself, and I made the decision—no one else." Now at sixty-three, Angelo Roncalli held the Vatican's most prestigious diplomatic position. He humbly responded that "where horses are lacking, the donkeys trod along," a supposed reference to himself as a second-level diplomat.[30]

While in Paris, he sensitively dealt with the government's demands that thirty allegedly pro-Vichy bishops be dismissed, getting that number reduced to three; dealt gingerly with the left-wing priest-worker movement that put clergy into the factories mainly in suburban Paris to continue their pastoral work; and advised the Vatican on nominations for bishops and three cardinal positions. Roncalli was criticized then and later for not having the sparkling wit and conversational veneer that is so appreciated in French intellectual life. Jesuit Robert Rouquette judged that Roncalli made a poor impression in Paris and was written off by many as a "clown." But Jacques Dumaine reported that Roncalli "is more artful than subtle, he has had much experience and radiates a lively bonhomie." And the anti-cleric and former premier of France, Edouard Herriot remarked, "If all the priests were like Roncalli, we would have no trouble with the church."[31]

When confronted with Vatican charges against the Jesuit scientist Pierre Teilhard de Chardin for his philosophy mixing Christology, anthropology, and evolutionary biology, Roncalli pushed them aside. He simply asked, "This Teilhard fellow...why can't he be content with the catechism and the social doctrine of the Church, instead of bringing up all these problems?" Roncalli was never a great admirer of theological distinctions and complicated theories, which ironically may explain his toleration for avant-garde theologians during his brief term in office as pope. He was to conclude, "In France ideas are born with wings. Without a touch of holy madness, the church cannot grow."[32]

Roncalli was by temperament a man interested in faith rather than theological constructs.. He believed that the purpose of the Church was to help men and women reach salvation. Roncalli, the diplomat, still respected the pastoral life, the simple habits of clergy who minister to the souls and sensitivities of real people living in a world still in the aftershock of the last terrible war. Later, Maurice Cardinal Feltin offered a character sketch of him at that time. He found the nuncio always friendly, understanding and adept at smoothing out problems; but he was decisive, firm and strong in his actions. He thought Roncalli to be "subtle, perspicuous, and far-sighted..." and a person who could slip through "the grasp of those who sought to exploit him."[33]

While the Curia moved on implementing the conservative strictures in Pius' encyclical *Humani Generis*, some French theologians as well as others were put under the new microscope and denied teaching faculties. Roncalli basically stayed away from the controversy, and later he was to resurrect some of these discredited scholars who would play major roles in Vatican II.

In Venice

In 1951, he was appointed by Pius XII to be the official Vatican observer to UNESCO, a very different approach than that pope's predecessors had used in recognizing or usually ignoring international organizations. On November 14, 1952, Roncalli was asked if he would consider taking the prestigious see in Venice. He was seventy-one years of age. This would be his last post, he concluded philosophically. He had lived by the admonition of St. Martin who said that he "neither feared to die, nor refused to live." Finally, Angelo Roncalli would return to the pastoral life and would be able to undertake diocesan reforms similar to what his patron, Radini Tedeschi, had done in Bergamo a generation ago, or those the great saint Charles Borremeo had concluded four centuries before in Milan.

Venice is not just a city; it is a dream, a fantasy of art and architecture. And it was on such a decorative stage that the aging diplomat arrived from Paris. Roncalli was in many ways a traditionalist, and he loved ritual and ceremony. He came to Venice on March 15, 1953 in a procession of colorful gondolas, saying that he wished to humbly introduce himself. He recalled his family, quoted Petrarch, and praised Marco Polo, the great explorer of the Far East. And in characteristic rhetoric, Roncalli went on, "I commend to your kindness someone who simply wants to be your brother."[34]

He had been previously named a cardinal in January 1953 at Pius XII's second and last consistory. Twenty-four new men were selected in all, fourteen of them non-Italian. The internationalization of the College of Cardinals was beginning. The pope also named Alojzije Stepinac of Yugoslavia, Stefan Wyszynski of Gniezno-Warsaw, Poland, and also a brilliant young prelate, Giuseppe Siri, the Archbishop of Genoa since 1946. Some said that Pius saw the last as his heir apparent, although the pope never seemed to concur publicly.

In March 1954, the pope nearly died, and Roncalli wrote that while he owed much to Pius, he hoped that he would not die at that time since it would interrupt his pastoral plan to visit his parishes and the proposed diocesan synod. Also, rather surprisingly, he opposed adding another feast, *Regalitas Mariae*, the Queenship of Mary, to the Church calendar. He saw it as counterproductive to ecumenical efforts—a rare objection from a high-ranking clergyman in those days.[35]

Pius miraculously recovered and later, after a crude power play, he either personally instigated or simply allowed his Curia inner circle to transfer Monsignor Montini to Milan. He was not to be given a cardinal's hat either. Roncalli was dumbfounded at the harsh treatment of his friend. It has been argued that Montini was too liberal, too powerful, too close to the papal throne. Seeing their opportunity, the conservatives finally eliminated his influence and stopped him from being Pius' successor by denying him the red hat. Ironically, the conservative leaders laid the groundwork for a greater revolutionary—the amiable and aging Patriarch of Venice. It has been argued by several close associates of Pius that he himself made the decision to transfer Montini to Milan without a red hat. The pope had lost confidence in his closest associate because of his involvement with leftist leaning youth movements, and because Montini regarded Fascism, not Communism, as the greater threat to the Church. Also, Pius felt that his successor had to be a more decisive leader than Montini would be, realizing that the latter could be elected later—which is what happened.

In his diocese Roncalli focused on what he called spiritual renewal and the "perennial youthfulness of Christian and religious life." On the one hand, he was impressed by the liturgical reforms of the archbishop of Bologna, the liberal Giacomo Cardinal Lercaro. And at the other end of the spectrum, he invited conservative Cardinal Siri to talk to a Catholic Action group. In 1956, the Supreme Congregation of the Holy Office (the old "Inquisition") demanded that he respond to complaints concerning the pronouncements of the local Christian Democrat newspaper which advocated an "opening to the left" politically. Roncalli disliked engaging in condemnations, but he felt compelled by the Vatican to criticize what he called an opening at "any price," which was "a very grave doctrinal error and a flagrant violation of Catholic discipline." Several years later he himself would be criticized for just such a gesture toward the U.S.S.R.[36]

At the time, Roncalli also expressed some interest in creating a commission to focus on the ecumenical movement—a precursor of what would become during his term as pope the powerful Secretariat for Christian Unity to be headed up by Pius' former confessor, the Jesuit Augustin Bea. Back in Venice, Roncalli was preparing for a diocesan synod in November 1957. It was at this synod that he first used the term "aggiormento," meaning an updating or reform of the ways of the Church to fit in with modern society. At that session he denounced authoritarianism and paternalism—criticisms which were seen then as veiled references to Pius' style of administration.[37]

Even the easygoing Roncalli had some problems with the laity of Venice—a rather conservative group even noticeably so in conservative Italy. His modest proposal to remove the iconostasis in St. Mark's Cathedral, the marble Gothic screen, and wheel it away at Masstime so the faithful would see better, produced a firestorm of opposition, and he backed down. Roncalli was to remark on one occasion, "We are not honored as museum keepers, but to cultivate a flourishing garden of life and to prepare a glorious future." Later he recorded in his diary the major event of the day—Pius XII had died.

The Transitional Pope
Roncalli's reactions were rather restrained on learning of Pius' death, especially for a pontiff who both rescued him from the backwaters of Vatican diplomacy and treated him with more respect than Pius XI. When the College of Cardinals met, it would contain only fifty-one voting members, and the average age was older than Roncalli, who was a month shy of seventy-seven. There was some speculation of reaching outside the ranks of the cardinals, especially to Archbishop Montini, but that was not possible in the eyes of most, although he may have received several votes on the first balloting. Thus, the conclave would be left with a very divided convention of those conservatives wishing to continue the theological policies of Pius XII; those wishing some modest changes, especially in administrative organization; those advocating major reforms; those craving some spiritual regeneration; and those who really were not sure what they wanted.

In a universe of fifty-one people, such divisions make for a highly fractionalized group process in which consensus is difficult to reach. Of the fifty-one cardinals, seventeen were Italian, six French, three Spanish, and three were Brazilians among others. Of the seventten Italians, eleven worked in the Vatican Curia, and six governed dioceses. Roncalli was one of the three patriarchs of the western Church, a mildly progressive figure who had extensive diplomatic experience. He had had his run-ins with the Pacelli bureaucracy, but his placid personality was such that he had not alienated many people over the years.[38]

There was surely a feeling that the Church needed a change in style and tone—a Good Shepherd, who would also support the prerogatives of the bishops and cardinals. The conservatives at first supported the young Cardinal Siri; the progressives, Lercaro of Bologna, who was called by an acquaintance, Luigi Santucci, "an after-school cardinal, a holiday-excursion cardinal"—that is a not so serious fellow. There was much support for the cultured Armenian, Pietro Cardinal Agagianian, a Curialist "more Roman than the Romans," it was said. One critic remarked that he was "more doctrinaire at sixty-three than Pius had been at eighty." There was also some support for the seventy-nine-year-old aristocratic Benedetto Aloisi Cardinal Masella, the moderate prefect of the Congregation of the Sacraments, and an experienced diplomat himself. The successful candidate would need two-thirds or thirty-five votes.[39]

Before the conclave, Roncalli was a frequent visitor to influential clergy in Rome, especially cardinals and prominent individuals who were well connected in Church politics. He was seen initially as a dark horse, one likely to emerge only in a long drawn-out conclave. But actually he entered with a strong core of supporters, mainly former French colleagues and non-Curial Italians who were loyal throughout the balloting. After four days of inconclusive voting, Roncalli finally prevailed, in part because of the concurrence of the leader of traditional Curia cardinals, Alfredo Ottaviani. Although the proceedings are secret, Roncalli himself said that he and Agagianian bobbed up and down in the balloting like peas in a boiling pot. He must have understood what was happening earlier than most of his colleagues. When he was elected he pulled out a written statement for the secret conclave members and boldly announced, *Vocabor Johannes*, "I will be called John" to the surprise of the cardinals and later the Vatican experts.

Roncalli said that he took the name John because it was the name of his father, the name of the church he was baptized in, and the name of a variety of cathedrals throughout the world, most especially the Lateran Basilica, the pope's own cathedral in Rome. The last legitimate pope to use the name was John XXII, who reigned from 1317 to 1334. There had been a later John XXIII, Baldassre Cossa, who was an anti-pope and who was alleged to have been a pirate who killed, cheated, and tried to perjure his way to the papacy.[40]

Before that election, Roncalli was visited in his cell by Ottaviani and his conservative ally, Ernesto Cardinal Ruffini of Sicily, who talked of what "a beautiful thing" it would be to call a church council soon. They had in mind another Vatican I or Council of Trent to correct the errors of Church members and the sins of the world. Roncalli was to observe that "everybody was convinced that I would be a provisional and transitional pope," *papade passagio*. Mainly what was expected was that he would restore the papacy to a more normal state of affairs and end the neglect and decay of the later Pacelli years.

Before the conclave, he had been asked by concerned conservatives if his friend Montini would be returned to Rome as secretary of state if he became pope. Roncalli shrewdly responded that since he was not going to be pope, the question was moot. He met several times with Monsignor Tardini, still the pro-secretary of state and the man who had been over the years so critical of Roncalli for his alleged naivete as a diplomat. To the surprise of many and the comfort of the conservatives, he later prevailed on a reluctant Tardini to take the secretary of state's position, even though the latter protested that they had frequently disagreed in the past, that he was tired from previous years of service, and that he wished to focus on his orphanage project. John insisted and Tardini knelt down in obedience, later remarking on the strange turn of events, "Such is life." The pope was not a man of the Curia, and what he knew he generally did not like. However, he made major overtures to the bureaucracy, and in the process he may have forfeited the chance to bring about the very changes he was later to embrace.[41]

Almost immediately, he called a consistory to name twenty-three new cardinals, thus exceeding the rule of Sixtus V (1585–90) who set the limit at seventy. John named Montini and Tardini and also new cardinals from places like the Philippines, Japan, Mexico, and Africa that had never had cardinals before. Still a man of tradition in so many ways, he restored the fur bonnet used by the Renaissance popes in place of the white skull cap that kept slipping off his head. He even created a new coat of arms, but protested that the lion (meant to represent Venice) was too fierce, too Germanic-looking.[42]

At his coronation, he insisted on preaching a homily in a language, Italian, that many of his listeners could understand, and he told the Vatican newspaper to drop the august titles when they referred to the pope. When the mayor of Bergamo decided to name Roncalli's brothers "Knights of the Italian Republic," (*Cavalieri della Republica Italiana*) John demurred. After his coronation, they went back home to till the fields.

He met easily with the press, simply calling himself a shepherd and never sought to emulate the ways or the intellectual sway of his predecessor. One priest, Antonio Samoré, said that while meeting Pius was like taking a stiff oral exam, meeting John was like talking to one's grandfather. After that coronation, he received visits from various chiefs of state. To one, Prime Minister John Diefenbaker of Canada, the pontiff remarked, "Well, here I am at the end of the road and the top of the heap."[43]

Very quickly he also assumed the duties of Bishop of Rome, visiting its churches, the children's hospital, Gésu Bambino, and even the Regina Coeli prison by the Tiber River. The children at the hospital, many of them suffering from polio, called out *"Viene qui, viene qui, Papa"* ("come here, come here, Pope"). And he waddled along, replying, "Quiet now, I'm coming. I'm coming to see you." Among the midst of the worst elements of the city at the prison, John simply remarked that he was "Joseph, your brother." As he reached the sealed off section of the prison he asked that the gate be opened, "Do not bar me from them—they are the children of the Lord." Inside he embraced, among other felons, a convicted murderer. Later on the Feast of the Epiphany, the pope sent the entire prison population a complete chicken dinner with wine. The press loved this new pope as it followed him around. But John had a more carefree sense of himself. Once he looked at his figure in a full length mirror and laughed, "O Lord, this man is going to be a disaster on television." One of his more favorable biographers observed, "When Angelo Roncalli became John XIII, a new man seemed born in him; it was as if mediocrity had given birth to genius."[44]

John is supposed to have said that he had "flung open the windows of the Vatican" to let in the air. Perhaps he never said that, but he surely acted as if he had. Roncalli was made pope in part because important elements of the conservative Curia thought he was reliable. They hoped they could use him to regenerate the institutional church by reasserting their authority and the Vatican's magisterium. That is why they wanted the council. At first they were correct in their assessment.

The New Pentecost
In January 1959, John XXIII claimed that he had been inspired by the Holy Spirit to call a Church Council. Actually, it had been suggested to him by various people, although he probably forgot the authors and just incorporated the suggestions into his own. He had hesitantly proposed it to Secretary of State Tardini and was delighted when the conservative Curialist agreed. Five days later, on January 25, 1959, John announced

the idea to the eighteen Curial cardinals at the Basilica of St. Paul Beyond the Walls in Rome. They sat quietly, almost stunned. Later Tardini asked John to go more slowly, and the Vatican newspaper even buried the dramatic story inside the pages of its daily edition. Finally, John XXIII allowed the Curial apparatus to set the council agenda by having the traditional commissions and agencies serve the needs of the council. Progressive critics would conclude that the results were highly predictable. The initial drafts on the basic questions before the Council would contain the same defensive, traditional, triumphalist expressions of criticism of the world and stale reaffirmations of the righteousness of the Church. There were no surprises.

Actually both Pius XI and Pius XII had considered the idea of calling a council together. Pius XI wished to emphasize the unity of the church after the horrors of the First World War, but he became preoccupied with resolving the "Roman Question." As for his successor, Pius XII received a memo from Ruffini and Ottaviani in February 1948, advocating a council that would focus on traditional concerns: clarification of Church doctrine, the threat of Communism, the moral constraints on war, reform of canon law, ecclesiastical discipline, and a definition of the doctrine of Mary's Assumption. Pius XII hesitated though in having the bishops leave their dioceses for so long a period of time, but he did set up five secret commissions to prepare for such a council if he decided to call it after all. John had the benefit of that material.

Pius had decided that whatever the council could do, he could do better and faster, and so it never came about. He defined himself the doctrine of the Assumption of Mary and issued his encyclical *Humani Generis* that condemned various errors, heresies, and unorthodoxies. When John explored the idea of calling a council, Cardinal Spellman in New York concluded that the pope had "been pushed into it by people who misconstrued what he said." Cardinal Lercaro of Bologna, supposedly a progressive, judged that the pope was either "rash and impulsive," due to his inexperience and lack of culture, or that he was a man of "calculated audacity." Even Cardinal Montini in Milan privately said that calling a council was a mistake, that at least three more years of preparation were needed, and that "this holy old boy doesn't seem to realize what a hornet's nest he is stirring up." But Montini's friend, Oratorian priest Giulio Bevilacqua, responded, "Let it be, the Holy Spirit is still awake in the Church."[45]

Thus it seems that neither the progressives nor the conservatives welcomed the idea of a Church council, especially of the sort that John called. Later Sister Pasqualina, in a rare visit back to the Vatican, also warned the new pope that people looked to the Holy See for leadership, and that it could not and should not repudiate its authoritarian heritage. It would lead to "an ecclesiastical tragedy," she judged. John good-naturedly blessed her, complimented her beauty, and remarked "let change take care of the future."

They said it would take four years of preparation; the elderly pontiff gave the bureaucracy only two. While John was talking of opening up the windows of the Church, the Curia was continuing its policies of blacklisting theologians and authors. Such discontinuities led to the quip in Rome, "Tardini reigns, Ottaviani governs, John blesses." The pope at times seemed remarkably reticent, almost as if he expected the council to just happen. At one point he remarked, "I am only the pope around here." And when he was asked how many people worked in the Vatican, he concluded—"about half!"[47]

The appointment of Domenico Tardini as secretary of state and then president of the Ante-Preparatory Commission was meant to calm the Curia and also to place some real management skills in charge. Tardini in turn wished to use the reliable experts (*periti*) from the Roman universities rather than import non-native talent and alien ideas. Thus another safeguard for the Curia was in place, and John seemed either unaware or in agreement. Still, Tardini would make it clear that it was the pontiff who was insisting on changes not he. Privately he referred to John as "the one up there," until the pope remarked to his surprise, "'The one up there is the Lord God of all. I am only the one on the fourth floor.'"[48]

When he was cardinal, Roncalli was supposed to have said to Pius XII, "Holy Father, you will leave a difficult heritage for any successor who tries to emulate you in your role as teacher and master of the Word." Later, however, he remarked to Georges Cardinal Grente that one should simply do the opposite of one's predecessors to make one's mark. John was clearly aware of the Roman gossip, criticizing him as a man of limited abilities, especially in comparison to Pius. Again, Cardinal Spellman in New York was supposed to have said that John had the intelligence of "a simple banana man peddling his fruit." But John was a wily old cleric who lived by the maxim that one should notice everything, turn a blind eye to much, and correct a few things. Earlier in his career, he had observed, "Well, priests have to give up so much, marriage, children—so many pleasures forbidden. They must be allowed the greatest clerical sport: criticism of superiors."[49]

He decided early that the cardinals should relinquish the plurality of positions that some held which had created a sort of interlocking directorship of power and influence among the Curia officials. When some cardinals disagreed, a distraught Pope John reportedly said, "They have refused the Pope." After that refusal, he ordered the changes made, and then wrote a public letter accepting their resignations with gratitude.[50]

When he made his announcement concerning the council, he also pledged to call a synod for the diocese of Rome and to order a thorough review of canon law. He called a synod for his own new diocese because he recognized, as did Pius XII in his last year, that the city of Rome and its environs had undergone enormous social and economic changes since the war. There were now over two million people with 190 parishes, and while Rome had over 3,000 priests, most of them were not involved in pastoral work, but employed by the Curia or were religious assigned to Roman universities.[51]

In 1959, John the bishop actually devoted more time to the synod than to preparing for the council. But the results were predictable and disappointing. The synod ended up insisting that Roman priests had to wear the cassock or black soutane at all times; be marked by tonsure or shaven crowns; avoid the opera and races; not use cars unless absolutely necessary; never be alone with a woman; deal only in the most careful ways with Communists, Freemasons, and heretics; and beware of faith healers and psychoanalysts. The Synod was a bad dress rehearsal for a wide-open ecumenical council that the pope would advocate.

John magnanimously praised the Synod's decrees for their "beauty and inner coherence, with occasional delicate touches that result in an unexpected psalmody, bringing clarity to the mind and savour to the heart." Privately however, he observed that "nothing is perfect in this world," and that his successor could call a second synod. Still he observed, "It will always be the humble Pope John who celebrated the first."[52]

Changing Foreign Policies
While the pope was reviewing the work of the synod and also preparing for his council, John was beginning to effect a major change in the Vatican's policies toward Communism and the Holy See's basic foreign policy assumptions as well. For the first two years of his pontificate he seemed, however, to adhere to the policies of Pius XI and Pius XII toward Communism. Then he began to make a clear and calculated attempt to disengage the Vatican from Italian domestic politics and from its historic pro-West Cold War allegiances. When the leader of the Christian Democrats, Aldo Moro, tried to create a coalition government by forming an alliance with the Socialists (PSI), John proved sympathetic. This was the so-called "opening to the left" (*apertura a sinistro*) that the Curia had condemned under Pius XII and that Cardinal

Roncalli was forced to censor while in Venice.

John did not directly align himself with Moro at first, but on April 11, 1961 he received Prime Minister Amintore Fanfani and celebrated the 100th anniversary of Italian unification. He was sending the message that he and the Vatican would abstain from interfering in political issues. Then on April 2, 1962, the pope met with Moro and called him "an excellent Catholic, a statesman, a man of great social concern."[53]

The pope aroused suspicions in other ways. In his early attempts to reach out to the Orthodox churches, he came into contact rather quickly with the Russian leadership. His overtures to the Orthodox Christian community and their hierarchies, asking them to come to the council, were complicated both because of their age-old animosities toward Rome and of the influence of the U.S.S.R. John the diplomat was aware of the ancient jealousies between Athens and Constantinople, and between them and the patriarchate of Moscow, which was a department of the Soviet government. He issued a general invitation to his upcoming council and left it to the Orthodox churches to decide how they would be represented, but he received no response. At first, Athens had balked at the idea, then Patriarch Athenagoras of Constantinople (Istanbul) informed Cardinal Bea that he could not attend the council, later the Patriarch of Moscow would not agree to come either, probably because the initial invitation came through Constantinople.

The pope then changed course and on September 27, 1962, he sent Monsignor Johannes Willebrands to Moscow with an invitation; later the Kremlin agreed that two official Orthodox Church observers could go to the council. Then the other two Orthodox prelates protested about breaches of protocol and a divide and conquer approach being used by the Vatican. Years later Athenagoras finally met with Pope Paul VI in Jerusalem—the first such visit since the Schism in 1054.[54]

During this period the Soviet government and Premier Nikita Khrushchev had apparently decided to work with Pope John whom they saw as likely to abandon the staunch anti-Communist policies of Pius XII. As for John he stopped referring to "the Church of Silence" behind the Iron Curtain and also ceased characterizing many long-suffering mainland Catholic Church leaders in China as schismatics when he realized the difficult options facing them over the years.

In its overtures, the Vatican diplomats quietly assured Communist leaders that the council would not be attacking Communism or embarrassing any observers from Eastern Europe or the Soviet Union. John was personally delighted when Stefan Cardinal Wyszynski and sixteen other bishops from Poland, four from each Germany, three from Hungary, three from Czechoslovakia, and all of the Yugoslav bishops arrived to attend the Council. However the bishops of Romania and Albania were absent, and most of the Catholic bishops of Communist China remained imprisoned.[55]

The pope also began secret negotiations to free church prelate Josef Slipyi, the Archbishop of Lvov from jail, using among others the services of American magazine editor, Norman Cousins. Later Franz Cardinal König of Vienna would be allowed to visit József Cardinal Mindszenty who had been granted asylum and was still living in the U.S. embassy in Budapest. Eventually he would be allowed to emigrate to Rome. Pope John also took up the case of Archbishop Josef Beran of Prague who had been under restrictions from 1947 to 1964, seeking to better his plight.

The pontiff's positive relations with the Russians began when they responded to his statement during the Berlin crisis of August-September 1961. The dangerous confrontation between the United States and the U.S.S.R. over the latter's harassment of that divided city eventually led to the threat of military action by the nuclear powers and the building of the Berlin Wall. John appealed to all involved, including those who did not believe in God, or in His Christ as he put it, as he pleaded for peace. For some reason, Khrushchev was pleased with the tone of the message and praised the pope. The Soviets saw quite correctly a break in the policies of Pius XII. Later during the much more dangerous Cuban Missile Crisis, the pope with the prior approval of both sides appealed to the Americans and the Soviets to choose negotiation over war. His dramatic appeal was praised throughout the world, including by the Kremlin.

Later Khrushchev's son-in-law, Aleksei Adzhubei, the editor of *Izvestia*, visited the pope on March 7, 1963. The interview lasted only eighteen minutes and was a rather simple expression of hospitality on the part of the pope, but it was a major step in normalizing relations between Russia and the Holy See. The pontiff asked Adzhubei and his wife about their children and expressed delight that one was called Ivan or John. At one point, he poignantly observed, "You say you are atheists. But surely you will receive the blessing of an old man for your children." They fell quiet and left deeply moved.[56] John even began to study the Russian language in order, he said, to "show how much he loved that great people."[57]

But John's overtures brought increasing criticism in Italy where the pope had announced that he wished the clergy to stay out of partisan politics. When some of the hierarchy, including Cardinal Ottaviani, disagreed publicly, John uncharacteristically rebuked the dissidents and reminded them of their duty of obedience to the pope. The cardinal had openly criticized the left leanings of what he called "sacristy pinks." When John near the end of his life issued his universal call for peace and brotherhood in his encyclical, *Pacem in Terris,* the last remnants of Pius XII's foreign policy came tumbling down. President Kennedy, who was himself seemingly seeking to abandon some of the cliches of the Cold War, remarked, "This encyclical of Pope John makes me proud to be a Catholic."

Issued on April 11, 1963, the encyclical is addressed to "all men of good will," and begins with a ratification of the traditional Catholic view that by the use of natural reason all can understand the need for peace, liberty, and a moral order. John started off with a long history of the duty to respect the inalienable rights of people. Those rights include not just speech, religion, property, and association, but also the right to social services, medical care, employment, culture, education, and vocational training. He also emphasized the right to freedom of movement and expressed concern for the plight of displaced persons.

John then talked of the match of duties and responsibilities with rights and liberties. He argued that men have a right to expect a political order characterized by truth, justice, charity, and enlightened cooperation. John reminded politicians that they must adapt the laws to the conditions of modern life. He noted three great changes that have marked the era: the progressive improvement of the economic and social conditions of working men; the increasing awareness by women of their natural dignity; and the political independence of nations once subject to foreign domination.

He further expressed his disapproval of imperialism and foreign economic domination, asked for respect for minority rights, and strongly condemned the arms race. In a positive sense John urged assistance for underdeveloped nations, praised the United Nations and its agencies, and urged Catholics to cooperate with Christians "separated from the Apostolic See." Laying aside some of the old prohibitions on such joint endeavors, John simply observed, "a man who has fallen into error does not cease to be a man."[58]

That same month, April 1963, the Christian Democrats lost strength in the elections in Italy, and the pope was attacked for having made it fashionable to support socialism, to look the other way at Communism, and even to allow a visit of Khrushchev's brother-in-law inside the Vatican gates. The Christian Democrats were probably hurt more by the downturn of the Italian economy, but to some it did not seem to matter.[59] John had weakened the Church's historic resolve against the left.

Pope John's image as a fair and compassionate world statesman was enhanced in other quarters, especially after his appeals for mutual restraint during the explosive Cuban missile crisis in October 1962. He had stressed over the years what he called *convivienza* (living together), and as a recognition of his efforts he was awarded the Balzan Peace Prize on May 1, 1963. On May 10 he visited the Quirinale, the palace of the Italian president, to view the giving of that award to other people as well. "Peace is a house, a house for everyone," he explained.[60]

Mother and Teacher
On domestic social concerns, Pope John had earlier issued his controversial *Mater et Magistra* on July 15, 1961. That encyclical marked the seventieth anniversary of Leo XIII's *Rerum Novarum* and the thirtieth anniversary of Pius XI's *Quadragesimo Anno*. One of the longest papal letters, some 25,000 words in length, John's encyclical affirmed the recent papal tradition of support for private enterprise and private property and presented a critique of Communism and socialism. But the state must act in a positive way to promote a healthy economy and widespread prosperity. In such activities, the principle of subsidiarity should be honored, that is those activities undertaken by the state should be restricted to those efforts that private groups or individuals cannot accomplish themselves.

The letter introduced the concept of "socialization," defined as the "growing interdependence of men in society giving rise to various patterns of group life and activity and in many instances to social institutions established on a juridical basis." There are advantages in such an interdependence that promotes higher standards of living and the welfare state. There are disadvantages in that it makes it harder for individuals to exercise their freedoms, to work and think individually, and to enrich one's personality. The letter emphasized a need for a true living wage for a worker and his family, a fairer redistribution of wealth, a more disinterested assistance to poorer nations, and a sense of the brotherhood of man. And as befits a true son of the soil, the pope spent some time talking about the problems of farmers.

John criticized economic imperialism and strongly urged the laity to participate in an apostolate to the world for social justice. And lastly, he gingerly acknowledged some aspects of the population explosion, but denied it was a serious difficulty and put his faith in scientific and technological discoveries to find solutions. Some feared that his letter however was another opening to the left, especially with its concept of "socialization" which seemed too close to "socialism." In the United States, many conservative American Catholics agreed with commentator William Buckley when he said, "mater si, magistra no."

By the end of 1961, John would be celebrating his eightieth birthday.

He had observed earlier that when he was chosen in 1958, the idea was that he was a provisional and transitional pope. "Yet here I am, already in the eve of the fourth year of my pontificate, with an immense programme of work ahead of me to be carried out before the eyes of the whole world, which is watching and waiting." To those who compared him unfavorably to Pius XII, he responded that everyday language was the language that Jesus used, and that "simplicity contains nothing that is contrary to prudence." When he was approached by Cardinal Spellman about the possible canonization of Pius XII, he sidestepped the request.[61] Still he took no comfort from reading the lives of his powerful and rather unsimple predecessors: Leo the Great and Innocent III—men more attuned to Pius XII's style of leadership than John's![61]

The conservative Cardinal Siri, holding dearly to Pius' legacy, called Pope John's pontificate "the greatest disaster in ecclesiastical history"— that is, the last five hundred years in his litany. Later at the beatification process of Pope John, he indicated however that he had been wrong.[62] Not all of Pacelli's circle was as critical of John XXIII. John began to form a very close collaboration with the Jesuit Augustin Bea, a former confessor of Pius' and the person who helped Pius write his liberal charter for advancing biblical studies, *Divino Afflinate Spirtu* (1943), and a man who would help provide strong direction for a very unclear council.

Beginning Vatican II
As a preparation for the council, the Vatican had sent out questionnaires requesting topics for discussion, and over 76 percent of the prelates and Catholic institution leaders responded. Basically they revolved around minor reforms and a modest desire for more autonomy. The *voti*, as they would later be called, were extensive and would be published in fifteen huge volumes.[63]

Peter Hebblethwaite reported that John decided in the beginning that "the president of each subcommittee would be the prefect of the corresponding Roman Congregation, or the dicastery." Thus the conservative Curia, with John's approval, would provide tight direction for the council. Excluded were some of the major theologians of the time, men who would be important figures in Vatican II and much later. Those included Jesuits John Courtney Murray and John L. McKenzie from the United States; Karl and Hugo Rahner from Bavaria; Frenchmen Henri de Lubac and Jean Daniélou; and French Dominicans Yves-Marie Congar and Marie-Dominique Chenu.[64]

On June 5, 1960, Pope John noted in passing that the decision to use the Curia did not exclude the enlightened wisdom of churchmen from elsewhere, but his statement had little impact. He insisted that the council had its own structures and organizations that would be different from the Roman Curia, but the meaning of that observation was unclear. What was apparent was that the excitement over the council was eliciting a great deal of public discussion, media coverage, and scholarly attention. One prominent liberal theologian, Hans Küng, openly insisted that the purpose of this council was "reform" in its broadest sense. His book, *The Council, Reform, and Reunion,* stirred a great deal of attention on both sides of the Atlantic with its positive discussion of the Protestant Reformation, the role of the Bible in worship, the development of a people's liturgy, the use of the vernacular, the reform of the Curia, the divorce of the papacy from politics, and the end of the Index of Forbidden Books. Surprisingly, Küng portrayed the Council of Trent as a reforming council that ended the abuses of the Renaissance church and not as a defensive reaction to the Reformation. Roncalli had found out some of the same evidence in his work on St. Charles Borromeo, the great churchman of that council.[65]

In the midst of all this, the pope turned to his new friend, Cardinal Bea, to head up a special secretariat—one dedicated to Christian unity that would be the agency responsible for communicating in a positive way to non-Catholic Christians. Now with the appointment of Bea, John had reached into the closest circle of Pius' admirers and found an old man who represented a new way of looking at the world and thus at the agenda of the council. Some conservative Curia members recalled to each other that Bea had been the author of Pius' liberal letter on biblical studies, and that he seemed back in 1949 to ignore the Holy Office warning against too extensive ecumenical contacts. They never forgot an infraction—real or even just reported.

On December 2, 1960, the pope met Dr. Geoffrey Fisher, the Anglican Archbishop of Canterbury. This was the first time that a pope and an archbishop from that see had spoken since the Reformation. Fisher was somewhat cool at first and sought to lecture John that the world would perhaps never see a "return to Rome," or a reunion of Protestant and Catholic churches, especially on Catholic terms. John was hospitable as usual, saying later that they talked of St. Gregory the Great and St. Augustine's mission to Canterbury. No photographs were taken and the public announcements were low key. Fisher left charmed by the pope, and later the archbishops of York and Canterbury appointed Canon Bernard Pawley as their personal representative to the Holy See.[66]

Throughout all of this, Pope John was becoming an increasingly popular personality internationally. Then in the summer of 1961, Secretary of State Tardini died, and the pontiff quickly named Amleto

Cicognani, the former nuncio to the United States and a more moderate personality to take Tardini's place. Some historians of the papacy have seen this change as the beginning of Pope John's liberation as a reformer and as a leader in the ecclesiastical changes that came out of the council that he himself had called.

There is no question that Vatican II (1962–65) had a profound impact on the Roman Catholic Church, far beyond what its church fathers originally imagined. What exactly John XXIII's intentions were and what his view was of the first session, the only one that he lived through, is somewhat clouded historically.

As for the Council, the preparatory work had moved in the Central Commission to Eugene Cardinal Tisserant after Tardini's death. The Central Commission became not just a coordinating agency, but actually a watchdog that thought it could veto the work of the other commissions. In November 1961, archconservative Alfredo Cardinal Ottaviani proclaimed that the council should author a new Profession of Faith, which would repeat the anti-Modernist oath of Pius X and also condemn again the errors listed in *Humani Generis*, reaffirm the doctrine of Mary's virginity, reassert the primacy of the priesthood, and attack those who emphasized the sinfulness and guilt of the Catholic Church over the years. It was the same old conservative agenda, and immediately enormous resistance ensued. It appeared that the power of the Curia, even without John's intervention, was beginning to wane.

The pope praised the Central Commission several times for its work, and on February 22, 1962, he issued a letter *Veterum Sapientia* ("the wisdom of the ancients"). It was a rigid defense of the importance of Latin in the life of the Church. It was more conservative than even Pius' pronouncements on the topic. One consequence, that some foresaw, was that a council held in Latin would favor the Curia, which dealt with that language every day in its work. That prediction did not hold true.

When the Curia began a systematic attack on Bea and his Biblical Institute, the detached pope responded sharply and expressed support for the orthodoxy of the Institute and ordered Cardinal Pizzardo, who led the assault, to send a letter of apology to Bea. The conservative dean of the cardinals, Eugène Tisserant of the Biblical Commission, was also involved, and the pope wrote to Secretary of State Cicognani, "The time has come to put a stop to this nonsense." Either that commission would prove useful to the papacy or it would be abolished, he warned. Quite correctly, he began to conclude "reforms have to begin from above."[6c]

Then the pope ordered that the schemas be circulated to all the members of the Council early so as to invite debate and discussion. Cardinal Montini, speaking for the pope, opposed the constant negative tone of the conservatives. A distraught John had already looked at some of the drafts of the schemas, and is supposed to held up a ruler, and said, "seven inches of condemnation and one of praise: is that the way to talk to the modern world?" The conservatives had their own reservations. Ottaviani, observing the general drift of events, glumly remarked, "I pray to God that I am to die before the end of the council and that way I can die a Catholic."[68]

Pope John talked of his contribution to the council as being his "personal suffering" and seemed to have a premonition of his own death as he pushed for an earlier session than most thought possible. He rewrote his last will and testament, and calmly said that he awaited "the arrival of Sister Death." He also drafted an edict concerning the period that the Chair of Saint Peter was vacant, restricted photos of the pontiff on his deathbed, and prohibited people from living in the papal apartments during that period. It was clear that the experiences of the previous pope were what he had in mind. He also rejected the request of Josef Cardinal Frings of Cologne and his colleague Julius Cardinal Döpfner of Munich that the council be postponed—time was of the essence.[69]

On September 11, 1962, John gave a speech in which he heralded the advent of the council a month away to help it gain some focus. He accepted the distinction between addressing the Church internally (*ad intra*), and the Church addressing the world (*ad extra*)—a view popularized by Léon-Josef Cardinal Suenens of Belgium. Of the seventeen schemata being prepared, only two dealt with the outside world. John admonished that "we expect a contribution based on intelligence and experience that help to heal the *scars* of the two world wars that have so profoundly changed the face of all of our countries." Like all mothers, he observed, Holy Mother Church detests war. The thoughts of Cardinal Suenens were obvious in John's very different declarations. Two weeks later, on September 23, he received confirmation that he had stomach cancer, the cause of death of two of his sisters.

In the first two years of his papacy, before the passing of Secretary Tardini, Pope John's views on major Church reform seemed contradictory. Partly it was the complexity of this allegedly simple man. It must be remembered that there were several sides to the aged cleric who assumed the papacy in 1958. First was the young pastorally oriented priest who had been accused of Modernism and who later in fact embraced the need to relate the methods of presentation (but not, he said, the articles of faith) to the contemporary world. There was the easygoing diplomat who understood the non-Catholic world, especially that of the explosive Balkans and the Middle East more than most. Then there was the non-judgmental archbishop and later cardinal who seemed less worried about theological controversies and incipient heresies than losing the souls of simple people.

Yet Roncalli was really not in his heart as progressive or as liberal as Montini for example. In fact, Montini was very sympathetic to the more speculative theologians of the time such as Yves Congar, Henri-Marie de Lubac, Pierre Teilhard de Chardin, and Hans Kung; to the worker-priest experiment in France; and to the pro-left wing of the Christian Democrats in Italy. Montini was a man of ideas, more than his friend Roncalli, and as such he was more influenced by the unorthodox winds of change. In some ways even Pius XII at times was more receptive to those movements than his own archbishop-diplomat successor.

John actively introduced fewer reforms than Pius XII or even Pius X. On a personal level, he avoided using telephones and dismissed television, seeing it as promoting worldly values and saturated with effeminate programs. Overall he had little interest as Pacelli did in technology or advanced scholarship. And he issued one of the strongest reaffirmation of priestly celibacy of that time.[70]

Oddly, John praised the early drafts from the Curia, while he called for a positive aggiornamento—a true opening to the world. As noted, he is supposed to have said that he thought it was important that he open the windows in order to let the fresh air into the Church. Whether he said that or not, he exhibited a confusing behavior at times. Was he supporting the Curia, or was he supporting those who were asking for substantial change?

In addition, he originally placed great emphasis on the ecumenical nature of the council, one that would boldly aim at the reunification of Christianity. But quickly it evolved into a Catholic council with non-Catholic observers, not non-Catholic participants.[71] Some saw his behavior as a series of skillful Machiavellian responses: he kept the Curia on his side, but supported those who wished to undercut its very powers. The bishops, nearly all appointed by Pius XII and through the Curia process, were seen especially in the first session as docile and rather conservative. They were no more willing to recommend radical changes than the priests in the Roman Synod Council years before. The bishops were however displeased at times with the ways they had been treated by the Vatican bureaucracy and by Pius over the years, but they surely were not great reformers.

There is a myth that Vatican II tapped into tremendous popular discontent among the laity who saw their Church as hopelessly out of date. There may have been some of that feeling among segments of the native populations or clergy in Third World countries, but actually there is little evidence that the council rested on such broad popular unhappiness. For example, it has been estimated that in 1956, only ten out of 600 bishops in Latin America exhibited any strong social consciousness in an area of the world where one would have expected such a sense. By the time of the council, Latin America was a problem area for the Church and its bishops exhibited some cohesiveness in their caucus's influence. But they were not council leaders.[72]

The discontent in the Church was expressed mostly by members of the hierarchy who were weary of the tight controls of the Curia, by uneasiness in the religious orders against the restrictions of their superiors, and by the continuing threat to speculative theologians, especially in the non-Latin European faculties and seminaries. The council was not a popular revolution, as much as a revolt *at first* of the "out" clergy against the insiders, mainly those in the Vatican hierarchy.

Roncalli as pope was now the ultimate insider with recollections still of how he had been treated in the past. He was definitely not a man of vengeance, or a person preoccupied with paying back slights; but he still had an old man's memory. His successor would be even more sensitive to those slights by the Curia that he had once so skillfully navigated and later been humbled by. Roncalli left the Curia alone; Montini as Paul VI would begin in a limited way to reform it.

A second problem that the Catholic Church faced is typical to large and/or multicultural empires or realms. That is the relationship between the central city or capital and the provinces. That concern is especially important in a Church that continues to characterize itself as the "one, holy, Catholic and apostolic Church." Here the word "Catholic" means universal—that is an institution that transcends boundaries, tribes, and cultures. The Curia feared that changes in theological metaphors in liturgy and in patterns of authority would accentuate the powerful centripetal or decentralizing tendencies prevalent in the postwar world. Political colonization was already dying, and even Conservative British Prime Minister Harold Macmillan would later talk of those irreversible "winds of change" begun between the world wars.[73]

The previous pope had written a long lyrical encyclical on the Church as the Mystical Body of Christ, with Jesus and his vicar on earth at the head. Now the Church would in Vatican II change the metaphor and speak of the non-hierarchical "People of God." It is by our language that we define ourselves. In a world of decentralization and complexity, the "People of God" could quickly become a thousand peoples, and with the introduction of the vernacular in even the sacred canon of the Mass, the Catholic Church would speak in a thousand tongues. At the council, and often under John Paul II and Benedict XVI, the meaning of that metaphor "People of God" would be deliberately downplayed.

The progressives saw those changes as being responsive to the needs of the faithful. The conservatives saw the change as a new Tower of Babel. As for John, he issued a papal encyclical reaffirming the centrality of Latin in the life of the Church, although some said he did not mean to deny the use of the vernacular in the Mass. Still his immediate successor would deal Latin the greatest blow imaginable by rendering it essentially obsolete in the sacred liturgy of the Church.

Which was the real Pope John? When John spoke of his agenda for updating the Church, he enumerated three great projects: a synod for the Roman diocese, the council, and a reform of canon law. The synod was to be a sort of dress rehearsal for the larger and more complex council. As noted, the conservative clergy showed little desire or inclination to engage in major changes in that diocese, even at the instigation of the Bishop of Rome himself. Institutions without the danger of peril hanging over them rarely reform themselves democratically. Even John's pastoral intention to minister in a sensitive way to priests who had left the Church was generally ignored by the hierarchy. Although he was an admirer of reforming bishops, past and present, his experiences in the synods in Venice and in Rome should have taught him a lesson about the limits of rejuvenation from the bottom up. And as for the reform of canon law, that was only completed by John Paul II on January 25, 1983—twenty-two years to the day of John XXIII's original announcement.

On October 11, 1962, John XXIII called the twenty-first General or Ecumenical Council together, an occurrence that some would later say was the most significant religious event since the Protestant Reformation. There in St. Peter's Basilica above the remains of the first pope, and surrounded by Bernini's magnificent baldacchino, the council began. Over 2,600 Bishops attended, a marked increase in the number of participants from Vatican I where 737 were in attendance. The pope entered the Basilica of Saint Peter's, abandoning the *sedia gestatoria* (the portable elevated chair), which he disliked, saying it made him seasick, and walked up the main aisle, looking to the right at the impressive statute of his first predecessor, Peter the Apostle. He had decided to use a less pretentious throne to sit on, and in his opening address John emphasized the pastoral role of the Council. After the beautiful tones of the traditional hymn *Veni Creator Spiritus*, the Mass was said in Latin with some parts in Greek.

The pope's sermon which lasted for thirty-seven eventful minutes, struck a strong and reforming note. He called history "the great teacher of life," and criticized the "prophets of doom [misfortune]" who "are always forecasting disaster, as though the end of the world were at hand." John then went on to say that the Church "brings herself up to date where required," so as to spread her message to "all men throughout the world." While the Church never departs from the patrimony of truth, she has to look to "new conditions and new forces of life introduced into the modern world, which have opened up new avenues to the Catholic apostolate."[74]

He also pushed aside the notion that Vatican II should continue the judgmental and defensive tone of Vatican I. John argued that the fundamental doctrines of the Church were well known and that focusing on that approach was not necessary. He calmly observed "the substance of the ancient doctrine of the *depositum fidei* is one thing; the way in which it is expressed is another." Pope John observed that the world expected a leap forward in doctrinal insight and the education of conscience, and concluded that "errors often vanish as swiftly as they arise, like mist before the sun." He also observed "nowadays, the bride of Christ [the Church] prefers to make use of the medicine of mercy than that of severity. She considers that she meets the needs of the present day by demonstrating the validity of her teaching, rather than by condemnation." The Church is thus the "loving Mother of all." He then spoke of Christian unity, rather than of the need for outsiders to "turn to Rome."

During the Mass, the Sistine Choir sang Palestrina's *Missa Papae Marcelli*, and the cardinals then paid their homage or obeisance to the pope. Canon law required that Pope John read out the oath of Pius IV from 1564 with its declaration that "I confess and hold the Catholic faith" and that "outside of which no one can be saved." In 1887, Pius IX added a reference to "the primacy and infallible magisterium of the Roman Pontiff"—sentiments that did not exactly set the tone that Pope John had presented that day.

Appropriately, the Council opened with the question: *Ecclesia, quid dicis de te ipsa*—"Church, what dost thou say for thyself?" After the first day of the council was over on October 11, 1962, John appeared before a crowd of 500,000 people, mainly Catholic youth who were carrying torches that evening. There he called out from his window, "dear children, dear children I hear your voices... My voice is an isolated one but it echoes the voice of the whole world...now go home and give your little children a kiss—tell them it is from Pope John."[75]

In the days following, the pope then met with the diplomatic corps, the press, and with observer-delegates on the general themes of his council. His aides referred to "the brethren in Christ" or non-Catholic Christians. To the amazement of the council and others, the two delegates who had arrived from Moscow expressed their "unaffected friendship" for the pope.

Then the council began. Despite the offer from Richard Cardinal Cushing of Boston to pay for a simultaneous translation system, the Vatican refused, and so the proceedings of the entire council were conducted in Latin. In preparation for the council's deliberations, a survey had been done of the Church's leaders to ascertain the topics to be covered. Over 9,300 proposals had resulted, and then were submitted to preparatory commissions appointed by the pope. In June 1960, over seventy documents or schema were produced. In the months that followed, the council's major deliberations revolved around the liturgy, the sources of revelation, the importance and role of mass communications, Christian unity, and the nature of the Church itself.

The Curial Opposition
One of the most dramatic events of the council came at the very beginning during the first organizational meeting. Powerful members of the Curia, led by Cardinal Ottaviani, called for the election of sixteen members to each of the ten conciliar commissions, with the pope appointing eight more members to each group. Then in a startling departure, Achille Cardinal Liénart of Lille proposed a delay and argued that the Church fathers should meet in national and regional caucuses and agree on slates for each of those openings. Cardinal Frings of Cologne immediately seconded the resolution on behalf of other German-speaking cardinals. The applause was overwhelming, and after only fifteen minutes the first business session was adjourned by the president of the council, Cardinal Tisserant.

When the Italian hierarchy felt slighted by the results of the voting, John helped to redress the balance of it, mainly by including members of the Curia from corresponding congregations on those commissions. Generally the pope stayed out of the council's business. The first major debate was on the question of liturgy, and once again the overwhelming majority of the council participants rejected the Curia-prepared draft. Underlining that discussion, though, was the more contentious issue of the powers of the bishops to run their own dioceses and to be seen in a collegial way as the successors of the Apostles.[76]

Conservative Cardinal Ruffini argued that the draft or schema had to be judged by the precepts of the encyclical *Mediator Dei* which affirmed the supremacy of the papacy. The implication was to denigrate the national congresses or groups of bishops. Then there was a long discussion on the importance of Latin vis-á-vis the vernacular languages for use in the liturgy. Addressing the council, the Melkite Patriarch of

Antioch, Maximos IV Saigh ignored the Latin tongue and spoke in French to the council members. He admonished them that in the Eastern Church every language is liturgical if it glorifies God.

Cardinal Tisserant recalled for the council that Hebrew and Greek had been used by the original Christians, and that the Slavic languages and Chinese had already been recognized by the Congregation of Rites as permissible. But for many in the Western Church, Latin was still a powerful sign of unity. Cardinal Siri of Genoa reminded listeners of Pope John's own encyclical, *Veterum Sapientia*, celebrating the use and study of Latin which had just been recently issued. Some native bishops cited the problems of dealing with endless tribal dialects, although in the end the African bishops overwhelmingly supported the use of the vernacular.[77]

In the debates Cardinal Spellman spoke out against the giving of Communion under both species, bread and wine, and against concelebration. And Cardinal Ruffini raised questions of hygiene for those drinking from the same cup or chalice. Even Pius XII though had approved concelebration, and the practices of receiving communion under both species were already used in the Oriental Rites, said Paul-Emile Cardinal Léger of Montreal. Ottaviani warned "are these fathers planning a revolution?" Too many changes would scandalize the faithful. Then he was cut off from going way over the time limit. Infuriated, he boycotted the council for the next two weeks.

On November 1, the Feast of All Saints, Pope John preached in Latin and then moved into Italian to praise the Church and some of its historical reformers. He said that there was "only one art, but a thousand forms." With that upbeat observation, the council resumed its debates. The pope again generally stayed out of the discussions, but when the elderly Bishop Peter Cule of Yugoslavia pleaded for including St. Joseph in the Canon of the Mass, he was rudely cut off by Cardinal Ruffini. Then the pope unilaterally added such an insertion of St. Joseph's name three days later, showing that the Canon, which had not changed since 610 A.D., was also alterable.[78]

The council moved on to a controversial discussion about the sources of revelation which began with a discussion of a schema presented by Ottaviani's preparatory theological commission. The issues were fundamentally dogmatic and went to the heart of the alleged historic differences between conservatives and progressives and even between traditional Catholics and what they considered were the influences of the Protestant Reformation.

On November 14, the debate on the revelation draft began. It came down to a simple question: How is the word of God delivered to mankind? Individuals may come to know that there is a God, that He has certain characteristics or attributes, and that by the use of right reason we can arrive at those natural truths. But the dogma is that God has intervened in human affairs and given to us greater knowledge to obtain a deeper, richer faith. The question is simple, the answer is complex, and a source of great contention.

Since the Council of Trent, the Catholic Church has taught that revelation comes from two sources: Sacred Scriptures and the traditional testimony of the early Church. The Protestant Reformation was partly fought over the insistence of its leaders that the Bible, and the Bible alone, is the source of God's revelation. Thus, it reduced the importance of the Church, the patristic fathers, the medieval theologians, and the magisterium of the pope and the bishops. Cardinal Ottaviani warned against any radical departures and asked for the protection of "safe doctrine." It is best to accept the scheme prepared by his commission, he argued. But Cardinal Liénart insisted that there were not two sources of revelation, but only one, the word of God. Cardinal Siri brought forth the specter of a new expansion of the Modernist heresy if one did support the schema, but opposition to that document mounted. The Cardinal from Vienna, Franz König, observed that the schema had nothing to do with the pope's program at all. Cardinals Suenens, Bea, and Ritter of St. Louis added their agreement to that view.[79]

After hours of confusing debate and a controversial parliamentary move by the conservatives, the pope personally intervened. He withdrew the schema from discussion and appointed a special balanced commission to be composed of members from the theological commission and the Secretariat for Christian Unity. Cardinals Bea and Ottaviani were to be co-presidents. In effect, he had thrown his support against the Curia and its drafts.[80]

At times, the question was raised who was actually running the council. Pope John's answer was a nonreassuring, "no one." Candidly the pope explained to a group of Pakistani bishops, "nobody around here knows how to run an ecumenical council. After all none of us have ever been to one." Actually the council was supposed to be managed by a council of presidents of eight cardinals, but in reality that group rarely met, and the Secretariat for Extraordinary Affairs had the responsibility for oversight, with the Secretary of State Cicognani as president. More influential were Cardinal Montini and Cardinal Suenens who provided some of the intellectual focus for the Council.

On October 11, 1962, Montini proved to be remarkably prescient in his prediction of how the council would proceed. He laid out a plan that would eventually be followed: the council should focus on the nature of the Church itself; it should place great emphasis on the Church's relationship to the outside world; the council should acknowledge papal infallibility and primacy, but go on to discuss collegiality and the important role of the bishops; it should also acknowledge the legitimate roles of the hierarchy, the clergy, and the people. Its attention should be directed in the second session to the mission of the Church. The third session should emphasize the relationship between the Church and the outside world: non-Catholic Christians, civil society, culture and the arts, the world of work, and relationships with the Church's traditional enemies.

Throughout it all, Pope John remained somewhat detached. On November 19, he told the French bishops that he was like the biblical patriarch Jacob, who was simply watched his sons quarreling. "Yes, there is an argument going on. That's all right. It must happen. But it should be done in a brotherly spirit. It will all work out. I, I am optimistic." To the conservatives who complained about the actions of the progressives, Pope John philosophically recalled that the disputes were even worse at the Council of Trent. His view of the acrimony was simply, "We are not friars singing in a choir." When the controversies about the Roman rite and Latin ensued, the pope not too subtly expressed his admiration for the different Ambrosian rite used in Milan.[81]

The council then moved on to a discussion of the nature of the Church itself. On the fourth day of debate, December 4, Cardinal Suenens again argued for redrafting the schema by asking for a reconceptualization of the entire work of the council. He argued that more than seventy documents needed to be pulled together, apparently speaking with the encouragement of the pope. By the end of November, John was reportedly dying, and he was encouraging a speed-up in the work of those drafting the schemas between the sessions. The second session was scheduled on September 8, 1963, and a new coordinating commission was instructed to reduce the drafts to under twenty.

The council also dealt with a statement on the role of the communications media and also the question of unity with the Eastern Orthodox churches. The first issue was one on which it was comparatively easy to reach consensus. There was much criticism however that the tone in the draft schema on the latter issue was once again that the Orthodox churches should simply "return to the true fold" of Christ, that is the Roman Catholic Church. The patriarch of Antioch argued that the text before the Council would insult the Orthodox churches, and also that one had to realize the unique history and differences of the Oriental Catholic churches vis-à-vis the Latin church.

The patriarch vicar from the Egypt, Monsignor Elias Zoghvy,

speaking in French, explained the differences between eastern and western Catholics. He noted not only differences in liturgy and emphases, but also differences in theology, but not necessarily dogma. He also cited the long history of autonomy and decentralization that characterized that branch of Catholicism. Archbishop Asrate Mariam Yemmeru of Abbas Abba, Ethiopia, reminded his listeners that their rite, said in Gheez or classical Ethiopian, dated back to the fourth century and included a continuing dialogue between the celebrant and the faithful. The schema ended up being combined with another decree on ecumenism prepared by Bea's commission. In effect, the initial draft was defeated.

Cardinal Ruffini had defended the schema in its entirety, but Cardinal König noted that there was no mention of freedom of conscience. Cardinal Ritter also re-emphasized the need for a clear statement on the relations of church and state and freedom of conscience as well. The most remarkable speech was made by Bishop Emile-Joseph de Smedt of Bruges who, to rising applause, denounced the Catholic Church's proclivities toward triumphalism, clericalism, and judicialism. He argued that the schema on the Church conveyed too much the impression of an institution arrayed in battle garb, one that was a pyramid with the people on the bottom, and characterized by an excessive legalistic attitude.[82]

Meanwhile, *Osservatore Romano* noted increasing anti-conciliar activities, especially among right-wing groups in Italy and France. There were attacks on the so-called Modernist tendencies that Roncalli allegedly exhibited when he was a young priest, the supposed pro-Communist tilt of the Vatican's foreign policy, and the constant assaults on the Curial government.

At the council, the influential Cardinal Montini urged the fathers to state the mind and will of Christ by defending collegiality and by being more ecumenical. He also became increasingly critical of the Curia, from whence he himself had come, and of the delay in the council's work. Observers thought that he was speaking on behalf of the pontiff. Soon it would be Montini who would be setting the agenda and controlling the tempo of the Council.

Good Pope John
Since late September 1962, Pope John had been aware of his precarious physical condition. Resigned and trusting in God as always, the pontiff concluded, "At least I have launched the big ship—others will have to bring it to port." On December 8, a recuperating Pope John seemed well enough as he ended the first session. When he was asked what he wished

to do after the council ended, he wistfully replied, "Spend a day tilling the fields with my brothers." Then for the next six months, he focused on foreign policy questions, especially the Vatican's relations with the Communist bloc and his call for world peace, enumerated best in his encyclical *Pacem in Terris*. He realized that his life was ending, and he seemed to plead with himself that he wished to die as a priest and as a pope, setting once again an example of the redemptive value of suffering. The Vatican observer Malachi Martin stated that at the end of his life Pope John realized what a terrible mistake the council was and he regretted it. If that is so, that record has never been clearly established.[83]

Stomach cancer can be a painful end, and Pope John simply remarked, "the first duty of a pope is to pray and suffer." He observed the irony of it all though: "Out there the world exalts me, while here the Lord rivets me to this bed." Gustavo Cardinal Testa, an old friend of Roncalli's, was consoled by the pope, "Dear Don Gustavo, we have to face things as they are. I have had a long life and served the Church and left some sort of mark on history. By God's grace, I haven't behaved badly."[84] On June 3, he died surrounded by his family and Vatican officials. And yes at this death, they tapped his brow to certify the end.

There is no question that Pope John XXIII was one of the most popular popes in modern times, one respected and loved both outside as well as inside his church. He was to them the good Pope John, the symbol of decency and good humor. As he once said, "All the world is my family." In his life, he was generally nonjudgmental, but not the simple fool of God that some people thought. His personal assistant, Monsignor Loris Capovilla, once observed, "Pope John was a father to everyone, but a friend to no one."[85]

But Pope John was also not the great manipulative leader, or the shrewd peasant visionary that some of his admirers seemed to herald after his death. As a good Catholic and as a good priest, he believed in the Church and in the moving directions of the Holy Spirit. The council of bishops was the successor to the Council of the Apostles, and he did not feel that he had to intervene daily in its deliberations. In some ways, he seemed to believe that the very idea of a Council, its introduction and its opening, was his contribution. He was never a great theologian preoccupied by dogma. He knew what he believed in and was comfortable with it. Pope John thought however the Catholic Church had to become modernized in the ways it expressed its message. He said to one ambassador, "We must shake off the imperial dust that has accumulated on the throne of Peter since Constantine," and he kept on referring to the need for a "new Pentecost."[86]

He was like most revolutionaries a traditionalist at heart. It was this pope also who so celebrated Latin, just before his successor nearly eviscerated it. It was this pope who was comfortable with the various drafts, until his council ripped them to pieces. Still he set the tone of openness, of aggiornamento that emboldened the bishops who, for reasons of pastoral concern and also probably plain old-fashioned revenge, tried to humble the once arrogant Roman Curia.

As noted, Cardinal Siri of Genoa once called John's papacy the most disastrous since the corrupt Renaissance popes 500 years before, although he later recanted. The post-Vatican II Church with its modern bishops and priests has come to accept the assumptions and the practices of the council. It is over, and one must live with its consequences, they seemed to be saying. The majority opinion, however, is positive toward the Council and its legacy and its patron, John XXIII.

The fussy, arrogant Curia was routed. Good for the Vatican fathers, the historians and newspaper reporters of the time seemed to say! But in reflection, some of what the traditionalists warned against came about. The Roman Catholic Church had been an authoritarian institution with a sense of unity, a well-recognized ritual, and a clear line of boundaries. Its orthodoxy, especially since the Council of Trent, had been rigid, but effectively passed on to each generation, socializing people in the ways of Holy Mother Church. [87]

Vatican II and the more radical forces that it unleashed caused considerable damage to that unity and continuity. Reforms of ongoing institutions are extremely difficult, and reformers inevitably have problems with providing balanced leadership that does not open the floodgates of extreme behavior. People do not revolt usually against conservative or even authoritarian governments as much as they do under the easy mantle of change. Thus reform is so dangerous to institutions and to leaders who believe that they can manage it.

But John would not know of those problems. He lived and died an optimist, and never had to bear the consequences of the revolution that he began. Thus he will be forever, "Good Pope John." In 2014, he was canonized a saint.

CHAPTER TEN
JOHN PAUL II, (1978–2005)

Before he passed away, John XXIII's successor Pope Paul whispered, "See, so the pope dies like any ordinary man." His last will and testament mandated a "pious and simple" service—as simple as a pope can probably request in any case. It was in August, the traditional vacation month of Italians, that his reign ended. Almost immediately some members of the Curia insisted that the next pope also had to be an Italian in order to deal with that nation's unique brand of politics. That demand was countered by a letter from Third World prelates supporting the election of a pastorally-oriented pope who could understand their increasing difficulties in the underdeveloped nations.¹

Choosing John Paul I
The Curia conservatives moved quickly to derail two major candidates who were being prominently mentioned: Sebastiano Cardinal Baggio, the head of the Congregation for Bishops, and Sergio Cardinal Pignedoli, from the Secretariat for Non-Christians. The former was portrayed as a committed progressive, and the latter had been criticized for being indiscrete in his dealings with the international pariah Colonel Muammar Gadhafi of Libya who had hosted a conference that attacked Zionism and Israel. The conservatives advocated instead Giuseppe Cardinal Siri—a staunch opponent of Vatican II, Pope John's papacy, and any rapprochement with the left in foreign policy matters. The normally very patient Pope Paul VI had on one occasion relieved Siri from the presidency of the Italian Conference of Bishops because of his obstinacy.

On the first ballot, Siri led with twenty-five votes; the only other candidate close to him was Albino Luciani, the amiable Cardinal Patriarch of Venice. Three times in the twentieth century, the College of Cardinals has turned to that ancient fabled city for a pope, and it was to elect from its citizenry the first pope to be born in that century. If the cardinals insisted on an Italian and wanted a moderate progressive from outside the Curia, there were really few other candidates of available age and pastoral experience from which to choose. Thus the assets of Albino Luciani seemed to become more obvious as the days passed by.

On the third ballot, Luciani received over sixty-five votes, and then he was elected with over ninety votes, while his own went to the liberal Alorsio Cardinal Lorscheider of Brazil. It was truly unanimity for a relatively unknown person. Before the conclave, the sociologist Rev. Andrew Greeley had remarked that the Church needed to name a "holy man who could smile"—and that is exactly what the cardinals got.

Albino Luciani was born on October 17, 1912 in Forno di Canalo (now Canalo d'Agordo) in the Dolomite Alps of northern Italy. His father was a migrant laborer and a committed socialist, but still he agreed to send his son to a seminary at the tender age of eleven. Later Luciani earned a doctorate in theology at the Gregorian University in Rome and was made vice chancellor of the seminary he had attended in Belluno. In 1958, he was named bishop of Vittorio Veneto where he was known for his strong pastoral orientation. Luciani generally supported the reforms of Vatican II, although he never played a major role in any of the four sessions of the Council.

In 1969, he was named the Patriarch of Venice and insisted that the people there abandon the triumphant procession of colorful gondolas and decorated boats that had so delighted Angelo Roncalli at his own installation. His admirers in Venice said that Luciani dressed in a simple priest's cassock and ate seaweed pizza with students. He soon sold his pectoral cross—a gift from John XXIII that had originally belonged to Pius XII. He did so to raise money, some $14,000, for the causes of the physically handicapped of the diocese.

In a trip to Venice, Pope Paul removed his own stole and placed it on Luciani's shoulders, an act of high approval that embarrassed the humble and unpretentious prelate. In 1973, he was named a cardinal, a normal honor for that ancient see. In his spare time, Luciani also authored a series of fictional letters titled *Illustrissimi,* addressed to famous "historical" figures, ranging from Pinocchio and Figaro to Charles Dickens, Mark Twain, and Empress Maria Teresa of Austria. The letters aimed at presenting the Catholic faith to common people in understandable formats.[2]

Once elected to the papacy, however, he glumly observed, "I have neither the wisdom of the heart that Pope John had, nor the preparation or learning of Pope Paul." On one occasion he had confided, "I am only a poor man, accustomed to small things and silence." Soon he was repeatedly asking his secretary, "Why did they choose *me*? Why on earth did they choose *me*?"[3] For the first time in the long history of the office, an incumbent took a dual name, in honor of the two pontiffs who had so influenced him and advanced his career. Also with that designation, he seemed to refuse to choose between those who respected John's memory and liberal legacy, and those who preferred Paul's more cautious style of reform.

What exactly his views were on the Church and the pressing controversies of post-conciliar reform is unclear because of the brevity of his term. Clearly he was pastorally oriented and even considered once, before finally dismissing the idea, that bishops should again be elected as they had been in the distant past. He seemed at ease with ecumenism, advised Paul VI not to issue any definitive statement on birth control, was privately critical of the increasingly controversial Vatican Bank, and was charmingly hospitable in welcoming to the world when he was still a cardinal the first "test tube baby," the pretty Louise Brown. Later however the Holy Office (renamed by Paul the Sacred Congregation for the Doctrine of the Faith) would formally condemn artificial insemination. Its theologians had never seen the lovely infant child.

The new pope showed his lack of experience in diplomacy on several occasions, most apparently when he warmly welcomed General Jorge Videla, the president of Argentina, a symbol of right wing Latin American regimes.[4] And despite his reputation as a progressive, he was really rather conservative in many ways. He had denounced "false moralism" during the Italian divorce controversy and had real concerns at first with the council decree on religious liberty. Luciani had been a student of Cardinal Ottaviani and had probably been inculcated in some of those rigid Romanist attitudes. In response to popular demand and despite his own inclinations, he restored the *sedia gestatoria* on September 23, and at St. John Lateran Basilica, the bishop of Rome's traditional church, he criticized those so overcome with creativity that they lead the faithful into "liturgical excesses." What his views were on other pressing questions would never be known. Five days later he was found dead in his bed.

For some reason, Vatican authorities insisted on maintaining that he was discovered dead earlier than he actually was, and that he had been reading that night the world-weary devotional work, *Imitation of Christ*, by Thomas á Kempis. Others said that he was absorbed over a distressing report on the abuses of the Vatican Bank or going over a mundane speech for the next day that never came. Rumors spread that "the smiling pope," as he was called, was murdered by various sorts of suspects. A book was even written detailing the alleged conspiracy, and one popular American film, *Godfather III*, had a pope poisoned by the Mafia. It appears though that the pontiff had had some serious cardiac problems and was not up to the demanding office he assumed and probably died of a pulmonary embolism.[5]

Pope John Paul I reigned for thirty-three days—a month in time—

and left only two marks on the Church: a remarkable smile that lit up his pictures and appearances and a genuine disdain for the once royal trappings of the office. At his funeral, some spectators sadly commented on how the soles of his new shoes were barely scuffed. Now a very shaken College of Cardinals had to elect a successor—as the faithful waited for their third pope in a year.[6]

A Man from a Distant Country
And so in October 1978, the College of Cardinals—some 111 in number—returned to Rome for a second conclave. It was increasingly obvious after the election of Luciani that there would be problems finding another acceptable Italian candidate who could carry the two-thirds plus one vote necessary at that time for election. Part of the reason was the clear split between Giuseppe Siri of Genoa, who at seventy-two was still seen as a protégé of Pius XII and who had been a consistent vocal critic of Vatican II and of Pope John, and Giovanni Benelli of Florence—the young, fifty-seven year-old hard-driving administrator who shook up the Vatican bureaucracy when he served Paul VI, and who emerged in this conclave as a candidate and not just a kingmaker. Three days before the conclave, fifteen Western European and Third World cardinals met to plot a stop Siri strategy. They put forth the names of Benelli, Ugo Poletti, the Vicar of Rome, and Giovanni Columbo, the Archbishop of Milan as candidates.[7]

At first Siri seemed to be very close to being the choice, but strong opposition developed especially from some Western European and Third World cardinals, and it proved in the long run to be an insurmountable obstacle. In addition, an Italian newspaper, *La Gazzetta del Popolo*, prematurely printed an ill-tempered interview with Cardinal Siri in which he again criticized the council in harsh terms. The interview was mysteriously delivered to the Roman residence of each member of the Sacred College. Privately the cardinal observed of John Paul I, "You can't govern with smiles or protestations of modesty and simplicity."

Since Pope John XXIII, and especially since Paul VI, the percentage of Italians in the College of Cardinals had markedly declined. In addition, in 1963, fifty-five of the eighty cardinals who elected Paul were Europeans; in 1978 only fifty-six of the 111 were Europeans. Also Paul VI had prohibited cardinals over the age of eighty from voting, thus eliminating nine cardinals, most of whom were probably conservatives, from having a role.[8] As a group, the cardinals wanted a man who was pastoral in his orientation, was in good health, and could exhibit a personal presence that appealed to the public at large. Some of the favorites of the previous conclave were no longer mentioned; they were in the Italian expression *bruciati*—burnt out cases.[9]

Before the conclave met, Cardinals Krol and König, both men with Polish roots, had a candidate—the Polish prelate from Krakow, Karol Wojtyla. Wojtyla was not well known outside of the College and the upper levels of the Vatican bureaucracy. Although he may have received up to ten votes in the previous conclave, his name was not mentioned prominently except in a brief reference in *Time* magazine. Years before, however, it was rumored probably apocryphally, that the mystic and stigmatic Padre Pio had fallen to his knees when he first met the young Wojtyla and had predicted that he would be elected pope and that his reign would be marked by an act of violence.[10]

After four ballots on Sunday—the first day of voting—it became more obvious that no Italian cardinal could be elected. Meanwhile between the rounds of balloting, Wojtyla spent some time reading a quarterly review on Marxism while waiting in the picturesque Sistine Chapel. On Monday afternoon, four foreign candidates emerged: Wojtyla, König (who did not want the position), Eduardo Pironio of Argentina, and Johannes Willebrands of the Netherlands who soon gave his support to Wojtyla.[11]

Still many of the Italian cardinals declined to support the Polish cardinal until Sebastiano Baggio of the Congregation of Bishops backed Wojtyla. In the end seventeen cardinals persistently refused to concur in his election on the eighth and final ballot. It has been rumored, but not confirmed, that Wojtyla was actually elected on the seventh ballot and refused, only accepting the office after Cardinal Wyszynski, the primate of Poland, insisted that he bow to God's will. After his election, he sat alone at a table beneath Michelangelo's *Last Judgment* in the Sistine Chapel, holding his head in his hands, and slumping down in his chair.[12]

Whether the speculation of his initial refusal is true or not, one of the cardinals there, Enrique y Tarancón, simply observed, "God forced us to break with history to elect Karol Wojtyla." To observers, Cardinal Benelli generously commented on Wojtyla's close ties to the Vatican Council, "His theological attitude is perfectly correct...what he says comes from his personal convictions. He is the right man at the right time. If there was one man who believed in the Second Vatican Council and had a firm will to carry it out it was Cardinal Wojtyla." Later the new pope would candidly admit that the conclave had taken a gamble in choosing him. There was indeed some concern that at fifty-eight he was too young for the position—making him the most youthful pontiff since Pius IX in 1846. And most startling, he was the first non-Italian elected in 456 years, since the Dutchman Adrian (Hadrian) VI was chosen in 1522.[13]

Wojtyla wished at first to take the name of Stanislaus in honor of the Polish Catholic bishop and saint from Krakow who had been murdered during Mass by the knights of King Boleslaw the Bold nearly 900 years before in 1079. But in a more measured gesture, he announced his choice of a name—John Paul II in honor of his predecessors. When he addressed the crowd outside St. Peter's Square in the early evening, he remarked in Italian that the conclave had called him "from a distant country and yet [one] always close because of our communion in faith and Christian tradition." Then he asked their forgiveness if he made a mistake in "your—our Italian language." It was a calculated slip and the crowd loved his gesture. When he playfully continued, "If I make mistakes, please correct me," the crowd responded, "Yes, we will." He was to be the most consummate actor in the history of the modern Church.[14]

The next day he surreptitiously sent his red skull cap to the altar of the Polish Virgin of Ostrabrama in Vilnius in Soviet Lithuania—a special tribute to his people and their tribulations. And in the evening, he called home to Krakow, to say how lonely he was. "I am sad without my friends," he remarked. Later he was to call the Apostolic Palace, "a cage, a gilded cage." His schoolboy acquaintance, Dr. Karol Poliwka, was to characterize Wojtyla as "a man of loneliness."[15]

He was a mystery—a public man who commanded enormous audiences wherever he went, and yet retreated into private spaces filled with religious fervor, ascetic mysticism, and deep personal loss. He wore heavily his complex and difficult past. We are all formed in so many ways by our childhood and our adolescent years. For Wojtyla those were years of war, death, and deepening religious commitment.

The Making of a Pope
Karol Wojtyla was born on May 18, 1920 in the small drab city of Wadowice, fifty kilometers southwest of Krakow in the foothills of the Carpathian Mountains, at the end of the tragedy called the Great War. Once he remarked, "During my childhood, I listened to veterans of World War I, talking about endless horrors of battle." He continued to grow to manhood as the Nazis and the Soviet armies ruthlessly divided up Poland. His family roots were in the peasantry, although his father, a strict but loving and religiously devout parent, was a retired military officer in the then Austro-Hungarian Army's quartermaster corps and was an admirer of Polish Marshall Józef Piludski.

Before he was twenty-one he lost his entire family. His mother, a onetime school teacher, died when he was only eight and an older sister passed away as well early in life; his elder brother, a physician, died of scarlet fever when Karol was eleven; and his father of complications from a stroke when Karol was twenty. In 1984, Wojtyla recalled the night of his father's death, saying, "I never felt so alone." Sadly he observed years later, "At twenty, I had already lost all the people I loved and even the ones I might have loved." And he wistfully remarked that there comes a time when boys brought up by their fathers (no matter how well and tenderly) make the painful discovery that they have been deprived of a mother.[16]

Unlike most of his modern predecessors in the papacy, he did not seem to be committed at an early age to the priesthood. Wojtyla chose that vocation only a year and a half after his father's death, after he himself had been nearly killed in several freak accidents, and as his world was coming apart in the Nazi-controlled zone of violence. The Church was feeling the full weight of totalitarian oppression, and the cardinal prelate of Krakow, Prince Adam Stefan Sapieha, informed the Vatican that the Poles were being annihilated just as brutally as the Jews. In that horrible environment, Wojtyla wrote poetry, studied philosophy, gained a military exemption by working in a quarry and then a water purification plant, and spent his free time as an actor in the Rhapsodic Theater (Teatr Rapsodyczny, or the "Theatre of the Spoken Word"), founded by Mieczyslaw Kotlarczyk. He was to say that his time as a worker was of greater value to him than his two university doctorates. Those sentiments found expression in a line in his poetry: "How splendid these men, no airs, no graces." Later in 1982 he reflected on how his experience as a worker and his seeing the horrors of Polish deportation "have profoundly marked my existence."[17]

At one point he fell under the spiritual influence of a tailor named Jan Tyranowski who introduced him to the writings of the Spanish mystic, St. John of the Cross, as well as to the "Living Rosary" devotions and the Catholic Youth Association. Wojtyla was later to characterize him as a saint.[18]

One tale that gained some circulation after he was chosen pope was that Wojtyla was married and that his wife was killed by the Gestapo, a story that has been discredited. One woman student, a contemporary of his, said that Wojtyla "did not avoid feminine company as a colleague, but he did not seek it." In his autobiography he notes how he had female acquaintances but was preoccupied with the theater and literature. Another incorrect story spread after his election is that Wojtyla was imprisoned for a while at the Dachau death camp.[19]

A more dramatic account is that during those dark years, he was involved in the underground in Poland, which sought through the Christian Democratic organization, UNIA, to save Jews from the

Holocaust. Consequently he was put on the Gestapo's black list, and was labeled an "unwanted person." But he denied that he helped in such efforts, saying to a Polish Jew Marek Halter, "I cannot lay claim to what I did not do." He was anti-Nazi but rather apolitical, seeing liberation as coming through Christian values and prayer. In 1942 he enrolled in the theological department at Jagiellonian University, an action that was illegal and could have led to his arrest and death.[20]

Some time after his father's death, Wojtyla decided to become a seminarian, as the Nazis grew increasingly murderous, putting over six million Poles, or one-fourth the total population, to death in just six years. The Church was also continually attacked, and 1,932 priests, 850 monks, and 289 nuns were killed or murdered in concentration camps. The SS leader, Reinhard Heydrich, ordered that the nobility, the priesthood, and the Jews all had to be liquidated to protect the Reich's interests.[21]

On one occasion Wojtyla himself was arrested, only to be fortuitously let go. Cardinal Sapieha moved several seminarians to his episcopal palace, and there Wojtyla spent the rest of the war, largely unnoticed by the outside world. His absence from factory work was initially reported, but the influential cardinal intervened quietly and his name was never forwarded to the Germans. He had for all intents and purposes disappeared. Wojtyla had wanted to join the austere Discalced Carmelite monastic order, but his confessor insisted that he was made for greater things ("*ad maiores res tu es*"), and besides Poland desperately needed parish priests after the Nazi genocides. In his autobiography, he affirmed that Sapieha himself discouraged him from joining the order.[22]

In November 1946 he was ordained, and then sent to the Angelicum, the Dominican house of studies in Rome to do graduate work in philosophy. Up to then, Wojtyla's education was sketchy because of the disruption of local academic institutions and seminaries in Poland. One can only imagine the excitement of going to Rome for a student who had lived in a Polish city plagued by war time conditions, food shortages, and the stiff coldness of drafty rooms and endless winters. And above all, he must have endured the loneliness of a young man without any family in a foreign land.[23]

His counterparts found him to be very cheerful, pleasant, forthright, humble, highly intelligent, and generally nonjudgmental toward others. Wojtyla studied under the compelling influence of traditional Thomists, although his own scholarly research examined the mystic St. John of the Cross, the author who charted the *Dark Night of the Soul*. Wojtyla was also attached to the Catholic War Relief Services where he assisted Polish refugees outside their homeland, and he came into contact with a

Monsignor Giovanni Battista Montini who would become his mentor years later. On one occasion, he also visited Marseilles, France, to meet Father Jacques Loew, one of the founders of the controversial worker-priest movement.[24]

Wojtyla graduated with highest honors; ironically on his doctoral board were two future members of the College of Cardinals who would choose him to be pope. In July 1948, he returned to Krakow and was shipped off for a brief time to a desolate parish at Niegowizi in the Galician countryside thirty miles from Krakow. Then he was transferred to Lublin University to become the university chaplain and a faculty member. Having just survived the brutalities of the Nazis, the Church was now under attack from the Communist Party, and about 10 percent of its clergy would end up imprisoned.[25] The traditional Polish Church was becoming a heroic fortress of martyrs under totalitarian states of the right and the left.

Unlike most Catholic thinkers who are Thomists, Wojtyla gravitated toward the philosophical theories of German Catholic phenomenologist Max Scheler and the Polish thinker Roman Ingarden, as well as the personalist philosophers of the French Catholic existentialist movement, such as Gabriel Marcel, Maurice Blondel, and Emmanuel Mounier.[26]

On October 23, 1948, Pius XII named Stefan Wyszynski to be the prelate of Poland, archbishop of Gniezno and Warsaw. A canon lawyer by training, Wyszynski was involved with the Christian worker movement in his nation and had been a vigorous opponent of Nazism and later Communism. Wyszynski immediately moved to reach some rapprochement with the Communists, and he signed an agreement that was criticized in some offices of the Vatican. The basic provisions acknowledged that while the pope had the highest authority on matters of faith, morality, and Church jurisdiction, the episcopate pledged that it would be guided by the national interests of Poland. In the process, the Church's bishops would seek to carve out their own autonomy and identity, but had to do so without threatening the viability of the Marxist state. In exasperation at the Vatican's criticisms, Wyszynski observed, "You talk about the Church of Silence, but here in Rome is the Church of the Deaf."[27]

In 1947 Wojtyla had been awarded a doctorate in sacred theology from the Jagiellonian University, the alma mater of the astronomer Copernicus and the real Doctor Faustus. In 1951, Cardinal Sapieha died, but his successor Archbishop Eugeniusz Baziak continued Wojtyla's high level mentoring, advising him to take a two year leave of absence to complete still another doctorate. Responding to the diverse needs in his complex personality, Wojtyla also published, under at least four pseudonyms, major works of verse, including dramas revolving around religious themes.[28]

In the early 1950s, Wyszynski came under increasing hostility from the Communists and also from the Vatican. In Rome the Polish prelate insisted that he was not "soft on Communism," but that "I want my priests at the altar, at the pulpit, and in the confessional—not in prison." He and later Wojtyla would consistently insist upon the importance of protecting the flexibility of the Church, but they also usually avoided partisan politics. As Wyszynski was to find out, state officials however insisted on interfering in the choice of bishops, and several members of the hierarchy were arrested during this period. In November 1952, Pius XII named Wyszynski a cardinal in a clear show of support. In September 1953 he was arrested by the secret police, the first major Polish prelate to be arrested since the Prussians had imprisoned Archbishop Mieczyslaw Ledóchowski in 1866. Wyszynski was released three years later in October 1956 when a more conciliatory regime came to power.

The authorities also closed down the theological faculty at Jagiellonian University where Wojtyla had been teaching. At that time he was finishing his doctoral thesis on Christian ethics and the philosopher Max Scheler, enlarging his circles of friends, and engaging in rigorous recreation, especially hiking and skiing. He would continue that latter sport even while pope until at age seventy-four when he fractured his hip in a bathroom accident.[30]

In 1956, tensions further increased among the Polish government, nationalist liberals, and the Soviet Union. To calm matters down, Russian armies were withdrawn for a while, and Wladyslaw Gomulka, who himself had once been jailed by Stalinists, came to power promising "the Polish road to socialism." He immediately made overtures to Cardinal Wyszynski, then under house arrest in a monastery for three years, and allowed him to resume full episcopal powers.

During those difficult years, Wojtyla was teaching at the Catholic university in Lublin and climbing up the academic ladder, establishing himself as a prolific scholar and a well-regarded teacher.[31] Among other projects, he was interested in preparing a study of the *Decretum Gratiani*, the compilation of Church canon law done by the twelfth century scholar, Franciscus Gratiano. Through it all, he continued to express himself as a poet, usually under the pseudonym of Andrzej Jowién. Explaining the appeal of drama and poetry, Wojtyla insisted that art is "a companion to religion and a guide on the road to God." In 1957 and 1958, he was working on an essay on love and responsibility that would become important in understanding his later views on sexuality and contraception.[32]

In his book, Wojtyla argued that "sexual relations outside marriage always cause objective harm to the woman, even if she consents to or positively desires them." As pope, he would even criticize the sinfulness of men who looked upon their wives "with lust" in their hearts. He was widely ridiculed for that remark, but it is in perfect harmony with his view that to treat a person as an object is unethical and immoral. Such a view is a noble signpost in evaluating behavior. But life is so ambiguous at times, and sexual activities such a mixture of the physical and fantasy, that it often does not fit its robust expressions into such hermetically sealed categories. Even love is more complicated than that. The Russian playwright Anton Chekhov noted of love, "Either it is a remnant of something degenerating, something which had once been immense, or it is a particle of what will in the future develop into something immense, but at the present it is unsatisfying, it gives much less than one expects."[33]

Called to the Hierarchy

On July 8, 1958, an ailing Pius XII named Karol Wojtyla auxiliary bishop. It was a surprising nomination, for the priest and academic had no extensive pastoral or administrative experiences. The promotion was undoubtedly due to the intercession of Archbishop Baziak who may in turn have been following some earlier pledges made to the late Cardinal Sapieha. Wojtyla was only thirty eight years old at the time, and probably was not known except by reputation to even Cardinal Wyszynski. Indeed his nomination marked the first time the cardinal had been in effect bypassed in the appointment of a Polish bishop. As for Wojtyla, he never hesitated when asked if he accepted the nomination from Rome. And one of his first acts was to move his mother's remains from Wadowice to rest beside his father in a Krakow cemetery.[34]

When Baziak died, Wojtyla was elected Capitular Vicar of the diocese of Krakow. Traveling to Rome with the Polish delegation to the Vatican Council, he met for the first time the influential Franz Cardinal König who years later would be an important figure in his election as pope. König remarked that the friendly young bishop before him seemed to lack a sense of self-assurance, spoke German poorly, and was dressed in frayed clothes.[35]

Wojtyla was diligent in working on various commissions, even though at first he said little in the public debates. One Protestant observer to the council, George H. Williams of Harvard University, however, predicted that Wojtyla would become a pope. Much later in 1977, Basil Cardinal Hume of Westminster met him and concluded, "I was struck by the impression he gave of strength, determination and durability."[37] Even Wojtyla's biographer, Tad Szulc, disclosed that Wojtyla was one of the major authors of Paul's controversial encyclical *Humanae Vitae,* and in his own papacy he was its single most consistent supporter in the Roman Catholic Church. It has been speculated that some 60 percent of the encyclical was written by Wojtyla. It is unclear if the progressive cardinals such as König who supported his candidacy in 1978, were aware of his central role. Wojtyla, a member of the enlarged commission dealing with the birth control issue, did not attend any of the working meetings, but apparently played a major part in shaping the mind of the hesitating Pope Paul. In his own statements, Wojtyla never wavered, and as pope he allowed his subordinates to suggest that the ban on contraception approached an infallible declaration, a view that Paul would never have ventured to advance publicly, although he may have contemplated it.[38]

After Archbishop Baziak's death, Wojtyla was temporarily in charge of the Krakow diocese, but it was left to Cardinal Wyszynski to choose a successor. Under the agreed-upon procedures with the government, the primate was to submit a list of at least three names to the Communist regime, and it could accept or reject any of the nominees. Then the cardinal would forward a name to the Vatican for final approval. It is clear that Wyszynski opposed having Wojtyla named archbishop of Krakow, just as fifteen years later he discounted the idea that his younger colleague could be elected pope. In fact, he put his own name forward if the conclave decided to go "foreign." After the first session of the council, the cardinal submitted a series of names to the Communist government, and each was rejected, one after another, until finally the government received and accepted the name of Wojtyla. Clearly the cardinal did not wish him to become archbishop of Krakow; and just as clearly the Marxist government was responsible for putting in place a man who would become "the Slavic Pope," and a person who helped to end the Communist regime in his homeland. Such is the irony of history. The Polish Communists thought they wanted bishops like Wojtyla who had a reputation for being apolitical. After he was installed, however, he proved to be in many ways a tougher and more determined foe than they had expected.

And so, on March 3, 1964, Karol Wojtyla at age forty-three was solemnly installed by Pope Paul as the Metropolitan Archbishop of Krakow. At first he had some difficulties with the local clerical establishment and remarked on one occasion, "Well, what can I do? When Cardinal Adam Sapieha [a predecessor], who was born a prince, looked down on them from his lofty height, they were afraid of him. But

I simply can't impress them in the same way—not as a former worker." Indeed, he was the first prelate in the history of that see not to come from the aristocracy.[39]

A Son of the Council

He would speak more often in the later sessions than in the first session of the Vatican Council. Wojtyla addressed the People of God analogy, ecumenism, and religious freedom—all in a positive way. But his views were often traditionally oriented rather than progressive in tone, and he was still a major proponent of a strong papacy, even in discussions about collegiality. During the council, Archbishop Wojtyla appeared before some students of the Polish College in Rome to answer questions on Vatican II. In response to criticism of Pope John XXIII and his rather abrupt call for a council, Wojtyla insisted that the Church had to deal decisively with some immense challenges: the rapid development of technology, a society oriented toward consumption and lacking altruistic values, the population explosion, the wide extent of atheism, and the need for world peace. The Church was becoming less effective under modern conditions, and many contemporary forms of behavior were in conflict with traditional Church ethics.

He maintained that in four years the Church had undergone an amazing change. An enormous outpouring of valuable opinion had come forth from the upper echelons of the hierarchy and theologians. He acknowledged the important parts played by such eminent theologians as Henri de Lubac, Jean Daniélou, Yves Congar, Hans Küng, Riccardo Lombardi, and Karl Rahner. The Church also had come to understand better non-Catholic and non-Christian religions and to recognize that atheism's appeal often came from its claim to liberate man from feelings of alienation. He praised the healthy debates in the council and the salutary effects of pluralism of opinion shown in its sessions.

Wojtyla commented to a friend on the important changes in the relationship between the center and the periphery of the Church—the pope and the bishops, the clergy and the laity. He advocated greater decentralization and an emphasis on collegiality. Also in his view, there had to be an end to "Constantinism," the principle of a close alliance between Church and the political regime which had been so important to Catholicism since the fourth century.[40]

Most dramatically, though, in the last session, he was a major mover on the draft on the relationships with the Jews. Born and raised near the death camp of Auschwitz (Óswiecim), he lived in a town with a large Jewish population and had formed close friendships with Jewish students. Wojtyla was acutely sensitive on the issue of Jewish persecution, and called the Auschwitz camp "this Golgatha of the modern world." He was the first pope to visit a synagogue and finally approved the Vatican's recognition of the state of Israel in 1994.

At the council, he also opposed the attempt of some bishops to condemn Communism. Later he stressed the need for dialogue with atheists and warned, "It is not the Church's role to lecture to unbelievers... We are involved in a quest along with our fellow men... Let us avoid moralizing, or the suggestion that we have a monopoly of the truth. One of the major defects of this draft is that in it the Church appears merely as an authoritarian institution." It was difficult enough to deal with them back home without new provocations.[41]

On May 29, 1967, Paul VI named Wojtyla a cardinal, some said to balance the influence of Wyszynski, who was becoming more intractable in the pope's eyes. As for Wojtyla, he was rather deferential at first to the older man, trying to allay any appearance of differences. At the age of forty seven, the Polish intellectual and poet was the second youngest cardinal in the Church and had probably reached the apex of his ecclesiastical career. Celebrating his installation, Wojtyla humorously said to his clergy in Krakow, "I can't go any higher now." There was no other position a non-Italian could aspire to in the Catholic Church, or so it seemed.[42]

Biographer Tad Szulc related that the Polish secret police had files on both Wyszynski and Wojtyla. They recorded that the elder prelate was from a traditional Catholic family, and that he had built his ecclesiastical career on anti-Communist sentiments. His hard-line position during the Cold War was very significant in establishing the directions of the Vatican's foreign policies under Pius XII, but with the advent of John XXIII his influence diminished as the tenor of that policy changed significantly. The reports judged that Wyszynski was characterized by a "shallow, emotional, and devotional Catholicism."

Wojtyla, on the other hand, was presented as an intellectual, one of the few in the Polish episcopate. He was judged as having roots in the working class and leftist university circles, and his rise in the hierarchy was seen as due not so much to his advocacy of anti-communism, as to the high regard others had for his intellectual breadth. He was not engaged in "anti-state" political activity, the report stated, and he lacked organizational and leadership qualities. His "secular lifestyle" also brought him closer to young intelligentsia and students. Recognizing the differences between the two men, the report advocated that the authorities make additional overtures to Wojtyla.[43] Later the Communist authorities would regret their sanguine assessments.

The Vatican Council and its call for greater collegiality spawned more opportunities for participation, and Wojtyla was appointed to three major congregations of the Curia—the Congregations for the Clergy, for Sacraments and Worship, and for Catholic Education. He was also a consultant to the Council for the Laity and was chosen by the pope in 1969 to be a member of the Synod of Bishops.

A high point of his career was Paul VI's invitation in February 1976 to give the Lenten retreat sermons to the Roman Curia and the pope. Paul asked Wojtyla to deliver his lectures in Italian, indicating later to some that the pope was grooming a foreign successor to be the next Bishop of Rome. In fact, before the conclave that elected him pope in 1963, Montini was supposed to have commented that maybe it was time then for a non-Italian pope. To an associate, Paul much later remarked that Wojtyla was "a brave, magnificent man." Between 1973 and 1975, Wojtyla privately visited the pontiff eleven times, a sign of high regard indeed.

Wojtyla's homilies, published later in 1979 under the title *Sign of Contradiction,* presented a somber picture of the West and its values, although he was critical of the excesses of both economic imperialism and Marxism. Still he specifically denounced liberal regimes where "men are sick with affluence and an overdose of freedom." A very frail Paul listened to Wojtyla's spirited defense of his ill-fated encyclical, *Humanae Vitae*. In May 1978, Wojtyla paid his last visit to Paul, and in August he attended his funeral. It was time for another Italian; although as noted there has been some speculation that the Polish cardinal received a few votes in the conclave that named Albino Luciani pope. At the conclave, Luciani related that the Polish prelate was writing furiously—not taking notes it turned out, but working on his next publication![44]

On September 28, Wojtyla was celebrating the twentieth year of his consecration as a bishop in the Catholic Church; Pope John Paul I had just died in the Vatican apartments. Some have recorded that Wojtyla had a premonition that he would be elected pope this time; if so, he was one of the few who predicted that choice, although his godmother had foreseen such an occurrence years ago, and over a century before, the noted Polish poet Juliusz Slowacki insisted that there would be a Slavic pope. His friends recorded that the usually mild-mannered and even-tempered Wojtyla became fretful and preoccupied after news of the pope's death, almost as if he knew the direction the next conclave would take. Except for several years in Rome, he had spent his whole life in Poland. Whatever close human ties he had forged in place of his lost family were in that land.

Although John Paul II took the name of his predecessors, he quickly moved away from both the open style of John XXIII and the caution and hesitations of Paul VI. After making some important gestures of support to the Roman Curia and to the Roman people in his new diocese, the pope established his brand of rule. Although he was a new voice in the council, he was never seen as a leading progressive force in those sessions. Still he immediately committed himself to its full implementation. His first words seemed to summarize his life, "Be not afraid..."[45]

Rather than characterize Wojtyla as a betrayer of the council as his critics have, one can view him as having some of the same reservations that Paul VI expressed over the years. Although he was committed to the legacy of the council, at various times, Paul spoke of his concern about its diverse directions. On November 23, 1966, he denounced the view that the council had given the "go-ahead for any kind of arbitrary changes." In October 1968, he pleaded for a return to obedience, and in March of the following year, he attacked the "giddiness" of certain priests. In January 1969, the pope remonstrated, "How many things, how many truths are questioned or doubted? How many liberties are taken with the authentic patrimony of Catholic teaching?"

Commenting on the adverse reaction to *Humanae Vitae*, Paul wondered aloud on September 10, 1969 how the "most poignant pain comes to her [the Church] from the indocility and infidelity of certain of her ministers and some of her consecrated souls, that the most disappointing surprises come to her from circles that have been the most assisted, the most favored and the most beloved." He spoke frequently of a "crisis of authority and faith," and a year before his death, he concluded that "a non-Catholic mentality was increasingly dominant in the Church."[46]

The Church of Karol Wojtyla
There are major differences between Paul and his successor. Paul was a man who appeared cautious, tentative, and ambivalent. But actually he saw his role as implementing the policies of a council that he himself would never have dared to call in the first place. John Paul II has always praised the movement of the Holy Spirit in the council, and in his first major address after his election, pledged "our primary duty to be that of promoting with prudent but encouraging action, the most exact fulfillment of the norms and directions of the Council."[47] But his actions, and especially those of the Congregation for the Doctrine of Faith under Cardinal Ratzinger, at times seemed to many committed to roll back the new order or to reaffirm aspects of the old. It is not without reason that the era of John Paul II has been termed the "restoration."

Coming from a nation where the Church knew intense persecution and where the basis of piety was strong and far-reaching, the pope was not able to understand—or accept—the very complexities of the new Church he headed. The comparatively young pontiff moved quickly, perhaps at times a bit abruptly, to reassert the hierarchical model of the papacy. Occasionally, his role model seemed to be more Pius XII, without the aristocratic aloofness of that Roman cleric. His administration appeared often as unyielding as Pius XI. And in his search for orthodoxy he has somewhat paralleled Pius X's campaign against the assorted errors of Modernism. But this pope was above all a man of ideas, a person who moved easily with other intellectuals and theologians in a manner similar to the autocratic and well-educated Leo XIII.

The man and the movement came together in another way. The last part of the twentieth century was saturated with the electronic media, and John Paul II was immediately at home in that milieu. The once Polish actor exuded a sense of poise, timing, and command that added to the usual aura of the papacy. He was a genuine crowd pleaser, even with those who disagreed with his rigid theological views. It has been said in the United States that while many faithful disliked the message, they loved the messenger.

The sources of progressive discontent during this time were manifested in three major focal points, and the pope moved to exercise greater control over each. The new synods—the symbol of collegiality—became groups that were more often meant to help the pope administer the policies that he initiated and approved. The new episcopal conferences of bishops were also brought to heel and were watched by the Curia as they served John Paul's bidding. And the Congregation for the Doctrine of the Faith stepped up its warnings and criticisms of highly visible theologians, some of whom were welcomed in the Council and acknowledged by the Church Fathers to be *periti*.

At the very start of his tenure, the pope challenged the "liberation theologians" in Latin America, sometimes without fully understanding the complexities facing the Church there. His synods walked away from the expression "People of God" and its implications, which he himself had once praised, as some in the Church bureaucracy were trying to restore the old hierarchical metaphors. As the years passed, the pope both celebrated the virtues of women and yet moved almost belligerently to put them in their place, that is, outside the pale of the priesthood by his exercise of infallible teaching.

He denounced priests who engage in partisan politics, while he himself stage-managed Polish domestic affairs in major ways, and played a significant role in upending the Soviet empire. And no churchman before assuming the responsibilities of pope ever spoke so graphically of sexual union and pleasure, and yet he seemed so wedded to characterizing all forms of contraception as part of an "anti-life philosophy," associating it with war, abortion, and euthanasia.

This conservative pope filled stadia with the young, and was named in 1995 by *Time* magazine as its "Man of the Year" because of the surety and self-confidence he exuded in the service of moral values that that very organ of opinion and others so often ridiculed. This pontificate of an "outsider" became one of the most controversial in modern times, accelerating the phenomenon of selective denial of doctrine by a usually docile faithful, especially in the United States and Western Europe. How has this papacy been cast in such complex molds?

One explanation that has been posited was that Karol Wojtyla, despite his incredible intellectual brilliance, was really rather provincial. He spent nearly all of his life in an Iron Curtain country, a nation without much contemporary intellectual importance or flavor. Poland was and is a backward land in many ways, blessed with a sense of deep patriotism and intensive piety, but at the fringe in terms of Western culture. Thus Wojtyla, for all his exposure to the world of ideas, had very limited perspectives.

Perhaps that criticism was somewhat just, but no one is born a cosmopolitan; we all come from somewhere. As one of his friends observed, "He is not a cosmopolitan, but he does have a sense of 'cultural collegiality.'" Some close to Wojtyla would not agree with that sanguine assessment. Three years into John Paul's pontificate, the eighty-eight year-old Carlo Cardinal Confalonieri observed, "We Italians have a universal vision. As for the foreigner at present in the Vatican, he is out of his element, he needs to study the milieu, and he should seek advice through the properly constituted channels." Indeed the pontiff himself, on one occasion he remarked, "I don't think the eminent cardinals knew what kind of personality I am, and therefore what kind of papacy they were getting."[48]

Another view is that Polish Catholicism is very different from Latin Catholicism. One of the reasons why the Catholic Church has survived over the centuries is because it has been governed by Italians who tend to be more cynical, more world-weary, and less passionate about ideas, ideology, and religion itself. They regard human nature as somewhat fallen, and the Church as a very imperfect institution that helps sinners, as best it can, get a decent stab at salvation. But the path is slippery, life can be sweet, and we all fall victim to various temptations. So when that happens, one looks the other way, uses the sacrament of Confession, and covers up if the behavior of the Church and its clergy lead to scandal.

By contrast, Polish Catholicism is tinged with the celebration of martyrs. Wojtyla's speeches were very much cast in the heroic model, and his own life and tribulations bore witness to its demanding standards. Indeed he himself observed, "The younger generation grew up in *an atmosphere marked by a new positivism*, whereas in Poland, when I was a boy, *romantic traditions* prevailed."

For such people, compromises are counterfeit and great betrayals. However for popes like Della Chiesa, Ratti, Pacelli, Roncalli and Montini, who learned their leadership skills in wartime diplomacy, the world is not black and white, but filled with varying hues of gray. One must accommodate, build alliances, work with fools and even evil men. Sometimes the best one can do in life is to minimize suffering by making common cause with very objectionable types of people. Did not Montini imply that in his persistent defense of Pius XII; did not Roncalli live that way by working with the Nazi Ambassador Franz von Papen to save Jews in the Balkans? They survived, as Roncalli once bluntly observed, by bending and not breaking. And their moral vision of Catholicism and their role as pontiffs were much more complicated than Wojtyla's.

Then too, the role models of our lives are rarely our contemporaries. They are the heroes of our youth, and the pontiffs that Wojtyla knew in passing were Pius XI and especially Pius XII, neither of whom were good guides to the contemporary world. The first was a stubborn, obstinate, unbending autocrat who dallied with dictators and then exploded in righteousness and self-righteousness against them. And his successor was the epitome of the regal aloof pontiff. Wojtyla never knew Pius XII's agonies and hesitations, more akin to Paul VI's than to his own certainties. The popular view of Pius XII embraced respect, admiration, and high intellectual regard. He spoke on every topic imaginable, and like Wojtyla considered himself both a linguist and a philosopher. However, he never called for a Church council and never had to deal with the unleashed forces of dissent that so perplexed Paul VI.

Reform has its own hope and its own dynamics, sparking an exuberance that comes from upending the old order of things. But restoration has its own model as well, and it is based on a romantic interpretation of the past. Wojtyla seemed to be pleading for such a restoration of the papacy of Pius XII, without though the arched pomp that the latter engaged in. Wojtyla believed that if one could strip the papacy of its pretentious symbols and be more accessible to the media, one can restore the Church and the papacy back to the era of unquestioning obedience.

Once when he was discussing possible bishopric candidates for the

United States, he took off his papal ring, and uncharacteristically slammed his hand on the table, saying, "No, we need stronger men there." Strength, fortitude, authority, heroism—such was the worldview of John Paul II. As for himself, he once reflected, "I have received more graces than battles to fight."[49]

But the forces of dissent are powerful in the Roman Catholic Church, and they arose from complex causes that had little in common with the dreams of restoration. It was not a failure of will that the Church was facing; it was profound economic, social, and cultural changes. Pope John felt that intuitively. In the beginning, Paul clearly articulated it. Wojtyla denied it. In defense of the conservative position, however one can ask if the Catholic Church lost so much after Vatican II, how can one say that more accommodation with the world will work? The progressive response is that if the Church cannot change, it will not survive; and the rejoinder is obvious—if it changes, can it survive with its integrity intact? That was the central dilemma that faced John Paul II's entire papacy, and his answer was very clear: the Church will remain conservative in dogma and practice, but try to reach out to the concerns of the world by emphasizing social justice, while not compromising basic tenets of the faith. Under such a prescription, the universal Catholic Church may be reduced to a smaller but more hard core, militant and obedient faithful.[50]

Understanding this formulation should not lead one to the simplistic conclusion that the state of the Catholic Church was simply a conservative Polish pope versus a progressive reforming faithful. The history of the modern Church involves the basic problem of providing leadership in an organization that lives not by production or consumption, but by ideas, beliefs, and symbols of the most important and intimate experiences of our brief lives.

One can see this difficulty in Wojtyla's convoluted dealings with the Latin American church. Organizationally, the Catholic Church is essentially a bureaucracy, headed by Italians (until recently), funded by Americans and Germans, trying increasingly to convert restless peoples in the Third World. It is in Latin America, Africa, and also Asia, where the populations are increasing dramatically, that the Church must focus—thus Vatican II's emphasis on evangelicalism. The great opponents of Catholicism as expressed in John Paul II's speeches, are materialism, secularism, commercialism, and sexual exploitation. Catholics have always lived beside decadence, corruption, and hedonism, and the Church continues to survive. The real ideological challenge to Catholicism today is Islam, and the most profound problem facing the Church is the condition of teeming poverty-stricken masses across the non-industrial southern hemisphere, many of them practicing or nominal Catholics. The challenges there are more basic, more demographic, more explosive than many people realize.[51]

The Protestant Reformation came about not just because of the failings of priests and popes, but also because of the long-term consequences of the plagues that killed off the local clergy and left people unchurched and ignorant of the faith. In a similar situation, in the United States Catholicism has become more secularized in large part because of the dearth of vocations, especially of nuns who once rather ably controlled the schools and the hospitals—the beginning and the end of the life cycle. The Vatican's increasing alienation from many women has had deleterious consequences far beyond making American feminists unhappy. It very well may be that the Catholic Church will lose many women, in the same way that in the nineteenth century it lost much of the industrial workers in Europe. At times, though John Paul seemed to sense that he had gone too far; in March 1996 for example he urged that women, especially religious, be given greater power in the Church, but stopped short of talking about the priesthood.

In 1996, a Vatican spokesman had to admit that in 1970 the Czech Church during the Cold War had ordained several women and some married men because of the severe shortage of clergy at the time. The ordinations were simply dismissed by the Vatican as "invalid," and those individuals were not re-ordained in 1992 when the Communist regime was over.

The world Karol Wojtyla was born in was the aftermath of the profound breakup of the Great War, where old patterns of deference based on class, authority, and religion that had persisted since the Middle Ages, were destroyed.[52] The postwar period was unable to heal those wounds, and the Second World War advanced the chaos even further. The Catholic Church re-entered politics to stabilize some of the countries in Western Europe, but it must be remembered that it was basically the Catholic countries that fell to totalitarianism—Italy, Spain, Portugal, Vichy France, Austria, and the Catholic parts of Germany. Small wonder that Pius XII had a difficult time condemning the Fascist regimes in World War II, since so many of his co-religionists lived in those lands.

Still the Roman Catholic Church was remarkably resourceful in both wars through its humanitarian efforts and was solidly committed to defending its own religious liberty after the last conflict, becoming aligned by necessity with the United States. All of those dramatic expressions—the 1920s, the war years, the Cold War period—were a part of Wojtyla's background, just as the Napoleonic regime was a looming presence in the tenures of the popes in the late eighteenth and early nineteenth centuries.

Although those wars, the thirty years' war of the twentieth century, are over, the consequences have continued to be unsettling. The Catholic Church is mainly successful where its beliefs are supported by strong families, dependably funded Catholic schools, and a popular culture that respects tradition and piety. The economics of the postwar industrial states and their effects have upset much of those props of the first two; the communications revolution with its pervasive commercialism has upended the last one.

Liberation Theology

Pope John Paul II started his reign with a clear, confident agenda of restoration. In Latin America he moved from the very beginning to clamp off the growth of so-called "liberation theology." But the animosity he created and his own intelligent reappraisal led him to reassess what he believed at first and what the conservatives told him about that region of the world.

His predecessor, Paul VI, had gone to Medellín in 1968 and given his guarded support to what turned out to be the beginnings of a very radical turn to the left. Paul VI, for all his subtleties, clearly placed the tradition-bound Roman Catholic Church on the side of the poor. In his encyclical *Popularum Progressio* and his letter *Octogesima Advenienes*, he embraced the Third World and pledged that the Church "cannot plead for the status quo." The synods held in Rome in 1971 and 1974 further supported the transformation of unjust economic and political systems. Thus the Church, especially in Latin America, developed a "preferential option for the poor" and denounced the "institutionalized violence" of oligarchical rule as "a social sin."[53]

Although Paul spoke out against identifying the Church with any political party or ideology, elements of the clergy still became radicalized, and numerous murders and tortures of priests and nuns ensued on that continent. The People of God often became organized in ecclesiastical base communities, the Bible became a tract for revolution, and Jesus was celebrated as the greatest revolutionary of them all, whose gospels were interpreted in neo-Marxist rhetoric. The conservative Church, once aligned so closely with the Latin American ruling classes in the 1940s and 1950s, was becoming increasingly committed to the poor and the dispossessed. John Paul I had indicated a desire to visit that continent, seeking to replicate the trip of his immediate predecessor. Now it fell to Wojtyla to take his place, and the consequences would be clearly troubling to the progressive wing of the Church.

Before John Paul II arrived, there were reports that he had already condemned "liberation theology," which in fact was not true. Actually his views, which seemed so confusing at the time, were rather clear upon closer scrutiny. He opposed priests and nuns getting involved in politics, arguing that their true vocation was to teach the word of God, but he was also very much on the side of land reform, a just wage, and democratic changes. His attitudes toward Marxism were honed in his own longtime battle against the Communist state in Poland, and the last thing he was amenable to was any attempt to encourage a Christian synthesis with that atheistic philosophy. The Gospels' radicalism came from true liberation, which he maintained was the freedom to know and to appreciate God's workings. He also had some concerns about a nonhierarchical or horizontal church that some radical theologians had advocated.

The pope must have worried about the toll that revolutionary activities were taking on the Catholic Church in Latin America. By the end of the 1970s more than 850 priests and nuns had been martyred in that area. So when the Latin American Episcopal Conference (CELAM) and others met at Puebla de los Angeles, Mexico, in 1979, the pope faced a very difficult situation.

Initially the pope was advised by Sebastiano Cardinal Baggio of the Congregation of Bishops and Colombian Archbishop Alfonso López Trujillo, both of whom warned that base communities were threatening the authority of local bishops and had to be abolished. Puebla must correct the abuses of Medellín, the new pope was counseled.[54]

But the pope, for reasons of his own, turned away from such an irrevocable and drastic step that would condemn the directions of much of his Latin American Church. He vigorously supported the search for social justice, which he was always comfortable with, but criticized the assertion that Christ was a political figure, a revolutionary, or a subversive. The conservatives did not get a specific statement of condemnation, although they would work in the Curia to get censures of liberation theologians. As for the progressives, they were rather demoralized by the pope's lack of fervor in their cause.[55]

One of the figures in the more radical wing of the Church in Latin America was Archbishop Oscar Romero of El Salvador, who was actually a rather quiet, nonpolitical prelate at the beginning of his tenure. But swept up in the civil war taking place in his nation and the murders of clergy, he became an articulate spokesman for social justice and human rights. In May 1979, he visited the pope and asked John Paul to condemn the murders of priests and others by Salvadorian death squads. The pontiff recommended instead "great balance and prudence," and asked that Romero stay with defending basic principles rather than incurring risk from making specific accusations. The pope insisted on the need for "courage and boldness."

After another visit by the archbishop in January 1980, John Paul II expressed his personal sympathies for the plight of the Church in Latin America and was deeply concerned about the possibilities of more bloodletting and retribution from the left. Several months later, on March 24, 1980, Romero was murdered by agents of the military intelligence command as he said Mass in the chapel of a hospital. It was a modern St. Stanislaus; it was another St. Thomas á Beckett in the making. The Church thus added another martyr to its long rolls.[56]

The Polish born Wojtyla was himself a courageous man, not above using the fault lines of politics to advance the interests of the Church in his native country. But to be successful there, one had to have a nearby monolithic church willing to face the clumsy Communist client state that was indirectly under the control of the Soviet Red Army. But Latin America was very different. The continent was infected by Marxist guerrillas, decadent military or oligarchical regimes, and very weak nascent democratic states. And the level of poverty on that continent was not being alleviated in many areas by social reforms or state planning.

The religious faith in his land was and is conservative and pietistic. While the hierarchy, including Wojtyla, was on the right side of the river called Vatican II, in Latin America the Church was faced with aggressive Protestant evangelical sects, articulate Marxist ideologues, and revolutionary happenings. The Church moved quickly from being a prop of the local and national oligarchies to becoming the vanguard of revolution in some nations. As in Poland the progressive clergy looked to the Church for solace, but in John Paul the more radical Catholics seemed at times to find more of a critic than an advocate. That discomfort was accentuated by the pope's disastrous visit to Nicaragua and the Curia's attacks upon liberation theologians. Thus the revolutionary church of Latin America found danger at home and censure in Rome.

To John Paul the situation in Latin America was symptomatic of a larger problem—the unraveling of discipline in the Church since Vatican II. From his very strict perspective, he saw such dislocations everywhere: the liberation theologians of Latin America, the advocates of synchrentism in Africa, the easy ways of theologians and bishops in the United States and liberal Western Europe, the laxity of the Jesuits, and the general confusion of so many professors of Catholic theology.

Not since Pius X had a pope sought to exercise such authority over the way the faithful lived, thought, and prayed. Gone was the smiling tolerance of John XXIII and the nuanced hesitations of Paul VI. Their successor believed that by a determined exercise of his indomitable will and extremely charismatic personality he could restore the Roman Catholic Church, preserve its ancient doctrines, and prepare it for the third millennium. Will and faith and leadership by only one dedicated man could make the difference. It was an extraordinary agenda and as expected...it partially failed.

John Paul had read and understood the words of the liberation theologians, although he did not empathize with all their sentiments and their neo-Marxist vocabulary. Those theologians advocated basic Church communities, *communidades eclesales de base*, which had been defined as families that lived together and pondered what they can do in common according to the spirit of the Gospel. The leftist Brazilian priest and theologian Leonardo Boff argued "a commitment to faith must have its political manifestation." Thus it was understandable how some conservatives—Church leaders and secular politicians—saw these communities as having subversive implications.

In the decade from 1968 to 1978 the Church, especially in Brazil, was under considerable attack with a long list of assaults and murders of its clergy. In El Salvador the InterAmerican Human Rights Commission concluded that the Catholic Church was being "systematically persecuted." In Colombia, Camilo Torres, a priest and a guerrilla, was killed, and other priests were engaged in similar activities in Colombia, Nicaragua, and Argentina. At first the Church was just a haven for hope, then it became an agent of social and political change.[58]

As noted, before Wojtyla came to that continent, he was approached by conservative prelates, arguing that he had to stop the abuses of the liberation theologians and revolutionary priests. He was orthodox himself, but still he was cognizant of the fact that in his own words, "the future of the Church will be decided in Latin America."

On the evening before his arrival, the Sanctuary of the Virgin of Guadalupe in Mexico City was already attracting people waiting for the pontiff's visit. When the pope finally arrived in Mexico, he kissed the soil and welcomed the religious who were dressed in simple civilian black trousers. Mexican law prohibited priests and nuns from wearing their religious garb in public—a part of the country's long tradition of anti-clericalism. The road to the city was thronged with cheering crowds extended as far as eighty miles, with people crying out "Viva la papa," and scattering flowers and confetti along the way. In Zocalo Square, originally laid out by the Spanish conqueror Hernando Cortes, over 200,000 people waited, many of them dressed in rags and frayed clothing. "You are Peter," some chanted as he passed by; and above the cathedral square was a huge banner that tellingly read, *Marxismo no*.

True to his conservative leanings, the new pope criticized theological deviations and reiterated the need for fidelity to the Catholic creed and to his own office. Later at the airport he was presented with a blanket full of roses, the sign of the Dark Virgin of Guadalupe. According to religious legend, an Indian Juan Diego wanted to have a shrine built at Tepeyac where he claimed he first saw the Virgin. When the local Catholic bishop demanded proof of her visitation, Mary returned and had Diego pick roses from a nearby mountain. At the bishop's palace the Indian offered up his blanket, which had enfolded in it an imprint of the Virgin. Even today, the nature of the imprint is unexplained. For the pontiff, what he saw in that nation must have seemed a great resemblance in piety to Our Lady of Czestochowa whom he deeply revered. Everywhere John Paul II celebrated easily the special blessings of Mary.

At one point the virile and handsome pope stopped a cheering group of nuns, chastising them, "Remember you are the mystical brides of Christ." And he also insisted in his addresses that political action and radical ideologies were not a substitute for prayer, an obvious swipe at liberation theology. John Paul pointedly remarked, "You are priests and members of religious orders, not social or political leaders... Let us have no illusion that we will serve the gospel if we 'dilute' our charisma by showing an exaggerated interest in temporal problems."

The trip to Latin America was a distasteful chore in some ways—for the pope appeared to many as a rigid conservative, although a person with a committed sense of social justice. In a visit to Brazil in 1980, John Paul showed his personal sympathies by insisting, "The Church is on the side of the poor, and that is where she must stay." On March 9, 1983 in a very poor and exploited Haiti, the pontiff blurted out, "Things must change here." Addressing a group of students in that nation, he pleaded for a just society, and recalled, "In my youth I lived these same convictions... As a young student I proclaimed them with the voice of literature and art." Still he was not portrayed as a friend of the progressive impulses unleashed by Vatican II in Latin America. In that sense reality and appearance were indeed one.[59]

Poland—Mother of All Poles
But his second major trip was a return of the heart, an odyssey back to his beloved Poland. To the relief of the Communist regime, then headed by party boss Edward Gierek, the pope insisted that his visit was to be a religious and not a political event. The government added to that theme by saying that it was the Polish episcopacy, not the state that had invited him.

But in that nation, the political implications soon mixed with the spiritual, exactly the sort of behavior that John Paul II warned against elsewhere. Indeed his attitudes and activities were contradictory; while he has urged priests and bishops to stay out of politics in their own nation, Karol Wojtyla has been deeply enmeshed in political action, public policy debates, and even partisan intrigue in his own nation before and especially after his election.

In 1970 Gomulka had been displaced after violent riots in the Baltic area, and the party put in Gierek who promised some accommodation with the Catholic Church. By 1973 however the state demanded a unified socialist education system that made it impossible for children to attend church for religious instruction. The bishops denounced that step as a violation of freedom of conscience and proclaimed the new laws not binding on the faithful. In 1976, steep rises in the cost of food led to greater unrest and the Church supported the right to protest. In addition, Cardinal Wojtyla publicly denounced discrimination against Catholics in filling various offices and positions and maintained that atheism was not a legitimate political philosophy.[60] Before he became pope, Wojtyla also encouraged the so-called "flying university" to hold classes on Church property, and he vigorously criticized anti-Church propaganda. Most importantly, Wojtyla took state censorship to task, saying with other Polish bishops that "the spirit of freedom is the proper climate for the full development of a person."[61]

The situation facing the Marxist state was quite different. The government permitted the pope to return—what else could a Polish regime do? But he wished to go to Krakow in May to celebrate the 900th anniversary of the martyrdom of St. Stanislaus. That legendary bishop had been killed for criticizing the wicked ways of a Polish king, and as with the death of Thomas á Beckett in Britain, the king's knights had rid the monarch of that troublesome man. The symbolism was too powerful for the Communist party, and so they postponed the pope's visit until the next month—June 1979—a delay that probably meant more to the party cadres than to anyone else.

The Communist regime also prohibited the pope from visiting Piekary near the Silesian capital of Katowich, the site of a popular annual pilgrimage by Catholic men at the end of the month of May. The government was worried about the Church's growing influence among the workers of that region. Instead the pope could celebrate Mass at the more important shrine of Czestochowa on June 5, and workers would be shipped in from parts of Silesia to attend.

In addition, he was not allowed to say Mass in the new church at Nowa Huta, the site of Wojtyla's successful battle against government directives opposing the construction of new churches. In May before he came, an explosion ripped off the leg on a statue of Lenin—a portent of events to come in that uneasy nation. Then on a cloudless June 2, the pope's Alitalia Boeing 727 landed at Warsaw airport. The government had carefully kept the airport crowd size as small as they could. Greeting the pontiff were the thin Cardinal Wyszynski, dressed in a black cassock, and high ranking officials of the Polish nation led by President Henryk Jablónski, accompanied by a military band and guard of honor. The cardinal prelate entered the plane first and privately greeted his once younger colleague. Some time later John Paul II emerged and dropped to his knees to kiss Polish soil. To the surprise of Vatican observers, the Communist leader delivered a warm welcome, calling the pope several times "Your Holiness," not exactly an accepted Communist salutation. He was praised as his proud nation's son, embraced by Poland, the "Mother of All Poles." John Paul was deeply moved and extended his own warm greetings as well.

The first stop was Victory Square for an open air Mass before 300,000 people. It was there that the Russians had built an Orthodox Church in the nineteenth century; it was there that Czar Nicholas I had created a parade ground for his troops; and it was there that the Germans had constructed a monument to their 1939 successful invasion. Overlooking that square stood an imposing oak cross. Addressing the crowd, the vigorous pope remarked, "The Pope can no longer remain a prisoner of the Vatican; he had to become Peter the pilgrim once more."

John Paul went on to other ceremonies and services. At one point he visited Gniezno, the ancient see of the Polish primates, where the earliest Polish kings were crowned and prayed at the tomb of St. Adalbert, who was a missionary to the Baltic peoples and who was killed by Prussian pagans. The pope also stressed the saint's Czechoslovakian background, as he trumpeted the theme that he was not just a Polish pope, but a Slavic one as well. He sang with the crowds, embraced the enthusiasm of the young, and reached deeply into the chords of piety.

At the great folk shrine of Polish Catholicism, Czestochowa, the crowd held up signs proclaiming the coming of the 600th anniversary in 1982 of the Black Madonna's visitation. The Poles believed that the Virgin Mary saved Poland from invading Swedish armies in the battle of Czestochowa in 1655. At that site a small number of monks and knights forced the Swedes to retreat. The town has a revered monastery on a hill called Jasna Góra ("Luminous Mountain") which is the site of the shrine of the Black Madonna. The famed portrait of the Madonna housed there is an icon that has become darkened over the centuries, and is supposed to have been painted by St. Luke the Evangelist on a wooden plank from the actual table of the Holy Family in Nazareth. In 1430 a Hussite soldier scarred the face of the portrait with a saber.

The pope greeted the massive crowds with a simple exclamation—"I am here." They responded with the song *Sto Lat, Sto Lat* ("May he live 100 years"). The pope toyed with the crowd, saying, "If this Pope lives all those years, your grandchildren will be coming to see him, and what can be done with such an old Pope? I can see only one solution: he'll have to run away and live in a monastery." Shades of Paul VI's melancholy thoughts, and on such a fine occasion.

John Paul cited the Virgin Mary's role in Polish history and life, saying, "She is present here in some strange way." When he was entertained by a young woman musician, he engagingly remarked, "I had to come to Poland to learn to sing again." The pontiff later talked to a meeting of bishops at a local monastery and gave his views on the uneasy relationships between the Church and state, as he urged authentic dialogue and a respect for the rights of all citizens. It was estimated that three and a half million people saw him at Czestochowa alone, and some twelve million people, or one-third of the total population, came out to visit him while he was in Poland.

On another occasion he reiterated his earlier position that the priesthood is a gift to God, a gift forever. He noted in passing, "It has been suggested that the Pope was trying to impose the Polish model of priesthood on whole world," But he observed that only with a life consecrated to the Church could the Church survive in "today's secularized world." At the Catholic University in Lublin which he knew so well, he celebrated the development of human potential, and then observed that universities around the world seemed to be undergoing "some kind of deformation."

Coming back to Krakow, the pope praised his old associations, and sadly remarked, "I have discovered in Rome that it is not easy to leave Krakow behind." He continued, "My heart has not ceased to be united with you, with this city, with this patrimony, with this 'Polish Rome.'" That night he sought to retire from the hectic pace and stayed at the archbishop's palace on Franciszkanska Street where he had once lived. But the crowds would not let him go. He teased them, "Do you intend to sleep tonight?" And they shouted back, "No." The pontiff countered, "Well I am going to bed because tomorrow I have got to walk on my feet, not my eyelashes." Then he said the Angelus with them and a prayer for the dead and closed the window tightly.

On the sixth day of his visit, he returned to his birth place at Wadowice where he met his old teacher of religion and acknowledged the parish of his family. Then he went on to the death city of Auschwitz, called in Polish Óswiecim, which is now a gruesome museum, and which still has the wrought iron lettering over the gates that reads, *Arbeit macht frei*—"Work will make you free." Some four million people from twenty-eight countries and fifty nationalities had been exterminated in the Auschwitz and the neighboring Birkenau (Brezinka) complexes.

One of the priests murdered there, Father Maximilian Kolbe, had traded his life for a Polish father of ten children, and had been beatified by the Roman Catholic Church in 1971. The pope knew Auschwitz well, having been there before, and he walked quietly to Block Eleven, Cell 18, and prayed at the site of Kolbe's internment. Outside was the man, Franciszek Gajowniczek, for whom the priest had traded his life on July 30, 1941. Near the camp the pope saw the railroad cars that had led countless people to their death, the international monument to the victims of Fascism, and a large canopy with a cross that carried a coil of barbed wire and a striped flag with the letter P for prisoner, and the designation 16670, Kolbe's camp number.

The Polish pontiff had referred to Auschwitz as the "Golgotha of our times," and he called Abraham the father of all. He specifically cited the people of Yahweh and insisted that no one should indifferently pass by the memorial tablets written in Polish, Russian, and Hebrew. He reminded listeners that six million Poles had died in this war—one fifth of our "people"; he repeated Paul VI's powerful admonition at the United Nations against war, and then he left the crowd in tears. Pointedly, John Paul observed, "Responsibility for war rests not only with those who directly cause the war, but also with those who do not do everything in their power to prevent it."

The next day was more upbeat as the pontiff visited the mountains that he so loved. There he appeared at Our Lady of Ludzmierz, another Marian shrine. Colorful costumes of the mountain people dotted the crowd. Later that day he went back to Krakow and renewed old acquaintances with academics and clergy. He addressed a large audience of students and talked of his much valued ties to youth and contradicted those who saw them as materialistic and seduced by the consumer society. Sometime in the early morning, he walked incognito along the streets of Krakow to remember once again its sights and sounds.

On June 9 the pope finally got permission to go to Nowa Huta, the sterile state community planned without a church, the city of the Communist future—it was said. Karol Wojtyla had fought a long battle to erect a church there, and he consecrated it in 1977. The Communists finally agreed that he could celebrate a Mass, not though at that church, but at a Franciscan church nearby—another empty party prohibition.

Later the Polish trip ended with the pontiff unexpectedly kissing Polish President Jablonski on both cheeks, and whispering to him good wishes to his mother. Then rather remarkably Jablonski kissed the pope's hands. The picture of those events raced across the nation's newspapers. Thus it was that Karol Wojtyla, the one-time factory worker, seminarian-in-exile, quiet intellectual, and reluctant prelate came home to his beloved Poland. For him it was a sentimental journey, for the Communist state it was the beginning of the end.

The Soviet leaders had been less sanguine about the whole visit. When the Polish episcopate issued the invitation to the pope, the Russian premier Leonid Brezhnev warned Gierek, "I advise you not to receive him because it will cause you much trouble." He cited with approval Gomulka's refusal in 1966 to give Paul VI a visa for the Christian millennium celebration. But as Gierek knew, there was now a Polish pope. And besides he himself had been graciously received by Paul VI on December 1, 1977.[62]

The pope's visit resurrected a true sense of pride among the Polish people. Clearly their allegiances were more with the Catholic Church than with the Communist state. A little more than a year later, the Gierek government raised food prices by 80 percent and unrest boiled over. At the Lenin shipyard at Gdansk, the workers led by a thirty-six year-old electrician named Lech Walesa staged a sit down strike. From those activities Solidarity and Rural Solidarity were born, and the Communist government's eventual demise was in sight. After some hesitation, the Church supported the unions, and the Gierek regime was replaced by another Communist government headed by Stanislaw Kania. Polish dissidents demanded and eventually got the right to strike, a relaxation of censorship, an end to Communist monopoly on the press, a five day work week, more economic reforms and worker self-government, and some autonomy for the universities. In December 1981, the pendulum swung again to a crackdown on dissidents after the concerned Soviet government insisted that the Polish regime restore order to their homeland. Security forces began a series of arrests, transportation was disrupted, and communications were cut off. The new authority was called the Military Council of National Salvation, and was headed by General Wojciech Jaruzelski who declared martial law and announced that a "state of war" existed.

On June 16, 1983 with martial law still in effect, the pope re-visited his homeland. The pontiff was received by warm crowds again, but the context was more somber. Wojtyla the patriot appealed to figures of Polish history and recounted the nation's long history of torment and troubles, as if saying "this too will pass away." Subtly he spoke of the "solidarity" of the Church with the people, and it was taken by the cheering crowds and the regime as a code word for solidarity with the union. The Communist government angrily accused John Paul of political activity, and indeed in Ponznan the pontiff paid tribute to those who had died in 1956 during riots over escalating prices, before moving on to dedicate another new church at Nowa Huta.

The pope had met with Walesa, and the Vatican newspaper *L'Osservatore Romano* informed its readers that the pope had distanced himself from the labor leader in return for concessions from the Polish regime, including ending military rule. Clearly Walesa was offered up as a sacrifice. A distraught John Paul II fired the editor, but in fact the substance of the story was correct.[63]

Four years later he returned to Poland again and once more expressed his solidarity with his homeland. The pope again met with union leader Lech Walesa, and the pontiff also visited a suburban church where Father Jerzy Popielusko had been assigned. In 1984 the priest was murdered by the secret police because of his support of the Solidarity movement. The pope prayed at his grave and placed yellow and white flowers, the colors of the Vatican city state, on it.

The government eventually realized that it needed Solidarity's cooperation, and with Moscow's consent it sought to work with the union to better economic conditions. Free elections were held and Solidarity won handily. The Catholic Church was granted total freedom, and Jozef Cardinal Glemp approved of the formal separation of church and state in Poland.

The Slavic Pope
Watching these events was a major admirer of the pope, the new American president, Ronald Reagan, who suggested that CIA Director William Casey establish some closer ties with the Vatican on the Polish question. Reagan had been deeply moved by John Paul's reception in 1979 in his homeland. Rumor had it that in December 1980 the pope had already sent Leonid Brezhnev a letter warning him that if the Soviet premier decided to invade Poland, the pope himself would return and rally the people to resist the occupation. If true, it was a extraordinary communication.

In 1979, the pope had also appointed a cardinal *in pectore* (in secret), and word spread throughout Lithuania that it was their imprisoned archbishop. The Soviet press at that time called the pope's views "an infection" and accused the Vatican of trying to "extend its religious influence over the republic." In January 1981 Lech Walesa had visited the pontiff in Rome and was hosted by Luigi Scricciollo, a spokesman for the Italian Labor Conference. Walesa may have misplaced his trust, for the Italian intelligence agencies believed that Scricciollo was a source for Bulgarian intelligence and a conduit to the Communist regime.

Casey, a devout Roman Catholic himself, went to Rome to seek to establish some ties with the Vatican, to at least exchange information. His request for a formal meeting however was denied, and Vatican Secretary of State Cardinal Casaroli refused even to see him privately. Meanwhile, the U.S. government quietly moved to dry up investments that might help the Polish government, and the regime began to totter economically. Then in July 1981, the Reagan administration offered Poland $740 million in aid aimed at promoting reform and protecting Solidarity. In addition, the American labor movement, through the AFL-CIO, was providing advice, training, and financial support to Solidarity.

After the military takeover in Poland and with the pope's near assassination fresh in his mind, Cardinal Casaroli finally agreed to meet Casey. The Church, he insisted, could not play a covert role with the intelligence agency or serve as a cover for CIA operatives, but it would provide information and facilitate contacts within Poland. Admiral John Poindexter, a National Security Council staff person and later himself director of the CIA, summarized the relationship, "clearly in terms of gathering information as to what was happening and from the standpoint of talking to Solidarity and other supporters of Western objectives in Poland, the Vatican was very helpful." The Church was not a partner, but had "mutual objectives in Poland." The agency gave the Catholic Church a code name in its own jargon—"the Entity."

The Israeli intelligence services and the French counterespionage units were also involved in helping to provide information and protecting some Solidarity activists. CIA funds were transferred in and out of accounts in order to help Solidarity publish and distribute literature and to buy electronic transmitters. The Solidarity movement though was infiltrated with spies in the service of the military government, while the CIA in turn penetrated the Polish regime at least as high as the Deputy Minister of Defense.

Having recovered from an assassination attempt on his life in 1982, Reagan had promised to keep the pope informed of his administration's actions toward Poland. Casey was later to bring John Paul information about what was being done to help Solidarity, but what specifics he gave are not public. In 1996 a major biography of the pope maintained, undoubtedly with some exaggerations, that the pontiff was deeply involved in directing Solidarity, met personally with Casey, and in return avoided criticizing the Reagan administration's policies in Nicaragua and its decision to upgrade nuclear weaponry in NATO.

By July 1984, the Jaruzelski government tried to reach some accommodation with the dissidents and declared an amnesty, but its efforts were only partially successful. The KGB and Soviet intelligence officers had from the very beginning of John Paul's election watched the Vatican closely. One report concluded, "the anti-socialist bias of the Vatican's activities have [sic] become particularly marked with the arrival on the papal throne of John Paul II..." The KGB also charged that "the Vatican's principal interest is concentrated on the most 'promising' countries of Eastern Europe, from its point of view, Poland, Hungary and Yugoslavia." By 1985 the Soviet Union would be headed by a new sort of leader, Mikhail Gorbachev, whose liberalization policies would lead to a democratization of Poland and the ultimate demise of the Soviet empire. As for the Vatican, it sought to get the United States administration to end economic sanctions against Poland, arguing in the words of the pope that the people had suffered enough. Walesa and other Solidarity leaders agreed, but the sanctions continued until January 1987.[64]

Pope John Paul moved quickly in the late 1980s and early 1990s to regularize relations with Poland, Hungary, the former Soviet Union states, Czechoslovakia, Romania, Bulgaria, and Albania. In 1985 he had issued an encyclical, *Slavorum Apostoli*, which praised the Slavic peoples and their common roots. Once again a pope paraded out Saints Cyril and Methodius—the two Greek monks who had transported Christianity to the Slavic peoples a millennium ago. They were saints in the undivided church, that is, before the split with Eastern Christianity in 1054.

In 1985 the Communist regime in Czechoslovakia had prevented John Paul from going there. By 1990 the world had changed, and playwright and president Václav Havel remarked that he himself had been a prisoner of the state six months ago and now he was there to greet the first Catholic pontiff to visit his homeland in history. The pope in his youth had lived near the Czech border and acknowledged their common heritage, exclaiming, "Here are our roots." When he was asked by a reporter to characterize the collapse of Marxism throughout Eastern Europe, he confidently said that it was just "another tower of Babel."

Facing the Soviet State
After his first visit to Poland, the Soviet leadership had ordered a top secret worldwide smear campaign against the pope and the Vatican's foreign policies. On November 13, 1979, the Secretariat of the Central Council approved a six point program that was also signed off by men who would become future premiers of the Soviet Union: Yuri Andropov, Konstantin Chernenko, and Mikhail Gorbachev.

The plan included the mobilization of Communist parties of Lithuania, Latvia, Ukraine, and Byelorussia, and also of the news agency

Tass, the Soviet television, the Academy of Sciences, and other organizations that were to begin a propaganda campaign against the pontiff. The second point in the proposal urged an exchange of information and propaganda with various other Communist parties, especially in states with large Catholic populations.

The Ministry of Foreign Affairs was instructed to stress the Soviet Union's commitment to world peace, and the Ministry and the KGB secret police were told to upgrade their efforts in the struggle against the Vatican's Eastern European diplomacy. The fifth point enumerated in the plan had the KGB publicizing in various countries that the Vatican's policies were harmful, and that the pope was dangerous to his own Church. Special channels were to be employed in both Western and socialist countries to spread that alarm. Lastly the Academy of Sciences was to organize more studies on the benefits of scientific atheism.

The new pope was portrayed by the Soviet leaders as using religion in an ideological struggle against socialism, and of having encouraged the activities of what it called "disloyal priests." The Marxist state was pledged to encourage identification of tendencies in the Catholic Church that opposed the anti-Communist foreign policies of the Vatican. Oddly enough, this particular proposal did not mention Poland and the special consequences that a collapse of that Soviet puppet regime would bring. Later it would be charged that the party leadership had approved more than simply a propaganda offensive against the pope. As John Paul II prophetically observed to Archbishop Romero, political activity, especially in non-democratic states, can exact from the Church a terrible price—including the blood of martyrs.[65]

It was ironically fated that the other important political figure who would cross the pope's diplomatic horizon also would be a Slav, Mikhail Gorbachev. And in some ways, he shared some characteristics with John Paul: he came to power at the early age of fifty-four; had advanced rapidly with the aid of powerful mentors; was deemed charismatic; and sought to channel directly the powerful forces of democratization sweeping through an authoritarian organization.

Mikhail Sergevich Gorbachev was born in 1931 in the Stavropl territory of the Soviet Union. He studied law at Moscow State University, joined the Young Communist organization, and in 1971 was elected to the powerful Central Committee. In 1978, he was appointed Secretary of Agriculture—the traditional elephant burial ground for ambitious Soviet bureaucrats, but he succeeded in staying viable and became the youngest person promoted to the Politburo. In March 1985 he was named the leader of the Soviet Union, the youngest man to hold that position since Joseph Stalin. In 1988 he became the Soviet President, its chief of state.

As soon as he took office, he announced that he was intent on nothing less than a major overhaul of Soviet society. He called his policies *glasnos* (opening up) and *perestroika* (restructuring). He sought to overcome the increasingly obvious consequences of seventy years of Communist political oppression and economic stagnation by a profound transformation of the Soviet system. Gorbachev adopted modified open elections and advocated a modernization program to achieve a more flexible economic system—giant steps that would challenge total party control then held by the bureaucratic cadre and its props, the internal secret police and the Red Army.

While all his reforms at home did not satisfy the expectations that they aroused, still Gorbachev's initiatives were well received by Western foreign leaders, especially Prime Minister Margaret Thatcher in Britain. Even Presidents Ronald Reagan and George Bush entered into important arms limitations agreements that partially curtailed the nuclear arms race and led to disarmament on an unparalleled scale. Gorbachev also took the popular step of removing Soviet troops in Afghanistan by early 1989, thus ending one of the major points of contention with the West.

He met with John Paul, and there seemed to be a real understanding of the magnitude of the changes that the Soviet Union was facing, as they both seemed to enter into a sort of mutual admiration society. For some reason, Gorbachev publicly commented that he had informed the pope that he had been baptized as a Christian—in the Russian Orthodox faith! The pope correctly remarked that the Soviet leader's problem was to find a way "to change the system without changing systems," and privately he expressed the hope that Gorbachev could keep the Soviet Union together. In the process, Gorbachev permitted a lessening of Soviet pressure on its satellites, including the pope's beloved Poland. There the Communists finally allowed free elections which Solidarity handily won.

As is so often true, the tides of revolution overwhelm the forces of reform, especially in recent history. Modern reformers raise expectations that they cannot fulfill in time and are too often replaced by the forces of chaos and then repression. The course of modern revolution is the tale of eighteenth century France and not colonial United States. After the great uprising for liberation comes too often deep discontent, terror, and repression.

Although these two Slavic leaders lived in different worlds, still both faced some similar management difficulties. By 1990 John Paul was still dealing with the problems of trying to mobilize the Church in the face of the loosening tendencies unleashed by Vatican II. He was permitting crackdowns and admonitions, although generally to no avail. Vatican II had raised expectations in his own authoritarian system. But in the Soviet Union Gorbachev was facing even more serious problems at home because of the worsening economy. He insisted that the state had to remain socialist, that Communism could function with "a human face." He was being challenged not just by reactionary elements, but also by democratic forces ironically led by Boris Yeltsin, a flamboyant demagogue who had been a harsh Communist *apparatchik* at one time. As matters worsened, Yeltsin was elected the first president of the Russian Republic, still encased however in the Soviet system.

Gorbachev faced continued old-line Communist opposition, and on August 19, 1991 those elements staged an inept coup to remove him while he was on vacation. Yeltsin rallied the people of Moscow, and other cities followed in support, and the coup failed within seventy-two hours. Gorbachev was restored quickly, the Communist Party officially banned, and the Baltic states given their independence. By December 1991, the Soviet Union just collapsed. Eleven of the remaining republics formed the Commonwealth of Independent States, but Gorbachev was the president of no remaining nation, and thus went into retirement on Christmas Day. Later he observed, "Everything that happened in Eastern Europe those last few years would have been impossible without the presence of this Pope."[66]

John Paul must have watched the mind-boggling events with incredible attention. He knew the politics of Eastern Europe as well as anyone, but no one could have expected what happened. The Vatican diplomats and the Western intelligence agencies never predicted the quick demise of the Soviet Union. To some of the faithful, it also seemed as if the Virgin's predictions at Fatima on Russia came true, only a few years after John Paul's final dedication with the bishops of that nation on March 25, 1984 to the cause of Mary. The formidable empire crumbled like pie crust—to paraphrase Lenin's remarks. The pope however refused to see those occurrences as an act of God. Communism fell because of its own injustices, he concluded. As for his own role, the pope judged, "I didn't cause this to happen. The tree was already rotten. I just gave it a good shake and the rotten apple fell."

The peculiar events that took place later, especially in 1995, added another twist. Repudiated Communist Party adherents in Poland helped elect a president, Alexsandr Kwaswienski, who defeated Lech Walesa, the Solidarity hero! And Communists in Russia began to make remarkable inroads into the democratic parliament. In once tightly ruled Tito's Yugoslavia, the demise of the Communist state there led to enormous ethnic violence, especially genocidal attacks in Bosnia. The pope deplored such misery once again. What could one make of what had taken place in such a short period of time? The pope had laid aside his own admonitions that the Church should not be involved in secular politics, and now he was seeing that the ways of Mammon were not only sometimes evil, but increasingly fickle.

And as Poland was experiencing the problems of democratization, the role of the Church itself in that state began to lessen. There was an official separation of church and state, an increase in the number of divorces, and even reports of greater acceptance of abortion. A disillusioned pope watched as his own countrymen insisted on keeping abortion legal. He sadly remarked, "I was offended by the Poles. But I'm getting over it."

There was less talk about the so-called "third Rome," the role of Moscow in Christendom. The pope had always believed that "the light comes from the east," but it did not. There was also less rhetoric about the triumph of a Slavic pope and less success in promulgating the goals of reuniting an activist and diverse Roman Catholic Church with what was an increasingly ossified Eastern Orthodox set of national communities. The pope warned these newly freed nations that they must avoid the perils of the West, the emphasis upon profit, upon rampant personal liberty, and especially the excesses of consumerism. But to many the appeal of the West was not just its eighteenth-century Enlightenment legacies, its liberal political rhetoric, or its sophisticated financial institutions, but the creature comforts that it brought to people so long denied the most basic elements of life. Thus once again the pope seemed to be out of tune with the movement which, in this case, he himself had help to father—the demise of the Marxist-Leninist states of Eastern Europe.

In reflecting on the strength of his own Polish Catholic church, John Paul had often praised the unity of that congregation, the importance of tradition, authority, and obedience to the bishops and to Rome. But those conditions were not present in other Eastern European nations, or at times even in Poland. In many ways the pontiff lived in a pre-Vatican II world. And early in his pontificate, he seemed to believe that if only he wished it to be so and said it, that the Church in very different lands would restore the hierarchical model. But that was not to be.

Reasserting Papal Authority
It was that assumption that led the pope to turn the synods from consultative assemblies to another forum for implementing his will and his view of the Church. It was that assumption that led him to assert in the most vigorous, and at times intolerant ways the *magisterium*—the teaching authority of the Church—which in reality became the teaching

authority of the pope exercised over national congregations of bishops and over Church theologians.

John Paul II was an incredibly prolific pope in his written pronouncements—rivaling Pius XII, the last traditionalist in that office. Very early in his reign, he issued his first encyclical, *Redemptor Hominis*, obviously written by the pope himself, and not by a collection of Curial theologians and experts. Because of his very different personalist philosophical bent and his Polish background and language, the messages were rather complex if not convoluted. For example, that first letter was seen as a critique of atheism, a real preoccupation with this pope who had lived almost all of his life behind two Iron Curtains of totalitarianism. But was it also, some people asked, a critique of interfaith ecumenism?

John Paul II was fascinated by the benchmark year 2000 and hoped to be the pope at the third millennium of Christianity. Yet at times, he used the creaky Marxist vocabulary of alienation to talk about modern man's sophisticated ills. Because he was so very bright, so full of ideas, it appeared that John Paul had abandoned the slow, cumbersome processes characteristic of collegiality. Again like Pius XII, he knew that he could do it faster and say it better, which in many cases was true—for both of them. For example, he accepted in principle Vatican II's formulation of a common priesthood of the faithful, but his real interest was in the traditional sacramental priesthood of men. Referring to priestly vows, he abandoned the more flexible policies of Pope Paul and concluded, "One must think of all these things, especially in moments of crisis, and not have recourse to a dispensation, understood as an 'administrative instruction,' as though in fact it were not, on the contrary a matter of profound question on conscience and a test of humanity." The response of many liberal Catholics in France, Spain, and Germany was critical toward the pope's "Letter to the Priests." One theologian, Hans Küng, actually attacked the pope for "violating the human right to marriage."

On one level the pope insisted to a gathering of cardinals in November 1979 that the main task of his pontificate would be to implement Vatican II. Later he called a synod to give its participants a very candid and depressing review of Vatican finances, asked for their advice on how to reform the Curia, and discussed the relationships between the Church and culture, especially the gap between science and faith—two carryover topics from the Council. He was in so many ways though a son of that Council, and its broad reach made it possible for him to travel and be noticed, that is to become in the end, pope.

But he has criticized false notions of liberty and renewal, and opposed any reinterpretations of traditional dogma. And his strong assertion of Catholic identity made ecumenism at times less possible. As John Paul said, he opposed reducing dogmatic concerns to "a common minimum"—a strategy used sometimes in interfaith dialogues, especially in their initial stages. The pontiff's very intense devotion to Mary, which some attribute to being a substitute for the human mother he lost so early, also discouraged new approaches to Protestant Christianity that often had no strong traditions of worship and respect in that area.[67]

He resolutely moved against theological dissidents as well. For some time the Vatican had been looking closely at the work of one of Catholicism's best known theologians, Edward Schillebeeckx, a Flemish Dominican who taught at a Catholic university in the Netherlands. Even before John Paul's tenure, Schillebeeckx's work on Jesus had raised conservative eyebrows, especially when those unorthodox views in his complex books received wide currency. One of his volumes aimed to show how Jesus was experienced by his contemporaries—an approach that stressed his humanity rather than his divinity, the latter which the theologian did not deny.[68] Especially troubling to the Vatican was his view that in cases of extreme necessity the Christian community could provide itself with extraordinary ministers for consecrating the Eucharist. In December, 1979, he was summoned to Rome to appear before two judges and a defense lawyer appointed by the Congregation.

At about the same time the Congregation moved against Hans Küng, a Swiss theologian teaching at the University at Tübingen in West Germany. Among other controversial pronouncements, Küng has argued that the notion of Jesus as the Son of God was really not to be taken literally. He directly challenged the concept of infallibility, concluding that the Church, not the pope, was infallible and only in the sense that the Church persists in the truth of Jesus Christ. He further cited historical examples of alleged papal heresies that were later appropriately rejected by Councils, and he agreed with another author's conclusions that Pius IX was mentally unbalanced at the time of the first Vatican Council, having actually threatened the bishops into making their infallibility proclamation. In October 1979, Küng publicly attacked the new pope, picturing him as having repudiated the directions of the Vatican Council with its emphasis on freedom, ecumenism, and collegiality. Consequently Küng was stripped of his authority to teach as a Catholic theologian, but allowed to stay on at the university in another department.[69]

Thus his claim to be a Catholic theologian was denied to a man who once was brought to Rome and celebrated as one of the *periti* or experts. At the same time, the Congregation was also reviewing the writings of

American Catholic author David Tracy and the Latin American Leonardo Boff, the father of liberation theology, among others. Overall the Congregation's sanguine view was that the faithful "have a sacred right to receive the word of God, uncontaminated, and so they expect vigilant care should be exercised to keep the threat of error from them."[70]

In August 1979, the Congregation for the Doctrine of the Faith condemned a book on human sexuality brought out by a half-dozen members of the Catholic Theological Society of America, and in September the pope went after the Jesuits. In October the Holy See informed the Jesuit priest, Robert Drinan of Massachusetts, that he could not seek re-election for a sixth term to the U.S. Congress.[71]

Two additional episodes that received widespread publicity were the expulsion of Rev. Charles Curran from his teaching position at the Catholic University in Washington, D.C., and the controversial treatment of Archbishop Raymond Hunthausen of Seattle. Curran had speculated that sexual morality had to be viewed within broader contextual frameworks than the ones then current in Vatican theology, and his views over the years generated substantial concern in the Curia and with traditional Catholics. For example, he indicated that masturbation was not really sinful or important. He also argued that while homosexual actions were wrong, such acts might be the only way for some to achieve a degree of humanity and sexuality. He advocated a "theology of compromise" toward those acts as well, as toward premarital sex. In addition, he suggested that contraception was acceptable.

In his writings he was also tolerant of artificial insemination and sterilization. More pointedly, Curran refused to accept the view that abortion was synonymous with murder, and had gone on record supporting the *Roe v. Wade* decision in which the Supreme Court established a national policy in America permitting abortions within limits. His dissenting views included a more liberal attitude toward divorce as well, and he maintained that questions of morality were part of the "noninfallible" *magisteriium* of the Church, that is, they were open to dissent.

Curran had been under close scrutiny before. As early as April 1967, he was fired from Catholic University because of his statements on abortion, but a strike by students and faculty forced the administration to reinstate him. The next year he helped lead a petition drive among Catholic theologians who opposed publicly the pope's birth control encyclical. Once again the faculty supported the dissidents and Curran remained.

But in March 1986 Curran and Cardinal Ratzinger, prefect of the Congregation of the Faith, met in Rome, and the matter remained unresolved. By late summer of 1986, he was again dismissed from his position in the university, and over 300 fellow theologians protested the Vatican's condemnation. Finally the university trustees offered him an opportunity to teach elsewhere, but not in the graduate school of theology. Later he left for other institutions outside of the Church's purview.[72]

As controversial was the Vatican's treatment of one of its own bishops, Archbishop Hunthausen, a reputed liberal, who had supported pacifism and refused at one time to pay part of his income taxes as a protest against defense spending. The Vatican was bombarded with conservative Catholic protests that accused him of general permissiveness in running his diocese. It was alleged, for example, he had allowed a special Mass for homosexuals in the cathedral, had expressed his sympathy for them, and had tolerated weird liturgies featuring clowns, balloons, and dancing at a funeral. In addition, he had granted an imprimatur to a book on sexual morality that was somewhat outside of the Church's orthodox views.

Finally in late summer 1986, Hunthausen was instructed to turn over to Donald Wuerl, new auxiliary bishop, his decision-making authority in the areas of the treatment of former priests, the training of new priests, marriage regulations, the moral supervision of homosexuals, and the management of health care facilities in the diocese. The result was an enormous outcry in the diocese and outside for what was perceived as an insult to the bishop and also to the church in that region. Even the Canon Law Society questioned whether his treatment did not violate Church law. The Vatican was forced to back down this time, and a three-bishop commission was appointed to examine the various charges. By 1987 Rome reinstated the archbishop's authority, but it named a coadjuctor bishop with whom he should consult. Traditional Catholics and clergy waited anxiously for his coming retirement.[73]

The leading agent in these condemnations was Joseph Cardinal Ratzinger of Bavaria, a once well-regarded liberal who had cooperated with the progressive *peritii* at Vatican II. He had been an articulate critic of the Holy Office—the precursor to his own congregation—saying its behavior was detrimental to the Catholic faith. However reacting to the student unrest of the 1960s and post-Vatican II excesses, he felt that discussions had often led to "lies," and that the age-old truths of the Church were being threatened by the twists and turns the Council had taken. Pope Paul had named him Archbishop of Munich and Freising, and he met Karol Wojtyla at an episcopal synod a year before the latter's election.

As he admitted, he became more conservative after 1968 as he saw that the consequences of the council were leading to an unraveling of the Church. What the popes and the Council Fathers expected, he said, was a new Christian unity; what they got instead was dissension that seemed to pass from self-criticism to self-destruction. He advocated "restoration" as a way to achieve a new balance and not as a turning back. It would be a recovery of lost values, he insisted, within a new totality, and he cited St. Charles Borromeo who helped to rebuild the Catholic Church after the Council of Trent without retreating back to the Middle Ages.

The real crisis of the Church was above all else a crisis of priests and religious orders, he publicly argued. Traditional pillars of ecclesiastical reform—the great religious orders—had vacillated, lost vocations, and experienced identity crises. In addition, bishops in episcopal conferences often accepted group decisions instead of being strongly persistent in their convictions, Ratzinger explained.

He then went on to speak of the major challenge before the Church—the teaching of moral theology. Like Wojtyla, he had serious reservations about the cultural influence of the West, noting that "economic *liberalism* creates its exact counterpart, *permissivism*, on the moral plane." Theologians must choose between opposing modern society or opposing the *magisterium* of the Church. Even in women's religious orders, there was a "feminist mentality," especially in North America. Only those who had lived in cloistered contemplative orders had withstood the *Zeitgeist* because of their sheltered life and their clear sense of mission.

In other instances, John Paul himself took the lead in dealing with discipline problems in his Church. In January 1980 the pope invited the Dutch bishops to Rome to end their divisions and to bring to heel one of the most unorthodox churches in his realm. Unlike Paul he was clearly not willing to accept their unruliness. Meeting behind closed doors, the bishops ended up accepting the pope's criticisms and his prescriptions. They went home and curtailed liturgical innovations, ecumenism, intercommunion, and the use of pastoral workers instead of priests. They also terminated appeals to bishops for a relaxation of priestly celibacy. The Dutch church was brought in line, but deep resistance toward the pope by elements of the faithful was apparent in his later visit to that nation. The normal indices of Church participation also began to decline in the Netherlands. Thus it appeared that the progressive bishops were meeting the aspirations of what represented a good segment of their Church.[74]

Having finished that business, the pope called the Ukrainian bishops to the Vatican to resolve several long standing problems. In 1946 the Ukrainian Catholic Church with ties to Rome was declared illegal by the

Soviet Union, and its archbishop, Josef Slipyi, was shipped to Siberia for eighteen years. Finally Pope John XXIII's appeals to Premier Nikita Khrushchev to have him released were successful. The archbishop was later made a cardinal and lived in exile in Rome. On his own, Slipyi decided to declare himself a patriarch—a step that Pope Paul disapproved of, and he went on to criticize the pope's overtures toward Eastern European Communist governments as "an obscene insult to the blood of martyrs of the Gulag Archipelago."[75]

John Paul persuasively informed a suspicious Slipyi that he supported the right of religious freedom, including in the Ukraine, and that the Ukrainian Catholics were invited to give him a name for assistant bishop who would be the successor to the cardinal. The local synod chose a successor, and the pope had patched over an old quarrel.

Not all areas of contention lent themselves to such easy solutions. Two of John Paul's predecessors, Pius XII and Paul VI, both had reservations about the Jesuits at times, but they were still admirers of the order. During Vatican II, Jesuits such as Bea, Rahner, and John Courtney Murray among others, helped to set the impressive agenda; later though some members of the order were rather vocal in their reservations about Paul's encyclical on birth control.

Beginning in 1965, a Basque named Don Pedro Arrupe had led the order and advocated an opening to the left that included democratization of the Jesuits and an emphasis on its social calling. Conservatives saw that as a betrayal of its historic religious apostolate in favor of social activism, rabble-rousing, and Marxism. Paul began to become concerned about the order's loss of identity, and whether it was laicizing itself by becoming simply a humanitarian agency. In September 1973 Paul wrote a letter to General Superior Arrupe, condemning the intellectual and disciplinary tendencies he felt would injure the order. He also opposed the attempts to end the differences in the organization between priests and non-priests, and a proposal to allow Jesuits the right to object to certain commands, including those from the pope himself. He directly intervened when conservatives told him that there might even be a possibility that the Jesuits at their general conference would be moving toward ending their traditional fourth vow—that of strict obedience to the pope.

It is with this background that John Paul II acted quickly and sternly in dealing with the Jesuits. When Arrupe decided to resign, the pope refused to accept his resignation, arguing that under the order's bylaws such a decision required his prior approval. Arrupe stayed, but afflicted later by a stroke, he was finally permitted to resign, and he moved to name one of his lieutenants, American Vincent O'Keefe, to the position of Vicar General until a General Congregation could elect a successor.

The pope then surprised the Jesuits and decided to stop any such appointment. In a deliberate slap at the Society, the pope named his own "personal delegate," vested with full powers to lead and personally control the order. In September 1983, the Jesuits elected Father Peter Hans Kollenbach successor to Arrupe. Kollenbach proved to be a moderate and judicious leader as he toned down but kept the basic thrust of the Decree Four statement. John Paul, who had had no real close experience with religious orders or the Society of Jesus, may have over-reacted as he took the next logical step to Paul's warnings and applied shock therapy to a proud and often haughty company of men. In any case, after the controversy settled down, he went on to praise the Jesuits for their "docile harmony with the directives of the *magisterium.*" As for Arrupe, he had candidly indicated to the Society that the last three popes had serious reservations about the directions in which the Jesuits were going—directions he himself favored. Still it seemed to some that the conservative Polish pope was more at home with conservative organizations such as Opus Dei, an association that Pope Paul had kept at arm's length, than with the long-established religious orders, which included not just the Jesuits, but the Dominicans and Franciscans as well.[76]

The Assassination Attempt

Pope John Paul II was a leader of surety and tenacious purpose, but on May 13, 1981 he experienced an event that had profound personal impact on him, one that threatened his life, deepened his already intense spirituality, and turned him even more to the protection of the Blessed Virgin Mary. As the late afternoon sun was setting, the pope was riding in a Jeep through the crowds in St. Peter's Square. At a range of less than ten feet, Mehmat Ali Agca fired a Browning 9 directly at the vulnerable pontiff.

Two bullets entered the pope, one penetrating his abdomen and the second hitting his right forearm and injuring the second finger of his left hand. A nun from Bergamo, Sister Letizia, had deflected the aim of the professional assassin by pulling on his jacket, and thus probably saved John Paul's life. The pope sank down in the vehicle into the arms of one of his aides, losing blood profusely and exhibiting on his face a strange mixture of pain and almost tranquility as he prayed. In the hospital, he kept repeating, "Mary, my mother, Mary, my mother," as he came perilously close to death.[77]

Overnight the vigorous pope appeared less triumphant and desperately human and mortal. Once he had observed that when he was young sick people used to intimidate him.[78] He was now to come to understand that his pontificate was to be closely linked to martyrdom and to suffering, and that he was spared hopefully to lead the Church into its third millennium, while he was destined to endure more pain. In his hospital room he contemplated the intercession of Mary, and then later read the collected information on the apparitions at Fatima, Portugal.

He had been informed, as had others, that the nun Sister Lucy, by then the last living Fatima child, insisted that the Virgin's request had still not been met. She had mandated that Russia had to be dedicated to her, and that dedication had to be done by the pope *in concert* with the Catholic Church's other bishops. This he would do, as he prayed publicly for the conversion of Russia. At the time it seemed far-fetched, because the Western intelligence agencies reported the continuing strength of the Soviet regime.

It has been speculated that the professional assassin who wounded the pope was hired by the Bulgarian secret police on behalf of the Russian KGB. The Soviet leaders had begun a campaign to discredit the pope, and had been especially wary of his activities with the Ukrainians, and of course with the Poles. The argument that was made in some quarters was that the Russians had ordered the pope's murder and used their allies to pull the trigger. However the opening of some historical archives in previously Communist countries has not lent any verification to that charge. After his recuperation, John Paul visited his assailant in a Roman prison, and in one of the most impressive photos of the time, the world saw the pope, as if almost hearing a confession, listening intently to Agca. Lip readers claimed that the assassin asked him how he was still alive, and the pope responded that another hand had directed matters. Then John Paul bluntly asked the assailant who had sent him. The latter's responses to the pontiff questions are not recorded, although he had said that John Paul knew everything about the episode.[79]

The pope, who had experienced such a lamentable young adulthood, once again knew pain and loneliness, and also a sense of being specifically saved by God's direct intercession. That experience probably added to his heroic sense of mission, his willingness to ask more of his fellow co-religionists than they were sometimes willing to give, and enhanced his view of the Blessed Virgin's watchful care. He sent one of the bullets that had wounded him to Fatima to be placed in a crown on a statue of Mary. Privately he later observed of the new bulletproof, glassed-enclosed popemobile, "All these precautions are useless. As soon as I go out, dressed in white from head to foot, I'm a target they can't possibly miss."[80]

The pope had rushed his recovery and had to return to the hospital and deal with a serious infection. But gradually he seemed physically mended, and he continued to devote himself to a more intensive role in the life of Polish national politics, as he came to embrace even more the Solidarity movement and Walesa. The pope who had disapproved of liberation politics in Latin America, ended the career of a Jesuit liberal congressman from Massachusetts, and pushed against the Church's involvement in partisan battles, became in many ways a participant in the end of the Polish Communist state. That demise was the preface to the real curtain riser—the total collapse of the Soviet system. The Slavic pope would play a critical role, as did the United States administration in that turn of events. Even more importantly, the ethnic tensions and economic problems would unravel the reforming Communist state headed up by Mikhail Gorbachev.

For over a century there had been prophecies of a Slavic pope, but this one's impact on geopolitics in that area was truly beyond expectations. Karol Wojtyla became even more than he imagined, a man of great destiny striding the world stage. In some strange way, the pope who so rejected the extremes of the West seemed to take solace at first in the view that Moscow, the so-called "Third Rome" as it has been called, would play a special role in the changing nature of faith and religious allegiances in the third millennium.[81] It was an Eastern Europe romance, one that misjudged the nature of contemporary Russians and one that denigrated the true importance of the industrialized West in the world of ideas and ideologies.

The Heroic Pope
The pope demanded more of his faithful, but the peoples of North America and Western Europe were also weary of such sacrifices. They had been through two terrible World Wars and the Great Depression. They intended to enjoy prosperity and peace—and yes, wallow a bit in their consumer products. That self-indulgence bothered the pontiff, and he reached out to the children of the next generation, as he pleaded for faith and justice. Rather remarkably they seemed somewhat attuned to his admonitions and to his extraordinary charisma. They responded in lively ways to his personal appearances, but as a group they still prized their possessions and their sexual and creative freedom. Thus the great contradiction of public attitudes in the United States and elsewhere toward this pope.

That same dimension can be seen in the pope's treatment of Catholic universities. Since the late 1970s, Catholic educators in the United States, led by the respected president of Notre Dame University, Father Theodore Hesburgh, and Jesuit priest Robert Henle of Georgetown, departed from the Vatican's attempts to control Catholic colleges and universities. They argued that such a step threatened the tradition of trustee control (important to American concepts of incorporation), raised problems for academic accreditation, and might present hurdles in receiving federal aid. So they insisted on delaying revisions. In 1990 the pope issued a new apostolic constitution, *Ex Corde Ecclesiae*, which sought to impose a unified charter that would place Catholic institutions of higher education under local bishops. In November 1996, the American bishops brokered a compromise with the major Catholic universities' leaders.[82]

John Paul had moved easily with academics and intellectuals throughout most of his adult life, and he had been an articulate spokesman for freedom of expression. He argued that the Church in the modern world was really the champion of reason, freedom, and progress. Rather remarkably, he also insisted in 1979 that the Curia reopen the Church's condemnation of Galileo Galilei, and he finally rehabilitated that controversial astronomer in 1992; the Vatican would end up calling Galileo ironically a "man of faith." Galileo had been originally brought to trial before the Inquisition in 1633 and threatened with torture if he did not recast his view that the earth revolved around the Sun, a view advanced earlier by the Polish scientist Copernicus. Wojtyla had been an admirer of Copernicus and lamented the consequences of Galileo's trial that established the popular view that faith and science were inherently in conflict.[83] In October 1996, the pontiff lent his support to the theory of human evolution as well, thus separating Catholicism from fundamentalist Protestant thought.

The pope also reinvigorated the Pontifical Academy of Sciences and had its members focus on informing national leaders of the horrors of nuclear weapons.[84] In the industrial city of Turin, in April 1980 the pope once again criticized both liberalism and Marxism, and his views seemed to be remarkably similar to the long-standing complaints of the European Catholic right that somehow the West took a wrong turn back at the Enlightenment. Behind it all in the pope's eyes was the menace of aggressive atheism and its war on God. Later in 1981, he spoke of the need for "those great souls" in history, individuals committed to respecting the faith. Addressing the crowd, the pontiff exhorted simply, "Europe needs Christ!"

But it would be a mistake to view John Paul as a simple conservative. In fact, his statements were very critical of capitalism and its emphasis on unbridled wealth and consumerism. His first encyclical, *Redemptor Hominis*, was an affirmation of the dignity of workers written by the only pope who has ever worked in an industrial setting. While he supported the struggle for justice, he opposed class warfare and hatred of others, a clear critique of Marxism.

On March 19, 1981, he addressed a group of factory workers north of Rome and insisted, "Be assured that the Pope is with you, that the Pope is on your side, whenever justice has been violated, peace is threatened or the due rights of anyone and the common good need to be encouraged." He then walked with the workers, ate, and drank wine with them. The pope answered their questions, listened to their grievances, and remembered his own times as a worker during World War II. When a television reporter observed to someone that this was the first time that a pope had eaten with the workers, the pontiff overheard the remark. Quietly he responded, "and that's not the only novelty of this pontificate." To mark the ninetieth anniversary of Leo's *Rerum Novarum*, John Paul II issued in September 1981 his encyclical *Labortem Exercens*. In it he supported joint ownership of the means of work, stressed the need for unions to be nonpolitical, and reiterated once again the idea of a Catholic social doctrine.[85]

The Restive New World
But his idea of social doctrine was very different from that taking place in Third World countries. The Vatican, with the pope's concurrence, had moved against the leaders of the liberation theologian movement in Latin America. The Congregation for the Doctrine of the Faith sent a letter to the Peruvian bishops listing objections to the writings of the theologian Gustavo Gutiérrez. The bishops were, however, divided, and Gutiérrez was invited to Rome for some private consultations. Then the Congregation went after the Brazilian Franciscan, Leonardo Boff. Instead of presenting his case to the bishops, the Congregation also called him to Rome. Two Brazilian bishops went with him in a show of support. In March 1985 the Vatican issued a document answering Boff's criticisms, and in May he was prohibited from publishing or teaching for a period of time. Later though the scrutiny continued, and a frustrated Boff left the priesthood altogether.[86]

In 1983, John Paul had made a controversial visit to Nicaragua, a visit that ended up being the nadir of his travels. The Nicaraguan revolution had expelled the Somoza family which for several generations had impoverished that tiny nation. Coming to power was a group of Castro-like Marxist guerrilla fighters called the Sandinistas. What made that situation difficult for the Vatican was that five of its major political leaders were Catholic priests, the most visible being the Minister of Culture, Ernesto Cardenal. Cardenal was a committed revolutionary and poet, a priest, and an associate of the gentle Trappist monk Thomas

Merton. He was to comment, somewhat sarcastically, that the pope was correct, clergy should not be involved in politics. "I used to be a poet. I became a priest, and the love of God led me to revolution. I have never gone in for politics."[87]

The position of the Vatican was that priests could not hold public office, and that if they did, they could not then exercise priestly functions until they resigned. The pope at first insisted that he would not visit that nation until that "irregularity" was resolved, but he decided on the trip anyhow. When he arrived at the airport, he publicly chastised Ernesto Cardenal while the priest knelt to receive the pontiff's blessing. John Paul uncharacteristically shook his finger at him angrily and insisted that he had to normalize his status.

Later, in front of a large crowd, the pope ended up in a shouting match with hecklers, probably planted there by the Sandinistas. When some people chanted, "We want peace!," the pontiff shouted back, "Silence," three times. In his visit he avoided mentioning the attacks of the anti-Sandinista Contras who were being heavily funded then by the Reagan Administration, and he demanded that Catholics support their bishops.[88]

It was an extremely distasteful episode. The Vatican insisted that the priests still in the government had to resign. One finally left the priesthood and became laicized, one left the Jesuits, and two were suspended from their priestly functions. In early 1996, the pope visited Nicaragua again. By then the Sandinistas had been voted out by the people, and the pope was greeted by enthusiastic crowds. In place of the strident guerilla leader President Daniel Ortega, who had once greeted the pontiff in military greens, the new president was Violeta Chamorro who was elected in 1990. She embraced John Paul and kissed his head as if she were welcoming a long lost uncle. As the pope proceeded down the major highway, lo and behold there was a billboard from previous president Ortega celebrating John Paul's visit. The pope had insisted that the Church be separated from the regime, and it appeared that in the longer perspective he was once again correct.[89] In October 1996, Ortega again ran for president—this time on a platform emphasizing God, forgiveness, and private enterprise. He lost a second time. In 1985 and in 2007 he again served as president.

Over the years, John Paul had made his position very clear—the Church "does not need to have recourse to ideological systems in order to love, defend, and collaborate with the liberation of the human being." As for liberation theology, one comes away with two very different impressions of that development. There is a genuine sense of righteousness against exploitation and a charming resurrection of the powerful image of Jesus' thirst for justice's sake. But overall the theology seems to be rather shallow, intellectually ragged, and often a collection of socialist slogans loosely wrapped in religious garb. By 1996, John Paul was dismissing liberation theology as irrelevant. And Cardinal Ratzinger was focusing his concerns on moral relativism.

Karol Wojtyla, the scholar of Marxism, probably had a better command of that ideology than did either its priest-advocates in Latin America or the Communist party bosses in Eastern Europe. Although the basic and primary problems of poverty, exploitation, and government violence remained, even the liberation theologians acknowledged that John Paul addressed those issues as well as they did. In fact, two such theologians, the Boffs, noted that while the pontiff put distance between himself and their rhetoric, he shared many of their legitimate concerns.[90]

It may be though that, once again, John Paul reacted too swiftly and too abruptly to a very complex problem in the Third World, where he himself had said that the future of the Catholic Church would be decided. By April 1986, the Vatican issued an "Instruction on Christian Freedom and Liberation," which took a more benign view, although, as noted, in a somewhat abstract sense, of the liberation theology movement. In the same month the pope had a friendly three-day meeting with the Brazilian bishops. The restrictions on Leonardo Boff, who had humbly observed the Vatican's limitations on his freedom, were at first lifted, although the criticisms were to be resurrected later.[91] Looking back at the pope's confusing journey into Latin American ecclesiastical controversies, one can appreciate more fully Pope Paul VI's carefully nuanced style; sometimes vigor and assertiveness are not unalloyed virtues. At times John Paul seemed to be too preoccupied with reining in deviating intellectual constructs, such that he gave the impression of a lack of sympathy to the very movements with which he himself was genuinely aligned. Unlike John XXIII, he insisted on setting everything right; unlike Paul VI, he could not live in a world filled with ambiguities.

After his first Polish trip, the pope also visited another historic Catholic country, Ireland. Again, John Paul warned against the prevailing materialism, self-indulgence, and consumerism that was so much a part of Western society in his view. At one point in Galway, he looked over a huge crowd of 200,000 people on a racetrack and cried out, "Young people of Ireland, I love you." Across the isle, the pope spoke out against moral shortcuts, the preoccupation with comfort, wealth, and pleasure, and the need to remember the kingdom of God. He supported the traditional bans on divorce and abortion and strongly opposed sectarian hatred in that island. In English, the pontiff proclaimed "violence is evil...violence is unacceptable as a solution to problems...violence is unworthy of man...violence is a lie"—references to the bloody sectarian wars so common in Ireland's life.

But as in Italy, Ireland would show signs of moving away from the traditions of the faith. In 1995, Ireland voted for a statute permitting divorce. That outcome was allegedly due in part to the revelations of a bishop living with his long-time mistress. Across the English Channel, in early 1996, even the saintly Mother Teresa seemed to approve of a divorce for the much publicized and estranged Prince and Princess of Wales in Great Britain. A continuous stream of soap opera headlines, taped lovers' conversations, and public confessions of infidelity on both their parts had taxed even her legendary patience. Thus at times the pope during his term in office had to face continuing deviations from the deposit of the faith—even among the usually faithful. He was especially embarrassed when the conservative cardinal he appointed to the see in Vienna, Hermann Grör, had to be replaced after accusations of pedophilia were made.[92]

Nowhere were the corrosive evidences of consumerism, hedonism, and excessive freedom more apparent in pope's eyes than in the United States. There too the effects of Vatican II and the birth control encyclical had contributed to a general loss of faith, to confusion in the seminaries, and to a massive decline in vocations. The pope was to observe that the Americans were nice people, but when it came to matters of religion, they sometimes followed outdated European trends. The pontiff sarcastically observed on one occasion that they had yet to "get past Bultmann"—a reference to the unorthodox Biblical scholar of the early twentieth century.

American Catholic attitudes generally reflected those of their fellow countrymen rather than traditional papal admonitions. For example, at the time of the pope's visit in October 1979, 66 percent of Catholics approved of birth control, 63 percent of divorce, 53 percent wished for priests to be allowed to marry, and 51 percent tolerated abortion on demand. The Church that the pope saw was not just one militant Church, but a host of groups, often speaking past each other. John Paul was concerned about the lack of Church discipline and the supposed weakness of some bishops, and he moved to change those directions.[93]

On his first visit his reception was enormously positive. In Boston, for example, the city and the neighborhoods turned out in force, even in the rain, and the pope graciously remarked, "America the beautiful, even when it rains." A six-foot poster in Boston quoted his words at his installation, "Be not afraid to open the door wide for Christ." In New York City he addressed the United Nations General Assembly where he pleaded for peace and insisted on the inalienable rights of every human being. That evening he said Mass before 75,000 people in Yankee Stadium, and spoke against "the frenzy of consumerism."

The next morning at Madison Square Garden, a youth concert exploded with football chants, "Rack 'em up, stack 'em up, bust 'em in two—Holy Father, we're for you." And the pope began to sing along, "Whoa—hoo—whoa—." In Harlem he consoled his predominantly black audience saying, "If we are silent about the joy that comes from knowing Jesus, the very stones of our cities will cry out. For we are an Easter people and alleluia is our song!"[94]

In Philadelphia, he reaffirmed his belief that "the priesthood is forever," and in Washington, D.C., on September 7, 1979 he had to face the forces of feminism within his own Church. Sister Mary Theresa Kane, the head of the Leadership Conference of Women Religious, in an address to Pope John Paul spoke of "the intense suffering and pain that is part of the life of many women in the U.S. Church." She insisted that in supporting dignity for people, the Church must open up its own ministries to all as well. Later the pope maintained that women were excluded from the priesthood, not because the Church was making a statement about human rights, or because of any exclusion of women from the mission of the Church. Rather, the exclusion was due to historical tradition—Christ had not included any women in the first twelve apostles. John Paul went on to praise the Blessed Virgin Mary, noting that while she was not incorporated into the hierarchical constitution of the Church—"yet she makes all hierarchy possible."[95]

Later in other countries, the pope would face the same criticisms from other women religious. On June 3, 1980, John Paul met a crowd of 5,000 French nuns at the motherhouse of the Sisters of Charity where the Miraculous Medal was struck by Catherine Labouré in 1830. There Sister Daniéle Souillard spoke of the need to abandon the traditional garb of nuns in order to pursue their professional work. The pope had insisted that the nuns should "never be ashamed to recognize your identity as women consecrated to the Lord." But some of the religious thought the admonition ill-advised, if not trivial.

A third example occurred on November 20, 1980 in Germany where Barbara Engl, president of the Munich Association of Catholic Youth, was critical of the pope's homily on Satan. She contended that young people felt the Church was more concerned with perpetuating divisions with the Evangelical Church than in promoting unity. She also indicated that there was a real need for priests and chaplains, and that the celibacy ban made little sense, as did the limits on women's ministry.

The pope did not respond immediately, but in April 1980 he praised St. Catherine of Siena, the sometime advisor and sometime harsh critic of popes. He called attention to the fact that "her feminine nature was richly endowed with fantasy, intuition, sensibility, an ability to get things done, a capacity to communicate with others, a readiness for self-giving and service."[96] Thus the pope's attitudes toward women remained both respectful and traditional, seeing them primarily as helpmates. In 1995 the Congregation for the Doctrine of the Faith insisted that the pope's ban on women as ministers had the force of an infallible declaration, increasing in some a sense of second class membership in a Church dedicated ironically to the special intercession of the Virgin Mary.

The most doctrinaire of the pope's addresses in the United States came in a Chicago seminary to 350 American bishops. There he proceeded to outline the sacred deposit of Christian doctrine that had to be safeguarded and taught. He extolled Pope Paul VI's encyclical, *Humanae Vitae*, and asked the bishops to give witness to the truth, thereby serving all of humanity. He went on to indicate that it was the laity's right to receive "the word of God in its purity and integrity as guaranteed by the *magisterium* of the universal Church."[97]

Later he observed that he was not offended to be called a conservative, for "the pope is not here to make changes, but to conserve what he has received with his charge." Thus, to the pope, Catholicism remained a fairly rigid belief system with a strong disciplinary code. Even though many Catholics disagreed with the message, as has been noted, they still loved the messenger. Throughout his visits to the United States over the years, the public responses, especially from the young, was extremely positive and respectful.

After a year in office, John Paul was praised by *Time* magazine that called him "John Paul, Superstar."[98] In the article, that journal of opinion indicated that the pope lifted people above the drabness of their own lives and showed them that they are capable of expressing better emotions and performing better deeds than they may have thought. In 1995, the pope was proclaimed the "Man of the Year" for many of the same reasons.

John Paul's commitment to traditional Catholic dogma and its distinctive mission had another side effect. The day after his election, John Paul indicated that he was committed to overcoming the obstacles to Christian unification—a preoccupation of both John XXIII and Paul VI. But almost immediately he seemed less interested in such efforts, especially as it dealt with the churches in the West. He was not much influenced by the Anglican/Roman Catholic International Commission and its discussions on the nature of the ministry. In Washington, D.C., he said to an interfaith group, "Recognition must be given to the deep divisions which still exist over moral and ethical matters. The moral life and the life of faith are so deeply united that it is impossible to divide them."[99]

He clearly rejected ecumenism as a limited collaboration, and insisted the churches should avoid reducing matters to a doctrinal minimum or the lowest common denominator. The Congregation for the Doctrine of Faith had warned against glossing over problems inherent in any discussions of reunification and ecumenism, and John Paul concurred with that view. Still the pope spoke of "the great common treasury" of the various Christian faiths, and in November 1980 the pope visited West Germany and directly faced some difficult Protestant authorities and clergymen. Instead of confronting them and stressing their doctrinal and historical differences, John Paul referred to St. Paul's "Epistle to the Romans," which their Martin Luther had called "the heart of the New Testament." He even quoted Luther approvingly in that regard, a neat rhetorical trick indeed.[100]

His interests in interfaith efforts were more oriented toward the Eastern Orthodox, as he continued his appeal as a Slavic pope to the peoples of the East. As early as February 1980, he talked of "the rearticulation of the ancient traditions of the East and West." As Pope Paul VI recognized, however, the papacy itself was a major obstacle—if not the major obstacle, for all non-Catholic Christians. John Paul spoke of the peterine ministry in October 1978 and stressed its relationship to the Church's internal unity and the need to guarantee its special mission. In his eyes, as in Pope Paul's, only the pontificate could safeguard those objectives. But much later in May 1995 in his *Ut Unum Sint* he seemed to praise ecumenism and solicit opinions about problems the papacy posed in that regard. As some commentators noted, the search for unity was also hindered by the addition of the doctrine of infallibility in the late nineteenth century and the newly promulgated Marian doctrines of the Immaculate Conception and the Assumption.

As the years passed, John Paul continued to insist on dogmatic rigor. When the pope came back to the United States in 1987, some of the American bishops tried to explain the differences between European and American cultures. Joseph Cardinal Bernardin told the pope, "It is important to know that many Americans, given the freedom they have enjoyed for than two centuries, almost instinctively react negatively when they are told they must do something. As a result the impression is sometimes given that there is a certain rebellious in American Catholics that they want to 'go it alone'." He continued, "When someone questions how a truth might be better articulated or lived today, he or she is sometimes accused (by the Vatican) of rejecting the truth itself or portrayed as being in conflict with the Church's teaching authority. As a result, both sides are locked in what seems to be adversarial positions. Genuine dialogue becomes almost impossible. They must be able to speak to one another in complete candor, without fear."

Archbishop Rembert Weakland of Milwaukee tried to explain even further, "The faithful are now more inclined to look at the intrinsic worth of an argument proposed by the teachers in the Church than to accept it on the basis of the authority alone." But the pope insisted, "It is sometimes claimed that dissent is totally compatible to being 'a good Catholic' and poses no obstacle to the reception of the sacraments. This is a grave error. Dissent from Church doctrine remains what it is, dissent; as such it may not be proposed or received on an equal footing with the Church's authentic teaching."[101]

The pope did what one would expect he would do in dealing with the American church. In 1980 he installed a Vatican papal nuncio in Washington, Archbishop Pio Laghi, to look closely at new appointments to that hierarchy, and he placed men in high profile American dioceses—Boston, New York, Washington and Los Angeles—individuals whom he knew shared his views and his insistence upon orthodoxy. Rumor has it that the new apostolic delegate was being given five years "to clean up the American Church." In 1985, he good-naturedly remarked, "They just gave me five more years."[102]

In order to guarantee orthodoxy throughout the Church, the Vatican, led by Cardinal Ratzinger, pushed for a new oath of fidelity, reminiscent of the Modernist hysteria of Pius X. The new oath, to be effective March 1, 1989, indicated that all parish priests, rectors, professors of theology in seminaries, and rectors of Catholic universities, as well as teachers of subjects dealing with faith and morals were to take a pledge. It read as follows: "I firmly embrace and retain all and everything which is definitely proposed in doctrine about faith and morals by the Church. In addition, I adhere by religious assent of the will and intellect to the teachings which either the Roman Pontiff or the College of Bishops declare when they exercise the authentic magisterium, even if they do not intend to proclaim them by definitive act." The Vatican gave its final judgment on any dissent from that instruction, saying that if Catholic theologians could not agree then they should in conscience be quiet or "suffer for the truth in silence and prayer."

The Dissenting Faithful
The pope also decided to reach some conclusion in dealing with rebellion on the right. He had tried desperately, as had Paul, to deal with Archbishop Marcel Lefebvre who at the age of eighty-two had moved to ordain four bishops and over four hundred priests from his followers,

individuals committed to the Tridentine Latin Rite and to the Church before Vatican II. He had named his seminary in a Swiss mountain valley at Econe, "The Fraternity of St. Pius X." By voiding an earlier agreement with the Vatican, Lefebvre in turn incurred automatic excommunication. Before a congregation of 5,000 supporters, he reasserted his continuous opposition to the changes that had taken place since the last Council. Three years later he died of cancer, still unrepentant, and the pope issued a statement saying that he hoped for a moment of repentance and would have been willing to lift the excommunication decree if there had been any sign of reconciliation. The pope, in a gesture to traditional Catholics, did permit the Latin Rite to be celebrated if the local bishop concurred, as long as it was not seen as a repudiation of the changes of Vatican II. When the vernacular Mass was criticized for not being very contemplative because of its excessive dialogue, and not much mystery, the pontiff simply remarked, "The Word is also a mystery." Eventually his successor, Benedict XVI, would re-establish the Tridentine Mass and encourage its frequent use, but by then few priests could say the Mass in Latin.[103]

Sometimes John Paul himself seemed to be uncomfortable with the extent to which he felt he had to go to protect orthodoxy. After his confrontation with the Dutch bishops and their decision to support him over the wishes of most of their faithful, the pope realized the consequences of his tough stand. In 1985, he made a trip through the Benelux countries and in the Netherlands; the streets were almost deserted in marked contrast to almost every other area he had gone. When there was strong protest against the pope's decision about nominating a new local bishop against the wishes of the faithful, he tried to explain his thoughts on the matter, saying, "In all sincerity, the Pope attempts to understand the life of the Church and the appointment of every bishop. He gathers information and advice in accordance with ecclesiastical law and custom. You will understand that opinions are sometimes divided. In the last analysis, the Pope has to make the decision. Must the Pope explain his choice? Discretion does not permit him to do so." On another occasion, he argued, "You cannot take a vote on truth. You cannot pick or choose."

The pope's recalcitrance in consulting with clergy and informed lay people in individual countries led him into another firestorm when he invited President Kurt Waldheim to the Vatican in June 1987. That invitation raised an avalanche of protest from Jews because of questions that had been raised about Waldheim's Nazi past that had recently been discovered. The Vatican's answer was that the pope had an absolute right to invite whomever he wished to the Vatican, and that Waldheim was then the president of Austria. As proof began to mount about Waldheim's complicity in some of the worst crimes of the twentieth century, the Vatican for unexplained reasons gave him a knighthood, the Order of Pius IX, almost as if to insist that it had no intention to listening to other people's judgments or the outcries from Jews and Christian alike.[104]

In his dealings with the African Church, the pope also sounded a sense of alarm. His predecessor, Paul VI, had asked for an African Christianity, and indeed that was being worked out to the chagrin of many traditionalists in the Vatican. The successes of early Christianity were due in part to its remarkable ability to synthesize, borrow, adapt, and twist pagan, Jewish, Greek, and Middle Eastern customs and cultic devotions into Christian channels.

At Vatican II, Cardinal Wojtyla had voted for enculturation, and as late as 1995 argued in favor of it, citing in fact the failures in China where the Church had refused to compromise with that nation's revered customs. In May 1980 however he had visited the African continent with a very different message. In Zaire, to the disappointment of many Catholics, he refused to attend a Mass featuring dancing and drums. He argued that the dangers of Africanization were especially apparent in worship because there had to be "a substantial unity with the Roman rite." The pope seemed to say that there was really only one dominant ritual, and that that was rooted in European tradition.

His real concern may have been expressed in his remarks to young married couples in Kinshasa when he seemed to indicate that if Africa Africanized the Mass, they would wish to Africanize their marriage customs as well, which would include trial marriage and polygamy. He insisted that monogamy was not a European but a Semitic idea, and that Africans were perfectly capable of that commitment. Being a Christian meant being converted, that is changing customs, he insisted.

Six months later at a general synod, forty African bishops continued to advocate that the Church should approve of African marriage customs in which it is believed that marriage unfolds progressively and is not fully sealed until the birth of the first child. In an environment in which sensuality seemed to be less repressed than in the West (or at least it is usually assumed), the pope faced another dilemma. It was reported that a considerable number of Catholic priests lived in various states of intimacy with women companions—another topic on which John Paul felt strongly. Thus even in the newly converted missionary fields, the pope saw the same challenges and the chaos due to a lack of discipline, loose ties of Church unity, and above all a failure of nerve.[105] The pope was in a peculiar position—he was the son of the council and in fact was genuinely committed to its implementation. But he and his closest advisors, such as Ratzinger, had to believe that its alleged effects were often disastrous for the Catholic Church, at least within the traditional framework. In a sense of collegiality, he called general synods, including one on the role of the family in the modern world. One hundred and sixty-one bishops were elected by their peers to attend. This time the agenda would be structured, as were the results.

The problem, of course, was that *Humanae Vitae* had hemmed in the basic contexts of the debate. The tone of the conference was set when the pope hailed a Chilean mother of seventeen children as a heroine. To listen to the married couples invited to the Synod, one would assume that everyone accepted Paul's ill-fated encyclical on birth control.

The pope was generally quiet during the synod, but his views were well known to all. And on October 8, he told a general audience in St. Peter's Square that husbands who looked at their wives with "concupiscence" had committed adultery in their hearts. That view, explainable within the context of his philosophical statements, drew sharp and often humorous commentaries—adding to the criticism that a celibate clergy, including its pope, really knew very little about the allures of sex. But John Paul was unbending. He had earlier expressed his frustrations with American bishops when he pointed to their 1968 pastoral letter on birth control and demanded, "Here's your own doctrine. When are you going to start insisting on it?"

That tone continued to be evident over the years in his treatment of the topic of sexual morality. Much later, John Paul would have to deal with sexual morality in a very different way. But for all his reflections on what he called "the theology of the body," this mystical and holy man could not deal with the greatest crisis of his papacy—the child abuse scandal in his own Church. John Paul had so celebrated the religious life, especially of priests, that he seemed unable at first to come to deal with the idea of priests sexually abusing children and adolescents. But as the scandal rocked the American Church (forcing the humiliation and resignation of Bernard Cardinal Law of Boston) and then the church in Ireland, in continental Western Europe, and even his own beloved Poland, he had to come to grips with it. Perhaps it was his age that prevented him from dealing expeditiously with the scandal. Cardinal Ratzinger was asked to investigate, and with disgust he perceived the threats of what appeared to be long periods of clerical abuse. And of further importance, it was obvious that members of the hierarchy had engaged in decades-long patterns of cover-ups of such behavior as they shuttled offenders from one parish to another, one monastery to another. Secular courts intervened, and the Church was left with enormous financial judgments that went to victims of abuse. Eventually, Catholic Church officials argued that since the peak of such activity was in the 1960s, it was obviously a reflection of the loosening of moral standards in that era. And since most of the abuse cases involved priests and boys, then it was another example of the evils of homosexuality, not the problems of celibacy, or the nature of an authoritarian Church.[106]

Dealing with the topic of divorced Catholics, the pope insisted that those who re-married could receive Communion only if they abstained from sex. Critics again charged that physical contact and not spiritual renewal was becoming the continuing preoccupation of the Vatican. One well-known conservative American monsignor, George Kelly, bluntly observed as early as 1981 that the Church "lost its people to contraception, and in a very few years." As for the pope, he dismissed a close friend's criticism of the contraception ban, concluding, "I can't change what I've been teaching all my life."[107]

By the mid and late 1980s the overall contours of the Wojtyla papacy were set. Despite his insistence that he was dedicated to implementing the Council's decrees, it was clear that he saw his papacy as a time of restoration, of a return to traditional values and discipline. He not only insisted on preserving the deposit of the faith as all popes are sworn to do, but he also moved beyond that obligation. John Paul came close to enclosing the teaching proclamations of his papacy with the near status of being infallible.

Infallibility is a loose and historically unclear formulation, which itself has never been fully defined, even at Vatican I. At times it seems that with mounting opposition to his restoration ideology, John Paul insisted on raising the ante and by doing so he made the Church and the papacy more vulnerable to attack in the long run, both inside and outside the fold. Even the extreme Pius IX never went so far. One good example was the Congregation for the Doctrine of the Faith's edict in 1995 that the exclusion of women from the priesthood was an infallible declaration. If that were so, some asked, why has it never been enunciated before by any pope, even by the most conservative ones. Infallibility was being used to quell debate rather than to preserve the faith.[108] And a few months later, the pope defensively stressed the need to open leadership positions up to religious women—excluding however the ministry of Christ.

The call to dialogue that this pope so celebrated, the invitation to intellectual freedom with which Cardinal Wojtyla so lacerated the Polish regime, were casualties of the march toward restoration. The second trend of this papacy was the increasingly frantic pace of the pope, almost as if he believed the alleged prophecy of Padre Pio that he would be both pope and also live an endangered life. He had faced enormous cheers in America, hostile reactions in the Netherlands, and nasty episodes in Nicaragua, but he continued on. Across the globe the pope brought his message and nowhere was he more insistent than in his denunciations of abortion.

The Culture of Life
Abortion, of course, is not new in Western history. The classical Greeks and Romans practiced it as did other cultures, but by the twentieth century the techniques of medical technology became more sophisticated and also safer in allowing women abortion as an option. In the United States the issue came to a head rather late in a Supreme Court case, which is the usual way that Americans deal with intractable issues—that is, by turning them into legal controversies. That decision in *Roe v. Wade* (1973) led to a Solomonic verdict that abortion was permitted in the first three months, was generally prohibited in the last three, and was a judgment call in the second trimester. No one was totally happy with the compromise, and the Court based its verdict on biological views of the human fetus' viability, rather than on any metaphysical or spiritual basis, a judgment one would expect in a pluralistic society such as the United States.[109]

The difficulty is that the definitions of viability at conception or potentiality are so complex that it is impossible to conduct public policy based on the latest monograph from a research laboratory. At times John Paul seemed to accept the biological basis for his condemnation, as when he had to acknowledge that medieval theologians such as the great Aquinas had said that human life does not begin until the "quickening period," or the beginning of the fourth month. The pope pointed out quite correctly that such observations were based on an obsolete view of biology.

John Paul reflected that "in the Middle Ages, it was thought that the developing being passed through a vegetable phase, then into an animate phase, and so forth, thus the responsibility for interrupting a pregnancy might not have seemed so serious to tender consciences as one might have believed that they were only putting an end to a plant or to an animal. Today that sort of rationalizing is no longer possible. The human being exists from the moment of conception. Modern medicine uses other ways to express that, but as for us we say that even an embryo, a baby is already marked with the image of God."[110]

The pope then explained that some people oppose abortion but support artificial contraception. "But to permit the use of artificial contraceptives is the same as to open the way for abortion, because the moral attitude is what counts in this instance. Human life is an absolute value, tied up with the creative power of God. It is not manipulatable."

But the positions of some Vatican theologians were and are more complex. The view or usual stereotype is that the Church believes that life begins at the very moment of conception—long before any definition of viability such as pain or neurological reactions are apparent to observers. Some theologians in the Congregation for the Doctrine of the Faith however have argued that the ontological status of the embryo has no bearing on the propriety of abortion. Respect for human life is called for from the moment that the process of gestation begins, and human biological life has value and must be protected whether it is considered to have a spiritual soul or not.[111]

That view is a little different from the general pronouncements of John Paul. Those theologians were saying that the prohibition against abortion from the moment of conception is "an intuition of faith." Those views free the questions of morals from the latest findings of laboratory scientists, but they also introduce elements of ambiguity that are less than persuasive in diverse societies.

Taking the advice of Cardinal Bernardin in the United States and others, the pope expanded his abhorrence of abortion into a full-length encyclical titled *Evangelium Vitae*. Arguing against abortion, birth control, capital punishment, and modern war, the pope proposed instead a seamless garment, a tapestry of respect for the culture of life against the culture of death. It is a powerful document even for those who may have reservations about its absolutist tone.[112]

The pope's commitment was not just limited to teaching the faith on the issue. In an old-time display of international power politics, the Vatican had in the past made common cause with Islamic regimes in order to oppose a U.N. conference in Cairo, Egypt meant to support reproductive freedom and world-wide abortion on demand. The Moslem theologians and many Protestant fundamentalists have opposed abortion as well, although John Paul II became at the time the single most articulate spokesperson against that accelerating practice. The then archbishop of New York, John Cardinal O'Connell, observed, "I see an alliance forming between the Catholic Church and the Muslim world against the west. It would really change an awful lot." It was a statement from a man who obviously did not know history or understand comparative cultures.

The Third Millennium
The pope continued his frantic pace on into his seventies. In addition to his travels, generally four major journeys a year, he continued to issue a

steady stream of letters and pronouncements. In 1983, he completed John XXIII's work by promulgating a new code of canon law. In 1985, he celebrated the twenty-fifth anniversary of Vatican II in his own way. In 1991, he used the occasion of a Church synod to celebrate the collapse of Communism. In 1992, a new catechism of the Catholic Church came out in Italy and France, and was followed in 1994 by a best-selling English edition for Britain and the United States. He had attended two colorful international interfaith conferences at Assisi, home of the beloved St. Francis, much to the chagrin of conservative Curia officials, and he expressed a desire to host a similar gathering at Jerusalem. Eventually, his successor removed the leadership at Assisi and never hosted another such event. In 1992, John Paul issued an encyclical called *Veritatis Splendor* which reiterated traditional Catholic moral theology and called for disciplinary action against dissident theologians. On October 19, 1994, John Paul became the first sitting pope to write a book, *Crossing the Threshold of Hope,* and two years later, after his sixth operation, he published his autobiography.

In September 1994, as noted, he spearheaded international opposition to abortion at the Cairo Conference on Population and Development, and sitting in a hospital bed on May 22, 1994 the pope signed an apostolic letter, *Ordinatio Sacaretodalis,* that said women could never be priests. In a radio address heard in Communist China on January 14, 1995, the pope offered to acknowledge that China's officially sponsored church, if it recognized the pope's authority over China's Catholics. In November 1996, after another serious operation and a short recuperation, he met with Fidel Castro and planned a visit to Cuba. The aging dictator exclaimed how as a boy he never dreamt he would meet a pope and dine with cardinals.

Still, at times the usual sensitive and humane pope seemed to become cavalier in his treatment of dissent. When on one occasion he was asked to reconsider seriously the question of a married clergy and female ministers, he recited the World War I tune, "It's a long way to Tipperary." It was an uncharacteristically flippant tone for a serious prelate to take.

There was also the way he dealt with Jacques Gaillot, the Catholic bishop of the diocese of Évreux in Normandy, a gentle and low-keyed individual who dressed in common street clothes. Gaillot had taken to television to talk about the problems of the dispossessed, supported the distribution of condoms to combat AIDS, and advocated a married priesthood, among other views. The pope decided that he should be named to a Sahara desert site called Partenia in Southern Algeria where there were few Catholics left.

It was a cynical display of papal power. But true to our times, the bishop turned Partenia into "a virtual diocese"—one linked up to the Internet. Thus the bishop's views were available to anyone with a computer connected to the World Wide Web! The bishop would answer questions, accept e-mail, and give out his unorthodox views while living in the comforts of France. When the bishop saw the pope again, John Paul asked him, "Why are you so *metitaque*?" Gaillot responded, "I am just trying to be like you."[113]

Popes live in real time too, and this pope was prone to slow down as the ailments of the advancing age caught up. In 1994, he lamented, "I'm a poor wretch." At times he even seemed frail, his hands shaking, his eyes glazed, and his legendary strength sapped. In addition to his wounds in 1981, and the subsequent viral blood disorder right after the shooting, John Paul was also been plagued with other ailments. In 1992, he had a large intestinal tumor removed, described as non- or pre-cancerous; in 1993, he had a shoulder injury after he tripped on a carpet; in 1994, he had a partial hip replacement after he broke his thighbone in a bathroom fall; in 1996 he had an appendectomy and was diagnosed with Parkinson's disease.

After his election, he had answered the complaints of some in the Vatican about the costs of building a swimming pool at Castel Gandolfo. He responded that the pool was cheaper than a new conclave! Into his seventies he still cut a graceful figure as a skier and kept up an exhausting pace, wearying his younger associates. As John Paul exhibited more signs of deterioration, however, there was speculation about what attributes the next pope should have. Rumors circulated that he turned over the managerial responsibilities to three senior cardinals Ratzinger, Secretary of State Angelo Sodano, and Giovanni Baptista Re, prefect for the Congregation of Bishops. As his Parkinson's disease became more serious, he considered resigning, but wondered how could a father resign? Usually the pattern of papal conclaves was to tilt to the other side—but this pope was a philosopher, a poet, a theologian, a pastor, and a diplomat. Which was the path to the future? The *New York Times* laid out a list of cardinals who were probable "papable," and those individuals characteristically praised the pontiff and celebrated his good health. As for John Paul, he insisted that with God's permission he would lead the Church into the third millennium, the beginning of a new time of the faith coming under the aegis of the Slavic pope. It seemed his destiny.

Since he was young he had been seen as a special, but never a pampered child. His uniqueness came from a real and true sense that he was a survivor of a family that died around him, of a genocidal war and brutal occupation, of youthful accidents, of Communist terror and intermittent persecution, of a near assassination. Whatever he tried his hand at, he had succeeded brilliantly. Popes rarely come to that office with such a record of genuine achievements, especially from a far-off nation. Apologists of the pope saw his election as a special sign of the Holy Ghost's inspiration for a Church in crisis.

Once there he seemed clear on his agenda, but at times even he appeared to have reservations that the conservatives were too willing to write off large segments of Catholics for a leaner, more militant Church. He preferred exhortation and example, and in those regards he had no peer. And he must have been weary of the ways of restoration himself. In fact at times his efforts were remarkably innovative and unpredictable. He made special efforts to reach out to Jews, Muslims, Anglicans, Lutherans, and especially the Orthodox Christians—showing that he was in many ways the heir to John XXIII and Paul VI. His Assisi meetings with religious of many faiths and sentiments were the most graphic testimony to those sympathies.

Despite his views on an exclusive male priesthood, the pope apologized to women for past slights. Indeed, as part of the new millennium celebrations, he delivered a series of apologies for the sins committed by members of his Church in the past centuries. It has been estimated that over the years, he issued some ninety-four apologies for the transgressions associatated with the Church. Some of those initiatives were poorly received by some of the College of Cardinals, but it is an extraordinary step by any pope. The pontiff observed, "The Church too must make an independent review of the darker side of its history."

On a personal level, Wojtyla was a man known for being mild-mannered, remarkably charitable, and almost nonjudgmental of people and their failings. He was uninterested in material possessions, including his own clothes, almost to the embarrassment of his friends. His companions were his books, his world ideas, and he was above all a skilled listener. The burdens of the papacy turned him into a very different symbol for millions. John Paul II will never be called "the good Pope John." He will be enshrined as a charismatic and formidable reactionary figure who began in earnest the process of reining in the Church and spurning the excesses of the modern world. He will be seen as having turned away from the spirit of Vatican II, while repeating the expressions of its rambling documents and religious cliches.

As noted, millions disliked the message, but they still loved the messenger. *Time* magazine, one of the major props of the superficial communications revolution in the United States, in 1995 named him the "Man of the Year." Why?—because it said he had the courage of his convictions in a world in which such a characteristic was rare. He was not a deal maker, an equivocator, an old time Vatican diplomat. He proclaimed to all, "We must never separate ourselves from the Cross. Never."[114] Although he must have had his own doubts at times, he insisted on protecting the traditional doctrines of his Church and of his right as pope to exercise its *magisterium*, its teaching responsibilities. His message was the same as the one he proclaimed at his instillation—*Non abbiate paura*. "Be not afraid." It was to be the hallmark, not just of his pontificate, but of his entire extraordinary life.

As he grew older and his disease advanced, John Paul became increasingly unable to do the simplest of duties, even blessing his beloved people. Still he did not resign. His admirers said that he had taught us how to live, and now in front of us he was showing us how to die. And so on the eve of the feast of Divine Mercy Sunday, this strong advocate of the mystic St. Faustina of Poland, went as he asked—to the Mansion of the Father. The huge crowds outside his window cried out that he should be declared by acclamation a saint, and that he was "John Paul the Great." In 2014, he was indeed declared a saint.

CONCLUSION

Of the 266 or so popes, we have chosen ten of the most important popes, not necessarily the holiest, in the two-thousand year history of the Roman Catholic papacy. We could easily have chosen some others, and indeed other authors of note have indeed done so. The fine English historian Eaton Duffy has labeled his history of the papacy *Saints and Sinners*, but most popes, even those who were important, were not really saints, that is they did not live lives that the faithful should venerate. The mere exercise of secular power, the making of unseemly alliances, and the humiliation of enemies do not characterize men of grace. But their actions have been important to develop and protect the Church as an institution.

What is remarkable is the Church so often takes on the secular characteristics of the world it lives in. The earliest Christian communities were run in many ways like the Jewish synagogues they came out of with their collegial leadership and deep respect for the written word. The established Church since Charlemagne and beyond took on the forms of the Roman bureaucracy and became legalistic, hierarchical, and precedent-driven. When the Roman Empire in the West collapsed, the popes took the place of the secular authorities in providing everything from food to security from the barbarians. It is no coincidence that we have chosen for our cover Pope Leo I who saved Rome by addressing the advancing barbarian chief Attila. For two thousand years, popes have addressed barbarians, especially in the twentieth century.

Popes make mistakes and many have committed major blunders: the refusal to acculturate with the Chinese and Asian ways of life is one of the most consequential. As noted, one can imagine a Latin Christianity side by side with Chinese Christianity. Other examples include the Protestant Reformation which was the product of the abuses of the hierarchy, the rise of the printing press, and the outbreak of nationalism. Before that the Church never recovered from the bereft of priests after the Great Plague, for people related to priests and not popes in their everyday life and death.

The modern Church has become interested in the Third World as the final vestiges of colonialism crumbled. The Church is now a strong presence in the Southern Hemisphere and Asia, funded by the U.S. and Germany congregations, praying in a Roman-originated rite. These ten popes have all had to deal with change, the change of physical environments, changes in democracy, and changes in ideas. After the Enlightenment, the Church was seen as an opponent of science and reason—a far cry from the optimism of Thomas Aquinas' theological work. But while it had its Galileo affair and the silencing of Vico, Tielhard de Chardin, and even John Rock (the father of the birth control bill), it ironically created schools, universities, observatories, hospitals, and staffed them for centuries.

The Catholic Church likes to see itself as one, holy, catholic (universal), and apostolic. But it also insists that doctrine cannot be changed, which of course is historically incorrect. In our own times we have seen the Church's attitudes toward slavery, capital punishment, imperialism, anti-Semitism, fasting on Fridays, participating in interfaith conferences, and even the presence of limbo upended. As John Henry Newman wrote, faith and doctrine develop, and sometimes new paradigms of thought, research, and presentation are reformulated, such that doctrines are indeed reformed. All of these ten popes were both innovators, and deep conservators.

The *magisterium*, "the teaching powers" of the popes and the councils, is not a collection of infallible words and phrases; it is reformulated, rediscovered, and held in the service of the Christ. Our book is not meant to teach theology or to convert souls; it is a historical study in diverse leadership styles in which we seek to find out how these men led a voluntary association of faith.

ENDNOTES

CONCEPT OF PAPAL GREATNESS

1. The third pope called "the Great" was is Nicholas I (440–461).
2. Michael P. Riccards, *Faith and Leadership: The Papacy and the Roman Catholic Church* (Lanham, Md.: Lexington, 2012), chap. 9. The last five popes are explored in this book and in Riccards' book *Vicars of Christ: Popes, Power, and Politics in the Modern World* (New York: Crossroad Books, 1998).
3. Riccards, *Faith and Leadership*, chap. 22.
4. Margaret MacMillan, *The War That Ended the Peace: The Road to 1914* (New York: Random House, 2014).
5. Robert K. Murray and Tim H. Blessing, *Greatness in the White House: Rating the Presidents, from George Washington through Ronald Reagan* (University Park, Pa.: Penn State University Press, 1994).
6. Eamon Duffy, *Ten Popes Who Shook the World* (New Haven: Yale University Press, 2011).
7. Richard McBrien, *Lives of the Popes: The Pontiffs from St. Peter to John Paul* (San Francisco: Harper & Row, 1997).
8. Avery Dulles, *Models of the Churches* (New York: Doubleday, 2000).

CHAPTER ONE

1. J. D. Crossan, *The Historical Jesus* (New York: Harper, 1992); John P. Meir, *A Marginal Jew* (New York: Doubleday, 1991); T. W. Allies, *St. Peter, His Name and His Office* (London: Richardson and Son, 1902); Constant Fouard, *Saint Peter and the First Years of Christianity* (New York: Longmans, Green and Co., 1892); Robert A. King, *A Biography of Saint Simon Peter the Apostle: From Fisherman to Martyr* (Kindle Edition) (NP: King and Associates, 2012); F. B. Meyer, *Peter: Fisherman, Disciple, Apostle* (Kindle Edition) (1919; reprint, NP: Titus Books, 2013); and Louis Duchesne, *Early History of the Christian Church: From its Foundation to the End of the Fifth Century*

(Volume I) (Kindle Edition) (1909; reprint, NP: Lex De Leon Publishing, 2013).
2. John 1:35–42.
3. Mark 1:16–18.
4. John 21:17.
5. Luke 5:1–11.
6. Matt. 16:1, Luke 9:21.
7. Michael Grant, *St. Peter: A Biography* (New York: Scribner, 1994), chap. 7.
8. Ibid.
9. Ibid., p. 69.
10. Matt. 16:17–19.
11. Grant, *St. Peter*, chap. 6.
12. John 2:7; 20:2–7.
13. Acts 15:25.
14. Galacians, 12:9.
15. Acts 15:7; 9:32–36; 10:5.
16. Bart Ehrman, *Peter, Paul, Mary Magdalene: The Followers of Jesus in History and Legend* (New York: Oxford, 2006). See also: Karen Armstrong, *St. Paul, the Apostle We Love to Hate* (Boston: Houghton Mifflin, 2015).
17. Acts 15:20.
18. Grant, *St. Peter*, chap. 13.
19. Acts 2:1–13, 214–41.

CHAPTER TWO
1. Bernard Green, *The Soteriology of Leo I* (New York: Oxford University Press, 2008), p. 10; Michael J. Walsh, *The Popes: Fifty Extraordinary Occupants of the Throne of St. Peter* (New York: Metro, 2013), pp. 28–31; and Susan Wessel, *Leo the Great and the Spiritual Rebuilding of a Universal Rome* (Boston: Brill, 2008).
2. Green, *Soteriology*, p. 7; Eamon Duffy, *Saints and Sinners: A History of the Popes* (New Haven: Yale University Press), pp. 33–36, with a copy of the beautiful bas–relief by Alessandro Algardi, "The Meeting of Leo the Great and Attila," p. 35.
3. Green, *Soteriology*, p. 3.
4. Trevor Julland, *The Life and Times of St. Leo the Great* (London: SPCK, 1941), pp. 48–49.
5. Julland, *Leo*, p. 53.
6. Ibid., p. 75.

7. Ibid., p. 99.
8. John Julius Norwich, *Absolute Monarchs: A History of the Papacy* (New York: Random House, 2011), pp. 232–36. Green, *Soteriology*, pp. 252, 293.
9. Julland, *Leo*, p. 298.
10. Ibid., p. 332.
11. Richard McBrien, *Lives of the Popes: The Pontiffs from St. Peter to John Paul* (San Francisco: Harper & Row, 1997), pp. 75–77; Julland, *Leo*, p. 358.
12. Ibid., passim.
13. Julland, *Leo*, p. 465.

CHAPTER THREE

1. Eamon Duffy, *Saints and Sinners: A History of the Popes* (New Haven: Yale University Press), p. 46; and R. A. Markus, *Gregory the Great and His World* (New York: Cambridge University Press, 1997).
2. Jeffrey Richards, *Consul of God: The Life and Times of Gregory the Great* (London: Routledge & Kegan Paul, 1980).
3. Michael J. Walsh, *The Popes: Fifty Extraordinary Occupants of the Throne of St. Peter* (New York: Metro, 2013), p. 19; Pope Damasus (366–84) was the major promotor of the cult of saints and martyrs.
4. Richards, *Consul of God*, pp. 23–28; Carole Straw, *Gregory the Great: Perfection in Imperfection* (Berkeley: University of California Press, 1988).
5. Richard McBrien, *Lifes of the Popes: The Pontiffs from St. Peter to John Paul* (San Francisco: Harper & Row, 1997), 96–98.
6. Richards, *Consul of God*, pp. 33, 49–50.
7. Ibid., p. 68.
8. Ibid., p. 80.
9. Ibid., pp. 87–89.
10. Ibid., p. 136; Michael P. Riccards, *Faith and Leadership: The Papacy and the Roman Catholic Church* (Lanham, Md.: Lexington, 2012); George E. Demacopoulos, *Gregory the Great: Ascetic, Pastor and First Man of Rome* (South Bend: Notre Dame University Press, 2015; Peter Brown, *Through the Eye of a Needle: Wealth, the Fall of Rome, and the Making of Christianity in the West, 350–550 AD* (Princeton: Princeton University Press, 2015.)

11. Richards, *Consul of God*, p. 197; Riccards, *Faith and Leadership*, p. 44.
12. Richards, *Consul of God*, p. 216.
13. John Julius Norwich, *Absolute Monarchs: A History of the Papacy* (New York: Random House, 2011), chap. 4.

CHAPTER FOUR
1. Arnold H. Mathew, *The Life and Times of Hildebrand, Pope Gregory VII* (London: Francis Grifiths, 1910); Glenn W. Olsen, *Beginning at Jerusalem: Five Reflections on the History of the Church* (San Francisco: Ignatius Press, 2004), chap. 2; H. E. J. Cowdrey, *Pope Gregory VII, 1073-1085* (New York: Oxford University Press, 1998); I.S. Robinson, *The Papal Reform of the Eleventh Century: Lives of Pope Leo IX and Pope Gregory VII* (New York: Manchester University Press, 2004); and Uta-Renate Blumenthal, *The Investiture Controversy: Church and Monarchy from the Ninth to the Twelfth Century* (Philadelphia: University of Pennsylvania Press, 1988), chap. 4.
2. Michael J. Walsh, *The Popes: Fifty Extraordinary Occupants of the Throne of St. Peter* (New York: Metro, 2013), pp. 88–89.
3. Eamon Duffy, *Saints and Sinners: A History of the Popes* (New Haven: Yale University Press), pp. 144–51.
4. Mathew, *Hildebrand*, p. 70.
5. John J. O'Malley, *A History of the Popes: From Peter to the Present* (Lanham, Md.: Sheed & Ward, 2010), pp. 89, 110, 122.
6. Mathew, *Hildebrand*, pp. 72–75; Richard McBrien, *Lives of the Popes: The Pontiffs from St. Peter to John Paul* (San Francisco: Harper & Row, 1997), p. 187.
7. Mathew, *Hildebrand*, pp. 77–81; McBrien, *Lives of the Popes*, pp. 87–93.
8. Mathew, *Hildebrand*, p. 87.
9. O'Malley, *History of the Popes*, p. 191.
10. Bernard Schimmelpfennig, *The Papacy* (New York: Columbia University, 1992); Norman Cantor, *The Civilization of the Middle Ages: A Completely Revised and Expanded Edition of Medieval History, the Life and Death of a Civilization* (New York: HarperCollins, 1993).
11. Mathew, *Hildebrand*, p. 117.
12. Schimmelpfennig, *The Papacy*, chap. 6.

13. Mathew, *Hildebrand*, pp. 192, 112.
14. John Julius Norwich, *Absolute Monarchs: A History of the Papacy* (New York: Random House, 2011), p. 106.
15. Ibid.; Mathew, *Hildebrand*, p. 231.
16. Michael P. Riccards, *Faith and Leadership: The Papacy and the Roman Catholic Church* (Lanham, Md.: Lexington, 2012), p. 66.
17. O'Malley, *History of the Popes*, chap. 11.

CHAPTER FIVE
1. Leonard Elliott–Binns, *Innocent III* (Hamden, Conn: Archon, 1968); John B. Pearson, *Pope Innocent III* ([Cambridge, England]: printed for private circulation, 1911); Kenneth Pennington, "The Legal Education of Pope Innocent III," *Bulletin of Medieval Canon Law*, 4 (1974), pp. 70–77; Maria L. Taylor, "The Election of Innocent III," in *The Church and Sovereignty c. 590–1918: Essays in Honour of Michael Wilks*, ed. Diana Wood, (London: Basil Blackwell, 1991), pp. 97–112; and Helene Tillmann, *Pope Innocent III* (New York: North Holland Publishing Co., 1980).
2. *Innocent III: Vicar of Christ or Lord of the World?*, ed. James M. Powell, 2nd ed. (Washington, D. C. Catholic University Press, 1994); Horace K. Mann, *The Lives of the Popes in the Middle Ages* (London: Kegan Paul,Trech, Trubner & Co., 1925), vols. 11 and 12; and C. H. C. Pirie–Gordon, *Innocent The Great: An Essay on His Life* (New York: Longmans, Green and Co., 1907).
3. Hans–Georg Beck, *From the High Middle Ages to the Eve of Reformation* (New York: Crossroad, 1986); Joseph Clayton, *Pope Innocent III and His Times* (Milwaukee: Bruce Publishing Co., 1941); Ferdinand Gregorovius, *History of the City of Rome in the Middle Ages* (London: George Bell & Sons, 1897) vol. 5, part 1.
4. Kenneth Pennington, *Pope and Bishops: The Papal Monarch in the Twelfth and Thirteenth Centuries* (Philadelphia: University of Pennsylvania Press, 1984); Donald E. Queller, *The Fourth Crusade: The Conquest of Constantinople, 1201–1204* (Philadelphia: University of Pennsylvania Press, 1977); and Brian Tierney, "The Continuity of Papal Political Theory in the Thirteenth Century," *Medieval Studies*, 27 (1965), pp. 227–245.

5. Brian Tierney, "Tria Quippe Distinguit Iudicia. . ." *Speculum* XXXVII (1962), pp. 48–59.
6. Kenneth Pennington, *Popes, Canonists and Texts 1150–1550* (Brookfield, VT: Variorum, 1993); I. S. Robinson, *The Papacy, 1073–1198: Continuity and Innovation* (New York: Cambridge University Press, 1990); Daniel Waley, *The Papal State in the Thirteenth Century* (New York: Macmillan, 1961); and J. A. Watt, "The Theory of Papal Monarchy in the Thirteenth Century: The Contribution of the Canonists," *Traditio*, ed. Stephan Kuttar et. al. (New York: Fordham University Press, 1964), pp. 179–318.
7. Penny J. Cole, *The Preaching of the Crusades to the Holy Land, 1095–1270* (Cambridge, Mass.: Medieval Academy of America, 1991); John Jay Hughes, *Pontiffs: Popes Who Shaped History* (Huntington, Indiana: Our Sunday Visitor, 1994), chapters 4 and 5; Elizabeth Kennan, "Innocent III and the First Political Crusade," *Traditio*, 27 (1971), pp. 231–49; Stephan Kuttner and Antonio Garcia y Garcia, "A New Eyewitness Accounting of the Fourth Lateran Council," *Traditio*, 2 (1964), pp 115–178; Jane Sayers, *Innocent III: Leader of Europe 1198–1216* (New York: Longman, 1994) Joseph R. Strayer, *The Albigensian Crusades* (Ann Arbor: The University of Michigan Press, 1971); and D. P. Waley, "Papal Armies in the Thirteenth Century," *English Historical Review*, 72 (January 1917), pp. 1–30.
8. Colin Morris, *The Papal Monarchy: The Western Church from 1050 to 1250* (Oxford: Clarendon Press, 1989). Sidney R. Packard, *Europe and the Church under Innocent III*, rev. ed. (New York: Russell and Russell, 1968); Phyllis B. Roberts, "The Pope and the Preachers," in *The Religious Roles of the Papacy: Ideas and Realities 1150–1300*, ed. Christopher Ryan (Toronto: Pontifical Institute of Medieval Studium, 1989), pp. 277–297; Joseph R. Strayer, *Western Europe in the Middle Ages* (New York: Appleton–Century–Crofts, 1955); and James Ross Sweeney, "Innocent III, Hungary and the Bulgarian Coronation: A Study in Medieval Papal Diplomacy," *Church History*, 42 (1973), pp. 320–324.
9. Francis S. Betten, "A Justification of Innocent III," *Catholic Historical Review* 16 (July 1930), pp. 145–163; Christopher R. Cheney, *Pope Innocent III and England* (Stuttgart: Anton Hiersemann, 1976). Kenneth Pennington, "Pope Innocent III's Views on Church and State: A Gloss to *Per Venerabilem"* in

Law, Church and Society, ed. Kenneth Pennington and Robert Somerville (Philadelphia: University of Pennsylvania Press, 1977), pp. 49–67; *Selected Letters of Pope Innocent III concerning England (1198–1216)* (New York: Thomas Nelson and Sons, 1953); and Charles Edward Smith, *Innocent III, Church Defender* (Baton Rouge: Louisiana State University Press, 1951).

10. Brenda Bolton, "Innocent III's Treatment of the Humiliati," *Studies in Church History, 8* (1971), pp 73–82.
11. Brenda Bolton, "Too Important to Neglect: The Gesta Innocentii PP III," in *Church and Chronicle in the Middle Ages*, ed. Jan Wood and G. A. Loud (London: Hambledon Press,1991), pp. 87–99; David Richard Gress–Wright, *The Gesta Innocentii III: Text, Introduction and Commentary* (Ph.D. dissertation, Bryn Mawr College, 1981).

CHAPTER SIX

1. Karl Otmar von Aretin, *The Papacy and the Modern World* (New York: McGraw Hill, 1970), pp. 78–79; E. E. Y. Hales, *Revolution and Papacy, 1769–1846* (London: Eyre and Spottiswoode, 1960); John Martin Robinson, *Cardinal Conslavi, 1737–1824* (New York: St. Martin's Press, 1987), introduction.
2. The long criticism is in E. L. Woodward, "The Diplomacy of the Vatican Under Popes Pius IX and Leo XIII," *Journal of the British Institute of International Affairs*, 3 (May 1924) p. 121.
3. J. Derek Holmes, *The Triumph of the Holy See* (Shepherdstown, W. Va.: Patmos Press, 1978), pp. 101–102. One profile of Metternich is in E. L. Woodward, *Three Studies in European Conservatism* (London: Constable & Co., 1929) part one.
4. E. L. Woodward, "The Diplomacy," op. cit. E. E. Y. Hales, *Pio Nono: A Study in European Politics and Religion in the Nineteenth Century* (New York: P. J. Kenedy, 1954), p. 27.
5. G. F.–H. & J. Berkeley, *Italy in the Making* (Cambridge: Cambridge University Press, 1968), vol. 3, p. 3.
6. Ibid.
7. Friedrich Nippold, *The Papacy in the 19th Century* (New York: G.P. Putnam's Sons, 1900), pp. 23–28; J. B. Bury, *History of the Papacy in the 19th Century; Liberty and Authority in the Roman Catholic Church*, aug. ed. (New York: Schocken, 1964); Martin, *Cardinal Conslavi*, passim.
8. Nippold, *The Papacy*, pp. 53–55; Burg, *History of the Papacy*,

op. cit.
9. Hales, *Pio Nono*, pp. 60–63.
10. Ibid.
11. Denis Mack Smith, *Mazzini* (New Haven: Yale University Press, 1994).
12. Hales, *Pio Nono*, pp. 67–68.
13. Ibid., p. 71.
14. Ibid., p. 90.
15. Nippold, *Papacy*, p. 102.
16. Denis Mack Smith, *Cavour* (New York: Knopf, 1985); William Roscoe Thayer, *The Life and Times of Cavour*, 2 vols. (Boston: Houghton, Mifflin Co., 1911).
17. Hales, *Pio Nono*, p. 121.
18. Ibid., p. 158–62; David I. Kertzer, *The Kidnapping of Edgardo Mortara* (New York: Vintage, 1997)
19. Smith, *Cavour*, pp. 78–79. The background on the marriage is in Smith, *Cavour*, pp. 142–43, and Thayer, *Cavour*, vol. 1, pp. 531–32.
20. Hales, *Pio Nono*, pp. 178 and xii.
21. Ibid., pp. 199–202.
22. Ibid., p. 206–11.
23. Ibid., p. 227.
24. Ibid., p. 244.
25. Ibid., p. 252.
26. Ibid., pp. 256–58.
27. Ibid., p. 261
28. Emil Ludwig, *Bismarck, the Story of a Fighter* (New York: Blue Ribbon Books, 1927), pp. 412–22; Otto Pflanze, *Bismarck and the Development of Germany*, vol. 2 (Princeton: Princeton University Press, 1990), chap. 7.
29. Hales, *Pio Nono*, pp. 137–48; Kelly, *Oxford Dictionary*, p. 310.
30. Hales, *Pio Nono*, p. 278; forty five French bishops were absent when the vote on papal infallibility came up: see McManners, *Church and State in France*, p. 1.
31. Hales, *Pio Pino*, pp. 290–95; Nippold, *Papacy*, p. 155; August Bernard Hasler, *How the Pope Became Infallible* (New York: Doubleday, 1981); David I. Kertzer, *Prisoner of the Vatican* (Boston: Houghton Mifflin, 2004).
32. Nippold, *Papacy*, p. 159–161; Johann Joseph Ignor von Döllinger, *Letters From Rome on the Council by Quirinus*, 2 vols. (New York: DaCapo Press, 1973); Wilfred Ward, *The*

Life and The Times of Cardinal Wiseman, 2 vols. (New York: Longmans Green and Co., 1900), chap. 30; *The Roman Question: Extracts from the Dispatches of Olo Russell from Rome, 1858–1870*, ed. Noel Blakiston (London: Chapman and Hall, 1962).

33. Hales, *Pio Nono*, pp. 299–306; Edward Cuthbert Butler, *The Vatican Council, 1869–1870, Based on Bishop Ullathorne's Letters* (Westminster, Md.: The Newman Press, 1962).
34. Hales, *Pio Nono*, pp. 320–21, and Pflanze, *Bismarck*, chap. 7.

CHAPTER SEVEN

1. Joseph E. Keller, *The Life and Acts of Pope Leo XIII* (New York: Benziger Brothers, 1879); Eduardo Soderini, *The Pontificate of Leo XIII* (London: Burns, Oates and Washbourne, 1934), vol. 1, chap. 1–3; William J. Kiefer, *Leo XIII: A Light from Heaven* (Milwaukee: Bruce Publishing Company, 1961); Justin McCarthy, *Pope Leo XIII* (New York: Frederick Warne & Co., 1896). Hartwell dela Garde Grissell, *Sede Vacante: Being a Diary Written during the Conclave of 1903 ...* (London: James Parker and Co., 1903), p. 2, argues incorrectly that there is no ceremony of striking the dead pope's forehead.
2. Rene Fülöp–Miller, *Leo XIII and Our Times* (New York: Longmans, Green and Co., 1937), pp. 53–54.
3. Those observations are in Fülöp–Miller, *Leo XIII*, pp. 56–60.
4. "Leo XIII," *The New Catholic Encyclopedia* (New York: McGraw–Hill, 1967), vol. 8, pp. 647–49.
5. Soderini, *Leo XIII*, vol. 1, pp. 71–72.
6. Ibid., p. 81.
7. Lillian Parker Wallace, *Leo XIII and the Rise of Socialism* (Durham, N.C.: Duke University Press, 1966), p. 80.
8. Ibid., p. 74.
9. Ibid., p. 87; Eduardo Soderini, *Leo XIII, Italy and France* (London: Burns, Oates and Washburne, 1935), part 1.
10. Soderini, *The Pontificate of Leo XIII*, pp. 108–09, 151; on Pius IX, see: Fülöp–Miller, *Leo XIII*, p. 82.
11. Ibid., pp. 113–20; *Leo XIII and the Modern World*, ed. Edward T. Gargan (New York: Sheed and Ward, 1961), frontpiece.
12. Otto Pflanze, *Bismarck and the Development of Germany*, vol. 2 (Princeton: Princeton University Press, 1990), passim; Lillian Parker Wallace, *The Papacy and European Diplomacy, 1869–1878* (Chapel Hill: University of North

13. H. W. L. Freudenthal, "Kulturkampf," *The Catholic Encyclopedia*, vol. 8, pp. 167–69; Wallace, *Leo XIII and the Rise of Socialism*, p. 131.
14. Soderini, *Leo XIII Italy and France*, part 1; S. William Halperin, "Leo XIII and the Roman Question," in *Leo XIII and the Modern World*, pp. 101–126; Humphrey Johnson, *The Papacy and the Kingdom of Italy* (London: Sheed and Ward, 1926), chap. 3; and S. William Halperin, "Italian Anti–Clericalism 1871–1914," *Journal of Modern History*, 19 (March–December 1947), pp. 18–34.
15. Bismarck's award is discussed in Wallace, *Leo XIII and the Rise of Socialism*, p. 134; Halperin, "Leo XIII and the Roman Question," p. 117; Francesco Crispi, *The Memoirs of Francesco Crispi* (New York: Hodder and Stoughton, 1912), vol. 2, pp. 393–94; Arturo Carlo Jemolo, *Church and State in Italy 1850–1950* (Oxford: Basil Blackwell, 1960), chap. 3; S. William Halperin, *The Separation of Church and State in Italian Thought from Cavour to Mussolini* (New York: Octagon Books, 1965); and Wallace, *Leo XIII and the Rise of Socialism*, p. 17. Between 1881 and 1891, Leo contacted the governments of Austria and Spain at least five times about leaving Rome. See: Philip Hughes, *Pope Pius the Eleventh* (New York: Sheed and Ward, 1937), p. 56.
16. Eric McDermott, S.J., "Leo XIII and England," in *Leo XIII and the Modern World*, pp. 127–58.
17. Ibid., p. 131.
18. Ibid., p. 136.
19. Ibid., passim, and John Jay Hughes, *Absolutely Null and Utterly Void* (Washington: Corpus Book, 1968).
20. Wallace, *Leo XII and the Rise of Socialism*, pp. 66–67, 103.
21. Ibid., p. 286; Soderini, *Leo XII, Italy and France*, part 2.
22. Wallace, *Leo XIII and the Rise of Socialism*, pp. 291–300; Soderini, *Leo XIII, Italy and France*, part 2; John McManners, *Church and State in France, 1870–1914* (New York: Harper and Row, 1972).
23. Halperin, "Leo XIII and the Roman Question," pp. 108–09; John J. Robinson, *Born in Blood: The Lost Secrets of Freemasonry* (New York: M. Evans and Co., 1989) on the Freemasons as heirs to the Knights Templar.
24. J. N. D. Kelly, *The Oxford Dictionary of Popes* (New York: Oxford University Press, 1986), pp. 311–13; *The Civitas*

Leonina refers to the area surrounded by a strong wall in the neighborhood of the Vatican and St. Peter's as far as the Castel Sant' Angelo, on the right side of the Tiber. Toward the middle of the ninth century Leo IV had enclosed that area, and it was a separate administrative unit until Sixtus V incorporated the district at the end of the sixteenth century as the fourteenth "rione," called Borgo. See: Daniel A. Binchy, *Church and State in Fascist Italy* (Oxford: Oxford University Press, 1941), pp. 256 and E. R. Chamberlain, *The Bad Popes* (New York: Barnes and Noble, 1969), pp. 8–9.

25. Thomas C. McAvoy, "Leo XIII and America," in *Leo XIII and the Modern World*, pp. 157–80.

26. Ibid., pp. 163–63. Robinson, *Born in Blood* argues that the Masons are the heirs of the Knights Templar in Britain who fled arrest and torture mandated by Pope Clement V and the King. They became a secret society of mutual protection that attracted great revolutionaries such as George Washington, Sam Houston, Giuseppi Garibaldi, and Simon Bolivar. See especially on Leo, pp. 307–11 and 345–59. This book has been called to my attention by Michael Nugent of the IBEW, Washington, D.C.

27. Especially informative on Leo's thoughts in this area are articles by John Courtney Murray, "Leo XIII on Church and State: The General Structure of the Controversy," *Theological Studies*, 14 (1953), pp. 1–30; "Leo XIII: Two Concepts of Government," *Theological Studies*, 14 (1953), pp. 551–567; and "Leo XIII: Two Concepts of Government, II. Government and the Order of Culture," *Theological Studies*, vol. XV, 1954, pp. 1–33.

28. Ray Allen Billington, *The Protestant Crusade, 1800–1860: A Study in the Origins of American Nativism* (New York: McMillan, 1938); J. P. Dolan, *The American Catholic Experience: A History from Colonial Times to the Present* (New York: Doubleday & Co., 1985).

29. Thomas T. McAvoy, *The Great Crisis in American Catholic History, 1895–1900* (Chicago: H. Regnery, 1957); Henry J. Browne, *The Catholic Church and the Knights of Labor* (New York: Arno Books, 1976).

30. Marvin R. O'Connell, *John Ireland and the American Catholic Church* (St. Paul: Minnesota Historical Society Press, 1988), chap. 13–16.

31. Ibid; McAvoy, "Leo XIII and America," passim; John Tracy

Ellis, *The Life of James Cardinal Gibbons* (Milwaukee: The Bruce Publishing Co., 1952), vol. 2, chap. 16 is on "Americanism"; James Gibbons, *A Retrospective of Fifty Years* (New York: Arno Press, 1972).

32. Quote is from O'Connell, *John Ireland*, pp. 462–63; John C. Fenton, "The Teachings of the Testem Benevolentiae," *American Ecclesiastical Review*, 129 (1953), pp. 124–33. The full text is an appendix in McAvoy, *The Great Crisis*.

33. McAvoy, "Leo XIII and America," p. 176. On one of the consequences of the development of the Catholic Church in the United States, see: Thomas F. O'Dea, *American Catholic Dilemma* (New York: Sheed and Ward, 1958); and Gerald P. Fogarty, *The Vatican and the American Hierarchy from 1870 to 1965* (Wilmington: Michael Glazier, 1985), pp. 190–94; James M. O'Toole, *Militant and Triumphant: William Henry O'Connell and the Catholic Church in Boston, 1859–1944* (Notre Dame, Ind.: University of Notre Dame Press, 1992), p. 104.

34. Raymond H. Schmandt, "The Life and Work of Leo XIII," in *Leo XIII and the Modern World*, pp. 15–50; Soderini, *Pontificate of Leo XIII*, pp. 130–33.

35. Thomas Bokenkotter, *A Concise History of the Catholic Church*, rev. ed. (New York: Image Books, 1990), pp. 300–301.

36. Wallace, *Leo XIII and the Rise of Socialism*, chap. 7 and 10.

37. *The Papal Encyclicals 1878–1903*,. comp. Claudia Carlen Ihm (Wilmington, N.C.: McGrath Publishing Co., 1981), pp. 241–61. A more convenient edition is *The Church Speaks to the Modern World*, ed. Etienne Gilson (New York: Image Books, 1954), chap. 8.

38. Leo had problems with party rivalries, see: Michael P. Fogarty, *Christian Democracy in Western Europe, 1820–1953* (Notre Dame, Ind.: University of Notre Dame Press, 1957), p. 10. In France the encyclical intensified the Catholic factionalism, see: Parker Thomas Moon, *The Labor Problem and the Social Catholic Movement in France: A Study in the History of Social Politics* (New York: MacMillan Co. 1921) pp. 172–193; the American experience is explored in Aaron I. Abell, "The Reception of Leo XIII's Labor Encyclical in America," *Review of Politics*, 7 (October 1945), pp. 464–95.

39. Wallace, *Leo XIII and the Rise of Socialism*, p. 40; Soderini, *The Pontificate of Leo XIII*, p. 139.

40. Schmandt, "The Life and Work of Leo XIII," p. 19; a more critical judgment of Leo than mine is in E. L. Woodward, "Diplomacy of the Vatican under Popes Pius IX and Leo XIII," *Journal of British Institute of International Affairs*, vol. 3 (May 1924), pp. 113–38.
41. Carlo Falconi, *The Popes in the Twentieth Century, from Pius X to John XXIII* (Boston: Little, Brown and Company, 1967), p. 2.

CHAPTER EIGHT

1. On Pius X's preoccupation with internal affairs, see Carlo Falconi, *The Popes in the Twentieth Century* (Boston: Little Brown, 1967), p. 91. Also of interest is Humphrey Johnson, *Vatican Diplomacy in the World War* (Oxford: Basil Blackwell, 1933), pp. 8–10 and John F. Pollard, *Benedict XV: The Unknown Pope and the Pursuit of Peace* (London: Burns and Oates, 2005). My note on the origins of the family name is from William Barry, "Benedict XV: Pontiff of Peace," *Dublin Review*, 170 (April–June, 1922), p. 162. The French press at first celebrated Cardinal Della Chiesa's alleged Francophile tendencies.
2. Henry E. G. Rope, *Benedict XV, The Pope of Peace* (London: John Gifford, 1941), Book 1. The Consalvi quote is on page 33; J. Van den Heuvel, *The Statesmanship of Benedict XV* (New York: Benziger Bros., 1923), pp. 16–17. A more recent discussion of the same topic is John F. Polland, *Benedict XV: The Unknown Pope and the Pursuit of Peace* (London: Burns and Oates, 2005).
3. Walter H. Peters, *The Life of Benedict XV* (Milwaukee: The Bruce Publishing Co., 1959), pp. 32–35.
4. Rope, *Benedict XV*, p. 30.
5. Peters, *Life of Benedict XV*, p. 39.
6. Rope, *Benedict, XV*, p. 43.
7. Barry, "Benedict XV," p. 164; Peters, *Life of Benedict XV*, pp. 45–48; Falconi, *Popes in the Twentieth Century*, p. 100 on quasi–secular Catholic journalism.
8. Peters, *Life of Benedict XV*, p. 68; William Henry O'Connell, *Recollections of Seventy Years* (Boston: Houghton Mifflin, 1934), pp. 341–42.
9. Peters, *Life of Benedict XV*, pp. 75–83; William Teeling, *Pope Pius XI and World Affairs* (New York: Frederick A. Stokes, 1937), p. 93. Published also under the title: *The Pope in*

Politics (London: Lovat Dickson, 1937).
10. Peters, *Life of Benedict XV*, pp. 90–92.
11. Ibid., p. 101.
12. Arturo Carlo Jemolo, *Church and State in Italy, 1850–1950* (Oxford: Basil Blackwell, 1960), p. 103.
13. *The Papal Encyclicals, 1903–1939*, comp. Claudia Carlen Ihm (Wilmington, N.C.: McGrath Publishing Co., 1981), vol. 3, pp. 143–151. Also of use is *His Holiness Pope Benedict XV on the Great War*, ed. Gabriel Martyn (London: Burns & Oates, 1916); and Falconi, *Popes of the Twentieth Century*, p. 115.
14. The origins and extent of World War I is taken in abbreviated form from my book, *The Ferocious Engine of Democracy* (Lanham, MD: Madison Books, 1995), vol. 2, pp. 64–68. The sources are: A. J. P. Taylor, *Illustrated History of the First World War* (New York: G. P. Putnam's Sons, 1964); Keith Robbins, *The First World War* (New York: Oxford University Press, 1985); Winston S. Churchill, *The Unknown War: The Eastern Front* (New York: Charles Scribner's Sons, 1931); George F. Kennan, *The Fateful Alliance* (New York: Pantheon, 1984); Norman Stone, *The Eastern Front, 1914–1917* (New York: Charles Scribner's, 1975); Denna F. Fleming, *The Origins and Legacies of World War I* (New York: Doubleday, 1968); Fritz Fischer, *Germany's Aims in the First World War* (New York: W. W. Norton, 1967); Graydon A. Tunstall, Jr., *Planning for War against Russia and Serbia: Austro–Hungarian and German Military Strategies, 1871–1914* (New York: Columbia University Press, 1993); John M. Blum, *Woodrow Wilson and the Politics of Morality* (Boston: Little, Brown, 1956); Sidney B. Fay, *The Origins of the World War* (New York: MacMillan, 1930); and Patrick Devlin, *Too Proud to Fight: Woodrow Wilson's Neutrality* (New York: Oxford University Press, 1975).
15. Robert Dell, "The Vatican and the War," *Fortnightly Review*, 103 (February 1915), pp. 286–95.
16. Peters, *Life of Benedict XV*, p. 113.
17. Ibid., p. 114; Denis Gwynn, *The Vatican and the War in Europe* (London: Burns, Oates and Washbourne, [1940], chap. 2, 3, 4.
18. Peters, *Life of Benedict XV*, p. 115; Henry L. Dubly, *The Life of Cardinal Mercier, Primate of Belgium* (London: Sands &

Co., 1928), part II; Augusta Pierre Lavielle, *A Life of Cardinal Mercier* (New York: Century Co., 1928), chap. 7, 8, 9.
19. Van den Heuvel, *The Statesmanship of Benedict XV*, p. 33.
20. Peters, *Life of Benedict XV*, p. 121.
21. Jemolo, *Church and State in Italy*, p. 163.
22. Denis Mack Smith, *Mussolini* (New York: Knopf, 1982), chap. 3; Martin Clark, *Modern Italy 1871–1982* (London: Longman, 1984), chap. 9.
23. Peters, *Life of Benedict XV*, pp. 127–38.
24. Johnson, *Vatican Diplomacy*, p. 18, 36; Clark, *Modern Italy*, p. 182.
25. Johnson, *Vatican Diplomacy*, pp. 20–21.
26. Anthony Brennan, *Pope Benedict XV and the War* (Westminster: P.S. King & Son, 1917), pp. 5–6; see also a summary of Friedrich Ritter von Lama's work in *Peace Action of Pope Benedict XV* (Washington, D.C.: Catholic Association for International Peace, 1936), and Diplomaticus [pseud.], *No Small Stir* (London: Society of SS. Peter & Paul, 1917).
27. Johnson, *Vatican Diplomacy*, pp. 21–21. For a different view see: Algeron Cecil, "Vatican Policy in the Twentieth Century," *Journal of British Institute of International Affairs*, 4 (January 1925), pp. 1–29.
28. Peters, *Life of Benedict XV*, pp. 140–41.
29. Johnson, *Vatican Diplomacy*, pp. 24–25; Peters, *Life of Benedict XV*, p. 143.
30. Peters, *Life of Benedict XV*, pp. 153–47.
31. Rope, *Benedict XV*, pp. 135–44.
32. Ibid., p. 153.
33. The speculations are from Johnson, *Vatican Diplomacy*, chap. 6.
34. Donald A. MacLean, *The Permanent Peace Program of Pope Benedict XV* (New York: Catholic Association for International Peace, 1931), p. 5.
35. Peters, *Life of Benedict XV*, pp. 192–93.
36. Johnson, *Vatican Diplomacy*, pp. 13–19.
37. Peters, *Life of Benedict XV*, pp. 182–85.
38. Ibid., p. 181; Daniel A. Binchy, *Church and State in Fascist Italy* (Oxford: Oxford University Press, 1941), p. 307.,
39. Peers, *Life of Benedict XV*, pp. 169–70, 177.
40. Ibid., pp. 193–94.

41. Clark, *Modern Italy*, p. 189; Peters, *Life of Benedict XV*, p. 195.
42. Peters, *Life of Benedict XV*, pp. 195–96.
43. Ibid., p. 197. On other initiatives toward a variety of ethnic and national groups see: Msgr. Batiffol, "Pope Benedict XV and the Restoration of Unity," *Constructive Quarterly*, 6 (1918), p. 209–25.
44. Philip Hughes, *Pope Pius the Eleventh* (New York: Sheed and Ward, 1937) chap. 3; "Pope Pius XI," *New Catholic Encyclopedia* (New York: McGraw Hill, 1967), vol. 11, pp. 411–14. For a more critical view of Vatican diplomacy during this time, see: Sergio I. Minerbi, *The Vatican and Zionism: Conflict in the Holy Land, 1895–1925* (New York: Oxford University Press, 1990).
45. Tad Szulc, *Pope John Paul II: The Biography* (New York: Scribner, 1995), pp. 13–14.
46. Peters, *Life of Benedict XV*, pp. 228–29.
47. Luigi Albertini, *The Origins of the War of 1914*, 3 vols. (New York: Oxford University Press, 1952–57).

CHAPTER NINE
1. Paul Hoffman, *O Vatican!: A Slightly Wicked View of the Holy See* (New York: Congdon & Weed, 1984), pp. 19–27; Carlo Falconi, *The Popes of the Twentieth Century* (Boston: Little, Brown, 1967), pp. 304–307; Barrett McGurn, *A Reporter Looks at the Vatican* (New York: Coward–McCann, 1962).
2. Francis J. Webber, "Pope Pius XII and the Vatican Council," *American Benedictine Review*, 21, pp. 421–24; William A Purdy, *The Church on the Move: The Characters and Policies of Pius XII and John XXIII* (New York: John Day Co., 1966).
3. Peter Hebblethwaite, *Paul VI, the First Modern Pope* (New York: Paulist Press, 1993), chap. 18.
4. Vittorio Gorresio, *The New Mission of Pope John XXIII* (New York: Funk & Wagnalls, 1970), p. 51. Roncalli was actually baptized Giuseppe Angelo, see Alden Hatch, *A Man Called John; The Life of Pope John XXIII* (New York: Hawthorn Books, 1963), p. 25. The only other patriarchs in the West are the Bishop of Rome and the Bishop of Lisbon.
5. Pope John XXIII, *Journal of a Soul* (New York: McGraw–Hill, 1965); Louis Michaels, *The Stories of Pope John: His Anecdotes and Legends* (Springfield, Ill.: Templegate

6. Richard James Cushing, *Call Me John* (Boston: St. Paul Editions, 1963), passim; Zsolt Aradi, *Pope John XXIII, an Authoritative Biography* (New York: Farrar, Straus and Cudahy, 1959).
7. Lawrence Elliott, *I Will Be Called John: A Biography of Pope John XXIII* (New York: E. P. Dutton, 1973), p. 15.
8. Ibid., p. 16; Meriol Trevor, *Pope John* (New York: Doubleday, 1967), chap. 1.
9. Cushing, *Call Me John*, p. 82; Zsolt Aradi, *John XXIII, Pope of the Council* (London: Burns & Oates, 1961), p. 4; Pope John XXIII, *Pope John XXIII: Letters to His Family* (New York: McGraw–Hill, 1970), p. 4; Ernesto Balducci, *John, "The Transitional Pope"* (New York: McGraw–Hill, 1965).
10. Hatch, *A Man Called John*, p. 47; Elliott, *I Will Be Called John*, p. 21; Giacomo Lercaro and Gabriele De Rosa, *John XXIII: Simpleton or Saint?* (Chicago: Franciscan Herald Press, 1965), part 2.
11. Peter Hebblethwaite, *Pope John XXIII, Shepherd of the Modern World* (Garden City: Doubleday, 1985), p. 54.
12. Hannah Arendt, *Men in Dark Times* (New York: Harcourt, Brace, Jovanovich, 1968), p. 68; E. E. Y. Hales, *Pope John and His Revolution* (London: Catholic Book Club, 1965), part 1; Giancarlo Zizola, *The Utopia of Pope John XXIII* (Maryknoll, N.Y.: Orbis Books, 1978).
13. Elliott, *I Will Be Called John*, p. 92.
14. Hebblethwaite, *Pope John*, pp. 63–78.
15. Hatch, *A Man Called John*, p. 67; Elliott, *I Will Be Called John*, p. 83.
16. Hebblethwaite, *Pope John*, pp. 113–15.
17. Elliott, *I Will Be Called John*, p. 96.
18. Cushing, *Call Me John*, p. 41.
19. Hebblethwaite, *Pope John*, pp. 121–29; Elliott, *I Will Be Called John*, p. 106.
20. Elliott, *I Will Be Called John*, pp. 101–103.
21. Ibid., p. 115; Hebblethwaite, *Pope John*, pp. 138–40.
22. Hebblethwaite, *Pope John*, pp. 133–36; Hebblethwaite, *Paul VI*, p. 104.
23. Hebblethwaite, *Pope John*, p. 143; Leone Algisi, *John the Twenty–third* (London: Catholic Book Club, 1963), chap. 6.
24. Cushing, *Call Me John*, p. 43; Gorresio, *New Mission*, p. 72.
25. Hebblethwaite, *Pope John*, pp. 149–152.

26. Elliott, *I Will Be Called John*, p. 156.
27. Hebblethwaite, *Pope John*, p. 169.
28. Ibid., p. 188.
29. Ibid., p. 195. On the Jews and the Good Friday prayer, see Elliott, *I Will Be Called John*, p. 284.
30. Hatch, *A Man Called John*, p. 126; Pope John XXIII, *Mission to France: 1944–1953* (New York: McGraw–Hill Book Co., 1966).
31. Cushing, *Call Me John*, p. 48; Paul Johnson, *Pope John XXIII* (Boston: Little, Brown, 1974), passim; Hales, *Pope John and the Revolution*, p. 18 claims that the demand was for the removal of thirty–three bishops.
32. Elliott, *I Will Be Called John*, p. 199; Hebblethwaite, *Pope John*, p. 218.
33. Hebblethwaite, *Pope John*, p. 227; Algisi, *John Twenty–third*, chap. 8–10.
34. Hebblethwaite, *Pope John*, p. 238; Algisi, *John Twenty–third*, chap. 11.
35. Hebblethwaite, *Pope John*, p. 249.
36. Hatch, *A Man Called John*, p. 148.
37. Hebblethwaite, *Pope John*, p. 265.
38. Bernard R. Bonnot, *Pope John XXIII, An Astute, Pastoral Leader* (Staten Island, N.Y.: Alba House, 1979), p. 6.
39. Elliott, *I Will Be Called John*, p. 243.
40. Hebblethwaite, *Pope John*, p. 286. A very different and more positive view of Cossa is presented in Nicola Fusco, *John Is His Name; A Survey of the Popes by That Name* (New York: Society of St. Paul, 1959), p. 11.
41. Hebblethwaite, *Pope John*, p. 291; Algisi, *John Twenty–third*, chap. 13.
42. Hebblethwaite, *Pope John*, p. 293.
43. Ibid., pp. 294–300; Michaels, *Stories of Pope John*, p. 61.
44. Cushing, *Call Me John*, p. 58; Elliott, *I Will Be Called John*, p. 272; Ernesto Balducci, *John "the Transitional Pope"* (New York: McGraw Hill, 1965), p. 24; Michaels, *Stories of Pope John*, p. 34.
45. Hebblethwaite, *Pope John*, pp. 310–24; Gorresio, *The New Mission*, chap. 10.
46. Paul I. Murphy, *La Popessa* (New York: Warner Books, 1983), p. 304.
47. Hebblethwaite, *Pope John*, pp. 326–30.
48. Elliott, *I Will Be Called John*, p. 268.

49. Murphy, *La Popessa*, p. 229; Elliott, *I Will Be Called John*, p. 188.
50. Hebblethwaite, *Pope John*, pp. 339–40.
51. Ibid., p. 348.
52. Ibid., p. 350.
53. Ibid., pp. 361–368; Hales, *Pope John and His Revolution*, part 4.
54. Johnson, *Pope John*, pp. 178–79.
55. Hebblethwaite, *Pope John*, pp. 427–28; Gorresio, *The New Mission*, chap. 8.
56. Elliott, *I Will Be Called John*, p. 276.
57. Norman Cousins, *The Improbable Triumvirate: John F. Kennedy, Pope John, Nikita Khrushchev* (New York: W. W. Norton, 1972), passim; Roland Flamini, *Pope, Premier, President: The Cold War Summit That Never Was* (New York: MacMillan, 1980); Michael J. Cimerola, "The Vatican and the Soviet Union: The Impact of Pope John," (M.A. Thesis, George Washington University, 1976).
58. Cushing, *Call Me John*, p. 65; *The Papal Encyclical 1958–1961*, comp. Claudia Carlen Ihm, vol. 5 (Wilmington, N.C.: McGrath Publishing Co., 1981), pp. 107–29; *The Encyclicals and Other Messages of John XXIII* (Washington, D.C.: TPS Press, 1964).
59. Hebblethwaite, *Pope John*, p. 229; Gorresio, *The New Mission*, p. 135.
60. Hebblethwaite, *Pope John*, p. 230; Gorresio, *The New Mission*, chap. 7.
61. *Mater et Magistra*, ed. Donald R. Campion and Eugene K. Culhane (New York: The American Press, 1961); Peter Rega, *John XXIII and the Unity of Man* (Westminster, Md.: The Newman Press, 1966); John F. Cronin, *The Social Teaching of Pope John XXIII* (Milwaukee: Bruce Publishing Co., 1963); Hebblethwaite, *Pope John*, pp. 389, 378; Hales, *Pope John and His Revolution*, part 2.
62. Hebblethwaite, *Pope John*, p. 368.
63. Ibid., p. 270.
64. Ibid., pp. 370–71.
65. Hans Küng, *The Council, Reform and Reunion* (New York: Sheed and Ward, 1961) published originally as *Konzil und Wiedervereingung*. Also see his later *The Council in Action* (New York: Sheed and Ward, 1963); and Robert B. Kaiser, *Pope, Council, and World; The Story of Vatican II* (London:

Burns and Oates, 1963).
66. Gorresio, *The New Mission*, chap. 9, pp. 383–84; Augustin Bea, *The Unity of Christians* (New York: Herder and Herder, 1963), chap. 5 and his *Ecumenism in Focus* (London: Geoffrey Chapman, 1969).
67. Hebblethwaite, *Pope John*, pp. 411–12.
68. Ibid., p. 414.
69. Ibid., p. 416.
70. Gorresio, *The New Mission*, pp. 92–93.
71. Hales, *Pope John and His Revolution*, p. 97.
72. George Bull, *Vatican Politics at the Second Vatican Council 1962* (New York: Oxford University Press, 1966), chap. 1 and 2; Melissa J. Wilde, *Vatican II A Sociological Analysis of Religious Change* (Princeton: Princeton University Press, 2007).
73. Harold Macmillan, *Winds of Change, 1914–1939* (New York: Harper & Row, 1966).
74. The following section on the first session of Vatican II relies heavily on Xavier Rynne, *Letters from Vatican City; Vatican II, First Session, Background and Debates* (New York: Farrar, Straus & Co., 1963). This section draws on pp. 70–71. Also: Hales, *Pope John and His Revolution*, part 3; Henri Fesquet, *The Drama of Vatican II; The Ecumenical Council, June, 1962–December, 1965* (New York: Random House, 1967), pp. 3–102; Bernard Häring, *The Johannine Council, Witness to Destiny* (New York: Herder and Herder, 1963); Carlo Falconi, *Pope John and the Ecumenical Council; A Diary of the Second Vatican Council, September–December 1962* (Cleveland: The World Publishing Company, 1964); Antoine Wenger, *Vatican II: Volume I: The First Session* (Westminster, MD: The Newman Press, 1966).
75. Hebblethwaite, *Pope John*, p. 435.
76. Rynne, *Letters*, pp. 87–97.
77. Ibid., pp. 100–109.
78. Ibid., pp. 114–29. On the Canon of the Mass, see Gorresio, *The New Mission*, p. 287.
79. Rynne, *Letters*, pp. 141–42.
80. Bonnot, *Pope John XXIII*, p. 255.
81. Hebblethwaite, *Pope John*, pp. 450–52; Elliott, *I Will Be Called John*, p. 281; Hatch, *A Man Named John*, p. 247.
82. Rynne, *Letters*, pp. 201–18.
83. Michaels, *Stories of Pope John*, p. 40; *The HarperCollins*

Encyclopedia of Catholicism, ed. Richard P. McBrien (New York: HarperCollins, 1995), p. 710.
84. Hebblethwaite, *Pope John*, p. 448.
85. Gorresio, *The New Mission*, p. 91; Howard Gardner, *Leading Minds: An Anatomy of Leadership* (New York: Basic Books, 1995), chap. 9; Hales, *Pope John and His Revolution*, p. 126; Eugene C. Bianchi, *John XXIII and American Protestants* (Washington, D.C.: Corpus Books, 1968), chap. 6; a more human picture is presented in Curtis Bill Pepper, *An Artist and the Pope* (New York: Grosset & Dunlap, 1968); Loris Capovilla, *The Heart and Mind of John XXIII : His Secretary's Intimate Recollection* (New York: Hawthorn, 1964); Michaels, *The Stories of Pope John XXIII*, passim.
86. Falconi, *Popes from the Twentieth Century*, p. 364.
87. Lercaro and De Rosa, *John XXIII: Simpleton or Saint*, part 1 deals with Roncalli in historical perspective. A critical judgment of the council as a majestic gamble that failed is Malachi Martin, *Three Popes and the Cardinal* (New York: Farrar, Straus and Giroux, 1972).

CHAPTER TEN
1. Francis X. Murphy, *The Papacy Today* (New York: Macmillan, 1981) p. 141.
2. Ibid., chap. 7; Albino Luciani, *Illustrissimi: Letters from John Paul I* (Bedford, England: Mount, 1978); Peter Hebblethwaite, *The Year of Three Popes* (New York: Collins, 1978), chap. 5–9; Andrew Greeley, *The Making of the Popes 1978: The Politics of Intrigue in the Vatican* (Kansas City: Andrews and McMeel, 1979); Malachi Martin, *The Decline and Fall of the Roman Church* (New York: G. P. Putnam's Sons, 1981).
3. Trevor Hall and Kathryn Spink, *Pope John Paul II: A Man & His People* (New York: Exeter, 1985), p. 7; David Remmick, "The Pope in Crisis," *New Yorker*, October 17, 1994, pp. 50–64.
4. Hall, *Pope John Paul II*, p. 8.
5. David A. Yallop, *In God's Name: An Investigation into the Murder of Pope John Paul I* (New York: Random, 1984) and the rejoinder, John Cornwell, *Thief in the Night: The Death of John Paul I* (New York: Viking, 1989).
6. Peter Hebblethwaite, "John Paul I" in *Modern Catholicism: Vatican II and After*, ed. Adrian Hastings (New York:

Oxford University Press, 1991), pp. 444–46.

7. Tad Szulc, *Pope John Paul II: The Biography* (New York: Scribner, 1995), p. 273; Nicholas Cheetham, *Keepers of the Keys: A History of the Popes from St. Peter to John Paul II* (New York: Scribner, 1983), chap. 25; Adam Bujak, *John Paul II* (San Francisco: Ignatius Press, 1992); Jef de Roeck, *John Paul II: The Man from Poland* (London: Geoffrey Chapman, 1979); George Huntson Williams, *The Mind of John Paul II: Origin of His Thought and Action* (New York: Seabury Press, 1981); and Carl Bernstein and Marco Politi, *His Holiness: John Paul II and the Hidden History of Our Time* (New York: Doubleday, 1996). The best biographies in English are George Weigel's, *Witness to Hope: The Biography of Pope John Paul II* (New York: Harper Perennial, 2004) and *The End and the Beginning: Pope John Paul II—The Victory of Freedom, the Last Years, the Legacy* (New York: Doubleday, 2011).

8. Szulc, *Pope John Paul II*, p. 272; Bernstein and Politi, *His Holiness*, pp. 159, 166.

9. Ibid., p. 274.

10. Ibid., p. 141, says that Wojtyla met Padre Pio in the 1940s, but in *The Pope from Poland: An Assessment*, ed. John Whale (London: Collins, 1980), p. 260, the time is placed in the 1960s, and it was predicted by Pio that he would have a short papacy terminated by violence.

11. George Blazynski, *Pope John Paul II: A Man from Poland* (New York: Dell, 1979), p. 3.

12. Peter Hebblethwaite, *Pope John Paul II and the Church* (Kansas City, Mo.: Sheed and Ward, 1995), p. 12; Hall, *Pope John Paul II*, p. 14.

13. Szulc, *Pope John Paul II*, pp. 271–81; Blazynski, *Pope John Paul II*, p. 106.

14. Mieczyslaw Malinski, *Pope John Paul II: The Life of Karol Wojtyla* (New York: Seabury Press, 1979), p. 4.

15. Szulc, *Pope John Paul II*, pp. 79, 283; Blazynski, *Pope John Paul II*, p. 3; Bernstein and Politi, *His Holiness*, p. 370.

16. Szulc, *Pope John Paul II*, pp. 17, 117; John Paul II, *"Be Not Afraid": John Paul II Speaks Out on His Life, His Beliefs, and His Inspiring Vision for Humanity* (New York St. Martin's Press, 1984), pp. 13–14; Blazynski, *Pope John Paul II*, p. 33 indicates that his mother died of a heart ailment; while Mary Craig, *Man From a Far Country: A*

Portrait of Pope John Paul II (London: Hodder & Stoughton, 1982), p. 3 indicates that she died in childbirth, and that the other female child, which died after living only one day, was born three years before Karol; Bernstein and Politi, *His Holiness*, says that his mother was not a teacher but a seamstress, p. 28.

17. Hall, Pope John Paul II, p. 16; Bernstein and Politi, *His Holiness*, p. 55.
18. Malinski, *Pope John Paul II*, p. 48.
19. Craig, *Man from a Far Country*, p. 24; Malinski, *Pope John Paul II*, p. 37; Pope John Paul II, *A Gift and a Mystery* (New York: Doubleday, 1996), p. 5–6.
20. Hall, *Pope John Paul II*, p. 17–18. On Wojtyla's underground activity, see Blazynski, *Pope John Paul II*, p. 49, substantiated by Dr. Joseph L. Lichten, the representative of the Anti–Defamation League of B'nai B'rith in Rome; a denial is in Bernstein and Politi, *His Holiness*, p. 60.
21. Szulc, *Pope John Paul II*, pp. 101–103.
22. Blazynski, *Pope John Paul II*, p. 51. Wojtyla has said that it was Cardinal Sapieha who opposed his joining the Carmelites, in John Paul II, *"Be Not Afraid,"* p. 32; and Pope John Paul II, *Gift and Mystery*, pp. 24–25.
23. Blazynski, *Pope John Paul II*, p. 58.
24. Szulc, *Pope John Paul II*, p. 147.
25. Craig, *Man from a Far Country*, p. 40.
26. Karol Wojtyla, "The Acting Person" in *Analecta Husserliana*, vol. 10 (Boston: D. Reidel, 1979); Kevin Wildes "In the Name of the Father," *New Republic*, December 26, 1994, pp. 21–25.
27. Szulc, *Pope John Paul II*, pp. 155–56; Craig, *Man from a Far Country*, p. 52.
28. The best known of Wojtyla's verse plays is *The Jeweler's Shop: A Meditation on the Sacrament of Matrimony Passing on Occasion into a Drama* (New York: Random House, 1980; appeared first in December 1960). A collection of his verse in English is *The Place Within* (New York: Random House, 1982).
29. Szulc, *Pope John Paul II*, p. 171.
30. Szulc, *Pope John Paul II*, pp. 19, 181; Malinski, *Pope John Paul II*, p. 42 says erroneously that the pontiff had a mild form of leukemia.
31. Szulc, *Pope John Paul II*, pp. 95, 190. Later the *L'Osservatore*

Romano listed Wojtyla as having published five books, 44 philosophical pieces, 27 essays, and a variety of poetry.

32. Andrew N. Woznicki, *A Christian Humanism: Karol Wojtyla's Existential Personalism* (New Britain, Conn.: Mariel Publications, 1980), p. 62; Malinski, *Pope John Paul II*, p. 113; Ronald Modras, "The Moral Philosophy of Pope John Paul II," *Theological Studies* 41 (December 1980, pp. 683–97; Bernstein and Politi, *His Holiness*, pp. 133, 144.
33. Karol Wojtyla, *Love and Responsibility*, rev. ed. (New York: Farrar, Straus, Giroux, 1995).
34. Craig, *Man from a Far Country*, p. 59; Bernstein and Politi, *His Holiness*, p. 88.
35. Szulc, *Pope John Paul II*, pp. 205–12, 223.
36. Ibid., p. 218.
37. Blazynski, *Pope John Paul II*, p. 170.
38. Szulc, *Pope John Paul II*, pp. 253–55; Robert McClory, *Turning Point: The Inside Story of the Papal Birth Control Commission and How Humanae Vitae Changed the Life of Patty Crowley and the Future of the Church* (New York: Crossroad, 1995).
39. Blazynski, *Pope John Paul II*, p. 83.
40. Malinski, *Pope John Paul II*, chap. 19.
41. Hall, *Pope John Paul II*, p. 33; Bernstein and Politi, *His Holiness*, p. 102.
42. Craig, *Man from a Far Country*, p. 83.
43. Szulc, *Pope John Paul II*, pp. 243–44; Bernstein and Politi, *His Holiness*, pp. 107, 162.
44. Karol Wojtyla, *Sign of Contradiction* (New York: Seabury Press, 1979); Malinski, *Pope John Paul II*, p. 42; Bernstein and Politi, *His Holiness*, p. 482.
45. John Paul II, *"Be Not Afraid,"* passim; André Frossard, *Portrait of John Paul II* (San Francisco: Ignatius Press, 1990), p. 15.
46. Peter Hebblethwaite, *Paul VI* (New York: Paulist Press, 1993), p. 7; James F. Andrews, "The Pope in an Age of Insecurity," in *Paul VI: Critical Appraisals*, ed. James F. Andrews (New York Bruce Publishing Co., 1970), pp. 14–15; Peter Hebblethwaite, *The Runaway Church* (New York: Seabury Press, 1975); George A. Schlichte, *Politics in the Purple Kingdom: The Derailment of Vatican II* (Kansas City, Mo.: Sheed & Ward, 1993).
47. Peter Hebblethwaite, *Introducing John Paul II: The Populist*

48. Hebblethwaite, *Introducing*, p. 21; Whale, *The Pope from Poland*, p. 27; Bernstein and Politi, *His Holiness*, p. 424.
49. On the romantic tradition, see John Paul II, *Crossing the Threshold of Hope* (New York: Knopf, 1995), p. 120; Frossard, *"Be Not Afraid,"* p. 35.
50. Szulc, *Pope John Paul II*, p. 23.
51. Peter Hebblethwaite, *The Next Pope* (San Francisco: HarperSanFrancisco, 1995).
52. Arno Mayer, *The Persistence of the Old Regime: Europe in the Great War* (New York: Pantheon, 1981); "Pope Sees Larger Role for Nuns," *Washington Post*, March 29, 1995, p. 2 from Reuters News Service. Information on women priests in Czechoslovakia was carried on the Associated Press wire and reported in the United States in November 1995.
53. Penny Lernoux, *People of God: The Struggle for World Catholicism* (New York: Viking, 1989), pp. 24–28.
54. Szulc, *Pope John Paul II*, p. 325.
55. The respected historian Jaroslav Pelikan in his *Jesus through the Centuries: His Place in the History of Culture* (New Haven: Yale University Press, 1985) argues that the images of Jesus have changed immensely over the years.
56. Szulc, *Pope John Paul II*, p. 327.
57. Whale, ed., *The Pope from Poland*, pp. 65–86.
58. Ibid; David Willey, *God's Politician: John Paul at the Vatican* (Boston: Faber and Faber, 1992), chap. 6.
59. Phillip Berryman, *The Religious Roots of Rebellion: Christians in Central American Revolutions* (Maryknoll, New York: Orbis, 1984), p. 275; John Paul II, *"Be Not Afraid,"* p. 142; Hall and Spink, *Pope John Paul II*, p. 331.
60. Hall, *Pope John Paul II*, p. 31; Willey, *God's Politician*, chap. 1.
61. Whale, ed., *The Pope from Poland*, p. 112.
62. On the Pope's visits to Poland see Szulc, *Pope John Paul II*, chap. 23; and Whale, ed., *The Pope from Poland*, passim. The quote on the war is in Whale's volume, p. 165.
63. Willey, *God's Politician*, pp. 40–43. A postscript on Poland is Jane Perlez, "Shrinking Gap between Church and State," *New York Times*, July 17, 1995, A3.
64. The ties to the Reagan Administration are presented in Bernstein and Politi, *His Holiness*, passim; Peter Schweizer,

Pope (London: Collins, 1982), p. 54; Bernstein and Politi, *His Holiness*, p. 482.

Victory: The Reagan Administration's Secret Strategy That Hastened the Collapse of the Soviet Empire (New York: Atlantic Monthly Press, 1994).
65. Szulc, *Pope John Paul II*, chap. 21.
66. Frossard, *Portrait of John Paul II*, p. 105; Remmick, "The Pope in Crisis," p. 54; Bernstein and Politi, *His Holiness*, pp. 351 and 476.
67. Whale, ed., *The Pope from Poland*, pp. 117–119, 229–31; John Paul II, *Crossing the Threshold of Hope*, pp. 130–31; Bernstein and Politi, *His Holiness*, p. 494.
68. Edward Schillebeeckx, *Jesus: An Experiment in Christology* (New York: Vintage, 1981); Bernstein and Politi, *His Holiness*, p. 48.
69. Peter Hebblethwaite, *The New Inquisition? Schillebeeckx and Kung* (London: Collins, 1980); *Contraception: Authority and Dissent*, ed. by Charles E. Curran (New York: Herder and Herder, 1969); John A. Coleman, *An American Strategic Theology* (New York: Paulist Press, 1982); Eugene Kennedy, "A Dissenting Voice: Catholic Theologian David Tracy," *New York Times Magazine*, November 9, 1986, pp. 21+.
70. Hebblethwaite, *Introducing*, p. 69.
71. Louis Baldwin, *The Pope and the Mavericks* (Buffalo, N.Y.: Prometheus Books, 1988), p. 45.
72. Ibid., pp. 71–99.
73. Ibid., pp. 101–103; Kenneth A. Briggs, *Holy Siege: The Year that Shook Catholic America* (San Francisco: HarperSanFrancisco, 1992).
74. Craig, *Man from a Far Country*, pp. 197–98; Joseph Ratzinger and Vittorio Messori, *The Ratzinger Report: An Exclusive Interview on the State of the Church* (San Francisco: Ignatius Press, 1985). See also his more moderate and scholarly *Church, Ecumenism and Politics: New Essays in Eccesiology* (New York: Crossroad, 1988).
75. Craig, *Man from a Far Country*, p. 158.
76. Jean Lacouture, *Jesuits: A Multibiography* (Washington, D.C.: Counterpoint, 1995), chap. 16–17; Malachi Martin, *The Jesuits: The Society of Jesus and the Betrayal of the Roman Catholic Church* (New York: Simon and Schuster, 1987), part 4; Henry Kamm, "The Secret World of Opus Dei," *New York Times Magazine*, January 8, 1984, pp. 38+; Bernstein and Politi, *His Holiness*, p. 422.

77. Szulc, *Pope John Paul II*, pp. 355–67.
78. Frossard, *Portrait of John Paul*, p. 68.
79. Paul B. Henze, *The Plot to Kill the Pope* (New York: Scribner, 1983); Claire Sterling, *The Time of the Assassins* (New York: Holt Rinehart & Winston, 1985). An unproven tale is that the pope and Leonid Brezhnev actually met on a Soviet warship in the Mediterranean, related in Luigi Forni, *The Dove and the Bear* (Kent, England: Midas Books, 1983.) Brezhnev said, "All that stuff about communism is a tall tale for popular consumption. After all, we can't leave the people with no faith. The church was taken away, the czar was shot, and something had to be substituted. So let the people build communism." *Washington Post Book World*, July 9, 1995, p. 3. On Fatima, see Timothy Tindal–Robertson, *Fatima, Russia and Pope John Paul II: How Mary Intervened to Deliver Russia from Marxist Atheism May 13, 1981–December 15, 1991*, 2nd ed. (Devon: Augustine Publishing Co., 1992).
80. Frossard, *Portrait of John Paul II*, p. 58.
81. Hansjakob Stehle, *Eastern Politics of the Vatican 1917–1979* (Athens, Ohio: Ohio University Press, 1981), chap. 9.
82. George A. Kelly, *The Battle for the American Church Revisited* (San Francisco, Ignatius Press, 1995), chap. 6; Andrew Greeley, *The Catholic Myth: The Behavior and Beliefs of American Catholics* (New York: Scribner, 1990).
83. James Reston, *Galileo: A Life* (New York: HarperCollins, 1994), passim.
84. Hebblethwaite, *Introducing*, pp. 89–91; Gordon Thomas and Max Morgan–Witts, *Averting Armageddon* (Garden City: Doubleday & Co., 1984); *Catholics and Nuclear War: A Commentary on the Challenge of Peace, the U.S. Catholic Bishops Letter on War and Peace*, ed. by Philip J. Murnion (New York: Crossroad, 1983).
85. Hebblethwaite, *Introducing*, pp. 99–113.
86. Phillip Berryman, *Liberation Theology: Essential Facts about the Revolutionary Movement in Latin America–and Beyond* (Philadelphia: Temple University Press, 1987), p. 109.
87. Whale, ed., *Pope from Poland*, p. 93.
88. Berryman, *Liberation Theology*, p. 108; Humberto Belli, *Breaking Faith: The Sandinista Revolution and Its Impact on Freedom and Christian Faith in Nicaragua* (Westchester, Ill.: Crossway Books, 1985); Robert Kagan, *A Twilight*

Struggle: American Power and Nicaragua (New York: Free Press, 1996).

89. Julia Preston, "Pope Returns in Jubilation and Triumph to Nicaragua," *New York Times*, February 8, 1996, p. A14; Larry Rohter, "Church Bombings Worry Nicaragua as Papal Visit Nears," *New York Times*, January 21, 1996, p. 3.

90. Some of the major works on liberation theology that I have reviewed are: Leonardo Boff and Clodovis Boff, *Salvation and Liberation* (Maryknoll, N.Y.: Orbis, 1984); Gustavo Gutiérrez, A *Theology of Liberation: History, Politics, and Salvation* (Maryknoll, N.Y.: Orbis, 1988); Leonardo Boff, *Ecclesiogenesis: The Base Communities Reinvent the Church* (Maryknoll, N.Y.: Orbis, 1986); *Liberation South, Liberation North*, ed. Michael Novak (Washington: American Enterprise Institute, 1981), especially Juan Luis Segundo, "Capitalism–Socialism: A Theological Crux," pp. 7–23; Richard Shaull, *Heralds of a New Reformation: The Poor of South and North America* (Maryknoll, N.Y.: Orbis, 1984); José P. Miranda, *Marx and the Bible: A Critique of the Philosophy of Oppression* (Maryknoll, N.Y.: Orbis, 1974).

91. Berryman, *Liberation Theology*, p. 110.

92. Craig, *Man from a Far Country*, pp. 166–70; Norman St. John–Stevas, *Pope John Paul II, His Travels and Mission* (London: Faber and Faber, 1982), p. 45; Bernstein and Politi, *His Holiness*, p. 510.

93. Ibid., pp. 173–77.

94. Hebblethwaite, *Introducing*, pp. 115–16.

95. Ibid., pp. 117–21.

96. Craig, *Man from a Far Country*, pp. 178–79.

97. Ibid., p. 181; Frossard, *Portrait of John Paul II*, p. 90.

98. Hebblethwaite, *Introducing*, p. 142.

99. Ibid., pp. 149–53.

100. Willey, *God's Politician*, pp. 85–6.

101. Kelly, *The Battle*, p. 9.

102. Willey, *God's Politician*, pp. 90–92; Frossard, *Portrait of John Paul II*, p. 113.

103. Willey, *God's Politician*, p. 88; Remmick, "The Pope in Crisis," p. 52. The Vatican would have usually given Waldheim the higher Order of the Golden Spur rather than the lesser Order of Pius X. Roberto Suro, "John Paul Holds Waldheim Meeting," *New York Times*, June 26, 1987, p. 1+.

104. Willey, *God's Politician*, chap. 7.
105. Janet E. Smith, *Humanae Vitae, A Generation Later* (Washington, D.C.: Catholic University Press, 1991); John Paul II, *Reflections on Humanae Vitae: Conjugal Morality and Spirituality* (Boston: St. Paul's Editions, 1984).
106. Robert Blair Kaiser, *The Politics of Sex and Religion: A Case History in the Development of Doctrine, 1962–1984* (Kansas City, Mo.: Leaven Press, 1985), chap. 11–12; Bernstein and Politi, *His Holiness*, p. 83.
107. Peter Steinfels, "Vatican Says the Ban on Women as Priests Is 'Infallible' Doctrine," *New York Times*, November 19, 1995, p. 1+; Peter Steinfels, "Wariness Greets Vatican Doctrinal Claim," *New York Times*, November 22, 1995, p. 24. The pronouncement followed the revelation that in 1970 women were ordained in Communist Czechoslovakia when the Church was forced underground. See the Associated Press report for November 13, 1995, and also Paula Butturini, "Vatican Move Raises Questions," *Boston Globe*, November 23, 1995, p. 2. Also relevant is Richard P. McBrien, "Ten Points on Infallibility," *Catholic Free Press*, April 12, 1993, p. 4.
108. James J. McCartney, *Unborn Persons: Pope John Paul II and the Abortion Debate* (New York: Peter Lang, 1987), pp. 83–84.
109. Frossard, *Portrait of John Paul II*, pp. 80–81.
110. McCartney, *Unborn Persons*, pp. 83–84.
111. Pope John Paul II, *The Gospel of Life (Evangelicum Vitae)* (New York: Random House, 1995).
112. Bernstein and Politi, *His Holiness*, p. 526; Hebblethwaite, *Next Pope*, passim; Roberto Suro, "12 Faiths Join Pope to Pray for Peace," *New York Times*, October 28, 1986, p. 3; John Paul II, *Crossing the Threshold of Hope*; on women, see: "Pope Sees Larger Role," p. 2. On China, Alan Cowell, "Pope Offers the Chinese a Deal on the Church's Role," *New York Times*, January 15, 1995, p. 3; on irresponsible behavior, Bernstein and Politi, *His Holiness*, p. 521.
113. Adam Gopnik, "A Virtual Bishop," *New Yorker*, March 18, 1996, pp. 59–63.
114. On the number of apologies, see Luigi Accattoli in Davaid Frossard, *The Rule of Benedict* (San Francisco: HarperSan Francisco, 2006); Frossard, *Portrait of John Paul II*, p. 111 Bernstein and Politi, *His Holiness*, p. 114.

ABOUT THE AUTHORS

Michael P. Riccards is a former college president at three institutions of higher education and a public policy scholar for the College Board and the founding executive director of the Hall Institute. He is the author of several major books on the American presidency and the papacy as a management problem, and has written 18 verse plays, some of which have been produced.

He is married with three children and has five grandchildren to whom this volume is dedicated.

Cheryl A. Flagg, the collaborator and editor of this book, is the Manager of Member Relations at the Council of Graduate Schools in Washington, D.C. She has been the collaborator with Michael P. Riccards on eight books and was the editor of a volume on Franklin D. Roosevelt and the New Deal.

PAPAL GREATNESS: THE TEN MOST IMPORTANT PONTIFFS

Made in the USA
San Bernardino, CA
21 November 2016